A LEOPARDI READER

A
LEOPARDI
READER

Editing and Translations by

Ottavio M. Casale

University of Illinois Press

Urbana   Chicago   London

*The preparation of this volume was made possible (in part) by a grant
from the Translations Program of the National Endowment for the
Humanities, an independent Federal agency.*

Library of Congress Cataloging in Publication Data

Leopardi, Giacomo, conte, 1798-1837.
A Leopardi reader.

Bibliography: p. 223
I. Casale, Ottavio M. II. Title.
PQ4709.E5A1 1981 851'.7 80-29068
ISBN 0-252-00824-3
ISBN 0-252-00892-8(pbk)

Al Conte Giacomo Leopardi
Recanatese

Contents

Foreword

————

The Introduction Professor Casale has provided for his balanced anthology of Giacomo Leopardi's writings is so thoughtful that it saves me from the temptation of trying too hard to impress readers with the significance of that poignant Italian voice without which the concert of European romanticism would sound incomplete. For that matter, I can just refer to the telling need of poets like Rilke, Lowell, Rexroth, Pound, or Heath-Stubbs to test their own artistry against Leopardi's by translating one or more *Canti*.

Besides offering in his own supple translation a substantial choice of Leopardi's uniquely melodic verse, Casale has made ample room for the superb prose, which he liberally samples from the various available sources: the huge Notebook *(Zibaldone),* the fervent Letters, the alternately mercurial and saturnine Moral Dialogues and Essays *(Operette Morali),* the aphorisms *(Pensieri).* Prose, with its free rhythms, translates with little loss of formal integrity; Casale's terse renderings of Leopardi's prose enable us to savor Leopardi's staccato hammerings, his ratiocinative convolutions, and his almost stream-of-consciousness notations.

Apart from the prose's experimental versatility, which is enough to insure its appeal to modern ears, its daring message will surely strike a sympathetic chord in the minds of moderns, who have weathered Victorian arrogance and the subsequent twentieth-century catastrophes and who now live in their uncertain aftermath. Leopardi saw through that hubris in advance, and he questioned the smug claims of positivist progressivism no less than the widespread belief in a dawning industrial millennium. Other exceptional minds of his time took a comparably dim view of triumphant bourgeois democracy—for instance Baudelaire, Kierkegaard, and then Nietzsche—but Leopardi alone did so without jettisoning those basic tenets of the Enlightenment which had heralded the democratic revolutions; we might even say that he criticized rising mass society in the very name of such tenets. Were not life, liberty, and *happiness* the touchstones of his critique, his cry of the heart in the face of all the disappointments—historical and personal—that the age held in store? Here was a protest against history past and present, against Nature itself—a Nature insistently personified as a cruel mother, or as a feminine power of enticing beauty who affords her helpless human captives a glimpse of possible happiness only to deny them any fulfillment.

With such a premise, it would prove hard to escape the paralyzing conclusion that life is a vanity of vanities, and all is vanity. And for Leopardi all is vanity, except the one certainty that survives all denials: the wounded consciousness that can conceive of infinity, the stubborn thought that reaffirms man's dignity, a voice in the desert. From the barren slopes of Vesuvius, that voice would make itself heard once more (in *Broom*) to confront nature's desolation and assert mankind's communal bond as the only viable response, the only possible salvation. At that point, Leopardi had managed to socialize his individual despair into what one might call the existential precipitate of the French Revolution—liberty, equality, and brotherhood having gone into temporary eclipse after Napoleon's excesses and downfall. Such was the reward of Leopardi's radical denials.

The eerie calm of the Stoic contemplator has thus replaced the passionate protest of the earlier *Idylls* poet; but there is fire at the center of that calm, for the poet by now has succeeded in tapping the deepest resources of his conscious and unconscious thought alike. The very manner in which he articulates his utterance, whether in prose or poetry, bespeaks the crossing of a barrier beyond which despair subsides into supreme lucidity, and language finds a new purity. When Leopardi says:

> Che fai tu, luna, in ciel? dimmi, che fai,
> Silenziosa luna?
> Sorgi la sera, e vai
> Contemplando i deserti; indi ti posi,

he is so utterly simple that diction almost skirts banality, and yet the voice sounds hypnotically mysterious, so intense is the rediscovery of each word's primal power. It would be impossible to capture in another language the flute-like wail of those long Italian vowels coupled with reiterated spirants and sibilants; however, Casale's transcription for the phonically different English instrument has achieved the best that could be done with such inviolable music, and he even echoes the "ài" effect by placing the word "sky" at the end of that first line in the *canzone Night-Song of a Wandering Shepherd of Asia*. The childlike questioning triggers a thoroughly disconsolate review of mankind's disabilities in an alien universe, hence the Beethoven-like effect of this *canzone.* In Casale's sensitive rendering, something of that effect is retained (or, better, reattained), especially since he pays close attention to the alternately lulling and driving rhythms of the original syntax. It can be said in general that Leopardi's shaping spirit of imagination, as directly conjured in *The Infinite,* reverberates into his translator's work to a heartening extent. Casale evinces a reshaping skill of the first order, and Leopardi's word could hardly hope for a better English embodiment.

Glauco Cambon
Storrs, Connecticut
January, 1980

Preface

——

This English edition of selections from Leopardi is directed not at the Italianist but at the general reader of world, comparative, or romantic literature who desires to know Leopardi as more than a name. Several features need comment. First, I have presented most of the selections chronologically so as to show development and connections rather than to honor genres. By weaving the prose around the poems, I hope to give the reader a richer, truer, and more interesting look into Leopardi's mind than is otherwise possible. The selections are numbered consecutively for reference, but titles of major works are listed in the table of contents. Readers wishing to consult the Italian originals of the poems can find them in an appendix at the back, where there are also a bibliography and notes. Second, I include more prose, and a greater variety of it, than have past anthologies. Although many would argue that Leopardi was chiefly a tragic or elegiac poet, the fact is that he expressed himself much more often, more variously, and perhaps more revealingly in prose. The reader who samples, let us say, the letters or *Zibaldone* passages will see what I mean. Third, I give more biographical and critical commentary than is customary in such a collection. I do so on the assumption that separated as we are from Leopardi in time, space, language, and ethos, such notations may prove helpful. This commentary appears in the General Introduction, in headnotes to the four basic sections and to important works, and occasionally elsewhere.

The translations are based on the comprehensive five-volume Italian edition *Tutte le opere di Giacomo Leopardi* edited by Francesco Flora. I do not usually give the location of an item in Flora as that would be superfluous both for those who read Italian and those who do not. The methods of identifying the five basic types of Leopardi's writing are as follows:

1. The Poems (or *Canti*). Each of the sixteen poems translated is listed in the table of contents and is dated and discussed in an individual headnote.

xiii

2. The *Operette Morali*. I have not translated this general title given by Leopardi to more than twenty dialogues, essays, and prose poems written over several years; the phrase "little works in moral philosophy" does not materially advance the cause of knowledge or of translation. As with the poems, I have indicated each of the ten *Operette* (or excerpts) by its separate title in the text and table of contents, and I date and introduce each piece in a headnote.

3. The *Zibaldone*. The word refers to Leopardi's massive "notebook" or "grab-bag." It is a good round word in Italian and will serve. The *Zibaldone* constituted 4,526 pages which Leopardi wrote between 1817 and 1832 and even indexed for himself. The seventy-one entries below, labeled Z, are of course untitled, but I indicate the date—when Leopardi gave one—and the page numbers used by Leopardi and cited in all reputable Italian editions.

4. The Letters. Leopardi left us 931 letters, of which I present the whole or parts of thirty-seven. The labeling system is self-evident.

5. The *Reflections* (or *Pensieri*). Thirty-one of these are given as a group in Section IV since we are sure only of the period when Leopardi assembled them. The roman numeral he intended for the item is given at the end of each.

In addition to these basic forms, I include a few miscellaneous writings which I identify as necessary.

In translating I have taken liberties—to each his language. I have tried to provide the modern English reader some of the lucidity and grace of the originals. In most of the poems, Leopardi used two line lengths. Sometimes he wrote eleven-syllable lines, or *endecasillabi*, throughout a poem, the Italian equivalent of blank verse. Elsewhere he experimented with the *canzone* form, using stanzas of different lengths which mingle the long lines with seven-syllable ones, or *settenari*. (Those interested in the technique of Leopardi's verse can find detailed English discussion in the notes and introduction to Bickersteth's translations.) Like Heath-Stubbs, whose work I admire, I avoid almost entirely the rhyme Leopardi sometimes uses. Almost exclusively I use iambic rhythm, the one most natural to English. In poems where Leopardi mixes short and long lines, I vary the lengths also, but not necessarily when he does. In both the prose and poetry I frequently change Leopardi's punctuation; provide different paragraph or section breaks; and even interpolate, exclude, or doctor a word or phrase if doing so seems salutary to me. My controlling assumption has been that to produce correct but obscure or dumpy versions would fail Leopardi, literature, and the English and Italian languages.

This volume owes much to certain persons and institutions. Kent State University and the National Endowment for the Humanities gave me grants to work on the project full-time during the spring of 1977 and the summer of 1979, respectively. Professor Glauco Cambon, now at the University of Connecticut, first taught me about Leopardi at the University of Michigan, and he has recently functioned sturdily as advisor, inspirer, and midwife: my debt to him is very great. Professors Olga Ragusa and Karl Kroeber of Columbia University gave me important psychological support along the way. I am also indebted to colleagues in the Romance Languages Department at Kent—Giuseppe Baglivi, Garrett McCutchan, John Kane, and Carolina Donadio Lawson—who advised me on knotty Italian and French passages.

Several phrases and ideas are echoed from the article "Leopardi, Arnold, and the Victorian Sensibility" by Allan Dooley and Ottavio M. Casale in the March, 1980 issue of *Comparative Literature Studies* of the University of Illinois.

Perhaps I owe most, however, to the following colleagues, friends, and family: to Robert Bamberg, Allan Dooley, Louis Paskoff, and William Hildebrand of the English Department at Kent; to my literate neighbor Nancy Abdo; to my wife, Linda Casale, and my daughters Laura and Elizabeth. For more than three years these persons offered me and Leopardi their ears, eyes, and opinions. I am grateful.

O. M. C.
Kent, Ohio
October, 1979

GENERAL INTRODUCTION:
THE MIND AND
ART OF GIACOMO LEOPARDI

General Introduction:
The Mind and
Art of Giacomo Leopardi

———

Giacomo Leopardi was one for whom words were special, primal, and chaste. In a life which reads like a devastating textbook on alienation, words were the instruments for reaching out, for tracing truth, creating beauty, affirming love, trying to touch other people, other times. And if no one else were listening, which was most of the time, he wrote to and for himself.

The urgency of Leopardi's desire to express is understandable. His body hunched and ruined by illness ("a walking sepulchre," as he phrased it), he knew early that the life of heroic action preferred by him and led by many of his cherished Greeks was out of the question. Indeed, a normal social existence including sexual love, marriage, and children was not possible. Words were a way to break through these limitations and those imposed by his parents' house, his parents' provincial town, the "abhorred" Recanati, and, worst of all, his parents' ideas. Besides the prisons of Leopardi's body, birthplace, and intellectual environment, there is another fact with implications for his expression: he denied to himself belief in God or any other comforting numinous reality, and he evolved as exclusively a humanistic and skeptical worldview as we encounter in the history of letters. This rejection may have taken a deep psychological toll of one who had been groomed to be defender of the faith (it certainly affected his reputation), but it also contributes to the deep and vulnerable humanity of his utterance. We see everywhere in Leopardi—explicit or implicit, direct or paradoxical—the importance of humans, their kinship, and their discourse; and this is so despite Leopardi's own frequent arguments to the contrary. Denied supernal aid, as he felt, he reaches out for humans, to learn from and teach, to feed off and to feed.

He had a habit of quickly outstripping teachers, and when the abilities of his tutors, including his father, Monaldo, were exhausted,

3

he began looking for new stimuli and friends, such as Giordani, Stella, De Sinner, and eventually Ranieri. When at the age of twenty-four he finally escaped Recanati for a few months at Rome, he was bitterly disappointed by the intellectual vacuum he found there, only to revive at discovering the learned German philologer-diplomats Niebuhr and Bunsen. The letters especially reveal the need for emotional and intellectual contact. Leopardi usually initiates a correspondence; he keeps track of answers and often asks explicit questions to insure response; and he always tries to answer promptly, even lengthily, himself. If his closest siblings, Carlo and Paolina, fail to write, he scolds them. Above all, when the correspondent leans psychologically on him, he temporarily suspends his own problems and tailors the topics and tone to the correspondent's needs.

Perhaps more impressive than Leopardi's words aimed at immediate communication, however, are those devoted to expressing himself to or about inert or distant realities, which come alive and close through his attention. Much of this utterance is melancholy, but undeniably he took pleasure in his solitary reading and writing. Leopardi had the literary intellectual's bent of being fascinated by linguistic facts, poetic and philological relationships, and sociological and philosophical connections, and he squirreled away his notations in a notebook for future use. The number of allusions in the *Zibaldone* to literatures and languages is in itself staggering. What is even more striking is that the erudition is in no way postured (as in Poe, for example). Rather it seems a vital outreaching for nutrition badly needed and for an objective world providing health and continuity to a mind worried over the precariousness of both. During the moments when Leopardi waited for a manuscript page to dry, it is said he would memorize the definition of one or two English or German words so as not to waste time. Even when he saw almost no personal future before him, he was projecting a *Letter to a Young Man of the Twentieth Century*. A good deal of the enormous amount of writing he did was obviously on deposit for his own future use and ours, but just as clearly he wrote to express a hermetic journey of the mind, a journey wherein the *process* of mind itself was as important as the discoveries made, the points achieved.

Nowhere is the hermetic aspect of Leopardi's commentary seen more sharply than in the poems, where he created an existential landscape all his own. Even the despairing conclusions of the dialogues in the *Operette Morali* seem tempered by the fact of conversation between humans or their surrogates. The poems, however, are loneliness made palpable. The poetic voice is variously that of a lone, alienated historical figure (Brutus, Sappho), an almost mythical spokesman for grieved

4

humanity (the wandering shepherd of Asia), or the poet himself re-membering former happiness and lamenting current or timeless fate (the speaker of *To Spring, To Sylvia,* or *Memories*). The entities addressed do not answer. They are usually mute forces or things in or behind the cosmos: nature, fate, the moon, the stars, a flock. If Leopardi does address individual humans, it is the departed Sylvia or Nerina (even the names indicate their unreality), symbols of his and perhaps everyman's lost vibrant youth. And, of course, there is the poem with the most barren landscape of all, *To Himself.* It is not only *"la donna che non si trova"* in these works, it is basic human contact we miss. If it were not for the exquisite language, the desire implied, and the beauty craved, these would be stark experiences indeed.

Leopardi expressed himself well enough to be considered one of the eminent writers in western literature (except possibly in our United States, where language barriers seem higher than elsewhere). Even if we were to set to one side his countrymen's opinion, which generally places him, with Tasso, Petrarch, and a few others, second only to Dante in the Italian tradition, there is the admiration of the greats from other lands. Sainte-Beuve seemed awed equally by the erudition and the art Leopardi displayed. Nietzsche was taken by the prose, estimating Leopardi one of the four great prose writers of the nineteenth century, along with Emerson, Merimée, and Landor. George Santayana, while acknowledging (as one must) that Leopardi's vision was narrowed by suffering, said of the poetry, "Long passages are fit to repeat in lieu of prayers through all the watches of the night." Matthew Arnold, that arbiter of touchstones, thought Leopardi one of the very greatest "modern" poets and compared him with Goethe, Wordsworth, and Byron. Schopenhauer, naturally enough, thrilled to the pessimism, bemoaning the fact that he and Leopardi never met.[1]

But the opinions of the great cannot make or keep a writer great. That prize can only be conferred by numberless readers over time, each confronting the literature on his own. In the confrontation with Leopardi, a problem instantly arises: how do we deal with the explicit pessimism or melancholy? The question is especially important to Anglo-American readers habituated for centuries to aggressively optimistic writing. And the issue is aggravated when the reader is at the mercy of translations of the poetry, when inevitably the bare idea communicates much more sharply than other poetic values. Consider how we might react to Keats's great opening line, "When I have fears that I may cease to be," if we were reading it for the first time in a translation beginning, "Every time I think I might not live long. . . ."

There are other questions too. How much of Leopardi's darkest substance has universal, objective force, and how much should we ascribe to individual and therefore untypical woe? (He himself was paradoxical on the issue, resenting the *ad-hominem* equation but also admitting to his Tuscan friends that with his poems he sought "to consecrate my pain."[2]) And how do we explain the seeming anomaly of a writer whose style sometimes approaches the sublimity traditionally associated with the most enraptured religious vision but which is linked in Leopardi to death, transience, and negation? After all, we expect our Miltons to be Miltons and our Jobs Jobs.

At the start of an essay on Leopardi, Francesco De Sanctis said, "Everyone forms his own God; and everyone forms his own Woman."[3] We can add that every reader forms his own Leopardi, approving or not, being moved or unmoved, fascinated or bemused, selective and even censoring, according to the different aesthetic and metaphysical tastes of the reader and his times and even according to the texts available. For example, whereas the publication of the complete letters generally invigorated interest in Leopardi, Croce admitted to being depressed at looking into what he saw as the personal workshop of a poetry he had thought objective.[4] The history of Leopardi's reputation is almost unique for the extent to which commentators reveal as much or more about themselves as they do about their subject. The relativist Leopardi might have shrugged his shoulders at the fluctuating spectacle.

Frequently, readers with a cause, religious or secular, theistic or atheistic, have simplified Leopardi and then discussed, rejected, or accepted their image whole. In addition to Schopenhauer, the English poet James Thomson, the auther of *The City of Dreadful Night,* admired the pessimism and devoted months of his life to learning Italian so as to translate the *Operette Morali.*[5] The patriot Giuseppe Mazzini, on the other hand, bent on carving out a new Italy and world, relegated Leopardi to the school of backward-looking classicists and aesthetes of no use to the struggle for nation and brotherhood.[6] The school of Lombrosian scholars in Italy accounted for Leopardi's darkness deterministically in terms of the physiological type to which he belonged.[7] The most summary view of Leopardi, however, was probably that of his contemporary Niccolò Tommaseo, an ardent Catholic and also the scholarly annotator of a Cicero edition crisply dismantled by Leopardi. For Tommaseo, Leopardi was a little count who croaked like a frog, "There is no God because I am a hunchback, I am a hunchback because there is no God."[8] (Hell hath no fury like that of a professor scorned.)

Perhaps the most tension-filled criticism of Leopardi is that of commentators excited by certain qualities and depressed by others. The complexity and paradoxes in Leopardi have bred their analogues in readers. The Italian biographer Ferretti, for example, agrees with Leopardi's priest friend, Vincenzo Gioberti, that Leopardi's denunciations paradoxically revealed his religious yearning, and says that Gioberti "understood the inner torment and the unconfessed need of God."[9] At the other ideological pole, the Italian Marxist critic Cesare Luporini, made somewhat uncomfortable by the more despairing ideas of his author, argues that Leopardi was actually "vitalistic" and "progressive" in his vision for humanity.[10] In a famous judgment, Croce found Leopardi's pessimism reprehensible, "a reasoned projection of his own unhappy state." To Croce, Leopardi was a great idyllic poet whose "pseudo-philosophy" vitiated many poems.[11]

For the student of British culture, the reactions of the English Victorians, assessing Leopardi in the full tide of empire and optimism, may have special interest. H. C. Merivale bluntly posed his problem in appreciation this way: "The translator, while anxious to introduce to the English-reading public a version of so fine a poem as the 'Canto notturno,' desires at the same time, happy as he is in his simpler faith, to disclaim on his own account all sympathy with the gloomy 'nihilism' which pervades it."[12] A more elaborate if similar reaction was that of William Gladstone, who wrote the first significant English essay on Leopardi.[13] Struck as he was by Leopardi's harmony, pathos, and even "majesty of expression," Gladstone deplored the absence of "the Gospel revelation; without which even while we feel the poet to be an enchanter, we cannot accept and trust him as a guide." Protecting the reader from the more questionable works, Gladstone gives the impression of someone carrying an infectious virus in a beautiful container. Matthew Arnold wrote of Leopardi late in his own career, at a time when Leopardi's name was being increasingly linked to philosophical pessimism rather than to art.[14] Arnold refocused English attention on the poetry, judging Leopardi superior in several ways to Arnold's favorite English romantic poets Byron and Wordsworth. The author of *Dover Beach* and staunch admirer of the classical world found much in Leopardi that resonated with his own mind and art (perhaps more than he could state), but he ultimately draws back. Leopardi falls short of the English poets because he lacks Wordsworth's sense "of joy in widest commonalty spread" and the positive strength into which both Byron and Wordsworth tapped from a superior force outside themselves. In short, though the terms and approach are so much more sophisticated, Arnold's view is Gladstone's cooled, refined, aestheticized. Despite the qualifications, Arnold's imprimatur boosted English interest in Leopardi: even though the Italian had died forty-four years before Arnold wrote, the spate of book-length translations in Britain begins just after the Arnold essay.

In the twentieth century, the study of Leopardi has increasingly abandoned the biographical and moralistic emphases of earlier times. With the basic life established and the illuminating *Zibaldone* available, Italian scholars have shown less interest in the relationship of Leopardi's work to his personal life or to absolutes outside it. While they have paid due attention to Leopardi's relevance to the modern world, they have also concentrated on intrinsic literary-intellectual qualities: on the sources and development of the writings; on the relation of the prose and poems; and—perhaps most interestingly—on the problem of unity, or the lack thereof, in Leopardi's thought. Although full-length studies in English are not numerous, they are high in quality and becoming more frequent. Since Bickersteth's volume of poetic translations in 1923, which featured an excellent scholarly introduction, we have had Iris Origo's impressive biography, Whitfield's probing study of Leopardi's humanism, Nicolas Perella's solid scholarly examination of Leopardi as poet and theorist of the sublime, G. Singh's focused study of the aesthetics, and Giovanni Carsaniga's analysis of the cultural relativism.[15] The trends here too seem clear despite healthy differences in emphasis and opinion. Leopardi is seen as a major romantic author whose art bears scrutiny and whose philosophical ideas, separately considered, are not as menacing as once thought. The rationalism so disturbing to the nineteenth century no longer demands apology. And the existential humanism Leopardi once represented so anachronistically seems highly relevant to a world which, after several apocalyptic wars, Dachau, and Hiroshima, seems less certain about ultimate answers, much less ultimate happiness. As with Emerson, we look to Leopardi not so much for the "correctness" of his responses to metaphysical questions as for the fact and the way that he posed those questions and the sheer, interesting dignity of his art and his search.

This is not to say that we need know little about the data of Leopardi's life. One need not be a Freudian or Lombrosian to wonder about the relation of Leopardi's life to his temperament and achievement. Some basic biographical facts will be given in headnotes throughout this volume, but a few highlights are in order here.

It was an aborted life in a sense, one which makes the painful circumstances of a Samuel Johnson or Edgar Allan Poe seem quite bearable by comparison. As he put it himself, Leopardi was born "of a noble family in an ignoble town of Italy." The date was June 29, 1798, and in his lifetime Leopardi was never to know an Italy free of foreign occupation. His parents, Count Monaldo and Countess Adelaide, were models of a displaced medievalism, raising their children to be defenders of the Church and monarchy. Count Monaldo, who would not go to the window to watch Napoleon ride by, was stubborn, over-protective, and unsympathetic to his children's desire for autonomy and fulfillment beyond their hearth and town. Clearly, however, he was usually well-meaning, and if the children received parental love during their formative years, it was from their father. Monaldo gave Giacomo, his oldest and favorite son, early access to his exceptional library and encouraged his studies, even to obtaining for Giacomo when the boy was fifteen a religious dispensation to read prohibited authors. Ironically enough, Leopardi was first introduced to the ungodly writers he came to love by being compelled to write essays denouncing their errors. The father and son, who eventually grew apart, were very close at first and shared many intellectual pursuits, although in ability Monaldo was to Giacomo roughly what Leopold Mozart had been to Wolfgang.

Countess Adelaide was another matter. Often striding through the house wearing men's riding boots, Adelaide was a stern, seemingly affectionless woman possessed of two major concerns. One was to repair the family finances bungled by Monaldo, the other to make sure that the children feared God, hated earth, and looked forward to heaven. Leopardi described his mother at length in the terrifying sketch of November 25, 1820, tucked away in his *Zibaldone* and thus not revealed until the latter's publication at the turn of the century. We must, however, look to other hints to appreciate the probable impact of his mother on Leopardi's mind: to the way in which he repeatedly portrays hostile, unresponsive forces or symbols in female terms, or to the fact that of his 931 letters only four are written to Adelaide, and even those seem mechanical. As for Adelaide's ultimate opinion of her son, she was unremittingly sure of her values and what constituted betrayal of them. Filippo Zamboni, an admirer of Leopardi, told a chilling story of his visit to the Leopardi palace after the poet's death. In the company of the "majestic" Countess, he rhapsodized toward a portrait of Leopardi, "Blessed be she who bore you." To which the Countess replied, "May God forgive him!"[16]

The early years were good, however. Giacomo, often wearing black clerical garb, was healthy, vivacious, and quickwitted, and he seemed to thrive on study and play. From Monaldo and family priests he learned rhetoric, mathematics, theology, much Latin, and basic Spanish and French. Later he was able to learn on his own much Greek, significant amounts of English and German, and enough Hebrew as a teenager to debate with learned Jews of Ancona. The boy was exceedingly religious—Monaldo was to say that the young Leopardi would not step on floor joints out of respect for the Cross. With his brother Carlo and other boys he played at war games, always taking the hero's part against the despot and bestowing ringing blows in the name of freedom. Alone, he indulged in animistic reverie, giving life and voice to trees and rocks he felt to be companions. Like other children, however, he seems to have fiercely resented being lied to in "real" matters. At about the age of ten or eleven, Leopardi began a "desperate" course of study in his father's library which led to his precocious reputation as a scholar of Christian and classical texts, but which also compromised his health. The amount of reading and writing the adolescent Leopardi indulged in was prodigious. Besides ingesting as many as several hundred pages of reading a day, he wrote dozens of translations of and commentaries on ancient texts, and he produced his own plays, essays, and verse. In 1812-13 (he was about fourteen), Leopardi wrote among other things a tragedy and a long *History of Astronomy* based on a bibliography of more than 300 titles. In 1815, he wrote many works, including the extensive *Essay on the Popular Errors of the Ancients* and a long commentary on the writings of Julius Africanus, and he translated Moschus's *Idylls* as well as a long Homeric satire. By the age of nineteen, he was skilled enough at Greco-Latin studies to concoct an allegedly discovered Greek *Hymn to Neptune* which recognized scholars accepted as genuine. In all the scholarly frenzy of these pubescent years, Leopardi was still his parents' pride, still an advocate of Christian dogma, although he was fascinated by the literature and mind of the pagan past.

Then came the "conversions," as Leopardi called them. Late in his teens and for various reasons—the collapse of his body, his own maturation, and the influence of Pietro Giordani, the skeptical Milanese intellectual and ex-priest with whom he corresponded and whom he eventually hosted at Recanati—Leopardi experienced a complex intellectual convulsion. One of the conversions was literary, the movement away from erudition and toward poetry and the glories of modern literatures, the condition of his eyes having much to do with the change. The other, overlapping transformation was definitely philosophical or theological, the abandoning of the faith of his fathers, a change which was to be permanent if confided at first only to intimates and suggested outwardly only by Leopardi's refusal to wear the priest's gown any longer. Although the divestiture was decisive and sincere, the reader will note evidence of a residual emotional attachment (if not more) to traditional Christianity. There is, for example, the frequent dating of notebook entries according to the church calendar and the frequent references to God and Catholic forms in Leopardi's letters to his father. Surely there is wistfulness as well as irony in these allusions, and we cannot attribute them, as Gladstone did, to hypocrisy.[17]

Anyone who has investigated medical diagnoses from earlier centuries will understand how Leopardi's physical condition is still a matter of doubt, with causes being confused with effects and genetic factors blurring into environmental ones. We do know that in 1819, the condition of his eyes became so bad as nearly to blind him for months then and sporadically afterwards. We also know that during his adolescence his spine curved until eventually he was a hunchback. Other afflictions biographers cite include a nerve malady, rachitis (defective bone growth usually caused by insufficient sunlight and vitamin D), asthma, kidney attacks, the coughing of blood, dropsy (or fluid retention), and, logically enough, bouts of severe depression. From this futile vantage point, we might isolate the scoliosis as particularly damaging in that spine curvature and the attendant shift in the rib cage progressively deteriorate the heart and lungs. But the years of seclusion, almost interment, during the formative stage must have done their part to bring out hereditary flaws: the young man purchased knowledge at an awesome price.[18] That Leopardi had, as often noted by those who met him, an incredibly beautiful smile is a testimony to human resilience.

The major motifs of the second half of Leopardi's life have a certain iron inexorability to them. Obsessed equally by the fear of early death and a Miltonic desire for literary greatness, he struggled to leave Recanati and reach the world of culture and intellect beyond. His eventual stays in such cities as Florence, Bologna, and Pisa brought him much of the desired contact and friendship. Curiously, however, he never met Byron, Shelley, or Keats; and unlike Melville and Wordsworth, who had Hawthorne and Coleridge, respectively, to charge their minds, Leopardi never found the extended company of an intellectual and artistic equal. There were other, more overt, disappointments. His search for a literary or church-related position which would free him from Recanati and money worry was never successful. When the Countess finally relented and issued him a monthly stipend, he was free, but only in a sense, and besides he was in the twilight of his years and energy. Leopardi's quest for sexual fulfillment was similarly doomed. Beyond his unexpressed attraction at the age of nineteen for his lovely but older and married cousin, Geltrude Cassi, he experienced two more strong passions, again for married women: that for Teresa Carniani Malvezzi of Bologna in 1826; the other and more anguishing, for Fanny Targioni Tozzetti of Florence in 1830-33.

A few words on Leopardi and love, which he seemed to need desperately to give and receive.[19] The question of Leopardi and women is a poignant one, characterized by an intensity of physical desire (it appears he was healthily sexed), a strong tendency to idealize women, his fears that they would either scorn his love or that the desired-dreaded fulfillment would inevitably end in disillusion, and the acute disadvantage of being physically repellent in a culture stressing personal beauty. Whether or not he died a virgin, as Ranieri claimed, seems unanswerable; that he never found a woman to love him is unquestionable. All the more reason to form strong attachments to men, which Leopardi did. On the basis of affectionate letters exchanged between Leopardi and Ranieri during a long winter's separation, some have sniffed out homosexuality, but this does not seem likely. As the biographer Origo notes, members of the same sex used extremely strong terms of endearment during the romantic epoch. (For that matter, the intensity of language and physical contact displayed even by Italians today is usually puzzling to the Anglo-American.) Furthermore, Leopardi was appalled by homosexuality, labeling it "infamous unnaturalness" in his notebook.

The largest disappointment, however, as Leopardi himself sensed and expressed it, was that regarding achievement and fame. The large amount of distinguished writing, translating, and editing Leopardi produced, despite his disastrous health, and the respect he generated in the minds of many contemporaries might have pleased him but it did not satisfy him. His desire always outran reality. For one thing his explicit world view was definitely out of tune with the brassy optimism around him. If at times he sounds querulous on the topic, it is understandable: like Melville and other dark prophets, he had trouble finding an ear for some of his ideas, much less honor. Further, the man who could say that the truly great measure themselves not against others but against themselves and the dimly seen possibilities of their art was bound to feel a sense of failure. Leopardi seems sincere when he says to Lebreton in the June, 1836, letter, "I have never done real work. I have made only attempts." These words were written at Naples, where his friend Ranieri had taken him to coax a few more years out of his life. When death came in June, 1837, it took an outstanding writer, who but for the opposition of the stars might have been even greater.

In the building of his *sistema*, [20] Leopardi drew nurture from his vast reading. From his study of ancient "superstitions," Leopardi learned to identify with the ancients; from reading ancient and modern rationalists and materialists in order to refute them knowledgeably, he grew to admire them. A mere listing of influences would take pages, as the *Zibaldone* index would show. Suffice to say that Leopardi's poetry and poetic theory owed much to Homer, Longinus, Virgil, Horace, Dante, Tasso, Petrarch, Burke and the English "graveyard poets," Alfieri, and Foscolo. Among the materialist or skeptical philosophers he respected deeply were Lucretius, Epictetus, Hobbes, Montaigne, Locke, Rousseau, Voltaire, Condillac, Chateaubriand, Helvétius, and d'Holbach. The tragic writings of Sophocles, Euripides, and of the authors of *Job* and *Ecclesiastes* played a part in his development, as did the speculations of Pascal, Vico, and Leopardi's beloved Madame de Staël. If one were forced to reduce this list to names of those who had the greatest impact on Leopardi's mind, one might choose Homer, Lucretius, Locke, Rousseau, and de Staël.

Like other romantics, Leopardi inherited the problem of belief, of "placing" man in a post-Cartesian universe where matter and spirit seemed at odds. The problem for Leopardi was probably exacerbated by personal factors. For figures like Blake, Coleridge, Emerson, and Shelley, the answer lay in differing versions of transcendental idealism which invested their worlds with benign spiritual presence and meaning. Even Poe, apparently such a materialist, held that the goal of poetry was supernal Beauty, and in his *Eureka* he outlined a cosmogony merging the physical and spiritual dimensions. As for Leopardi, many have attempted to idealize or spiritualize his meanings, but he himself attempted unblinkingly to create a system or mythos which would deliberately exclude the numinous. During and after his philosophical conversion, he embraces Locke and rejects absolutes: "There is hardly any absolute truth except that *All is relative.*" [21] And he self-consciously adopts the posture of Montaigne, asserting that "I by nature am not far from doubt even about things regarded undoubtable." With almost a dread of accepting supernal causation or facile explanations, no matter how attractive, Leopardi seeks to analyze man's practical and mental life in terms of a material cosmos. In a fallen world, with man uprooted and God gone or *"absconditus,"* as Pascal feared at times, Leopardi tries materially and systematically to justify the woes of man to men.

Such a task is not easy even for a great philosopher, which Leopardi was not, and the reader approaching Leopardi should arm himself with fruitful reservations about the ambiguities and tensions in the scheme at any point of Leopardi's development. In the first place, no system or program has ever accounted for the greatness of an artist, no matter how fond certain writers have been of their mythos. The riches and paradoxes of Yeats and Zola transcend gyres and chromosomes. With Leopardi, the philosophical ideas only begin to set up the impact of the art. Second, although for the sake of tidiness I will discuss the phases of Leopardi's thought, the truth is that for Leopardi almost no important idea or attitude is exclusive to one period; rather, a complex of attitudes bulges prominently in one phase of his life or another.

Leopardi's early system, heavily conditioned by Rousseau, is sometimes described as his "historical" pessimism because of the linear fall he ascribes to man, from a state of nature to one of civilization. In nature, man felt a unity with his cosmos, and though he was unhappy at times, nature supplied him with a rich imaginative life. The saving illusions granted to man tempered his pain sporadically, lifted him beyond self-love and self-immersion, fended off tedium and despair, and fulfilled his ingrained yearnings toward beauty, meaning, happiness, and the infinite. In the "denatured" or civilized condition, man has fallen into a world dominated by intellect, science, and truth, and he has no sure, continuing access to those "sacred" and vivifying illusions. The twin horrors which make modern life nearly unbearable are the vision of *nulla* and the experience of *noia*. Using his intellect or reason, man inevitably peers into the abyss of *nulla*, or nothingness, the void of his and the universe's purposelessness. More biting even than this vision is the enduring of *noia,* an untranslatable concept, indelibly associated with Leopardi, to which the English words "tedium" and "spleen" and even Baudelaire's "ennui" are inadequate. As the reader will see, Leopardi kept on expanding and refining the idea. (Words for things and states we constantly experience are, after all, the ones that become irregular or complicated in their usage.) At its root, *noia* is the *"taedium vitae"* described by countless writers over time, but Leopardi goes further. It is the psycho-spiritual paralysis which makes all physical, moral and intellectual activity or affirmation impossible and undesired, a kind of becalming reminiscent of Carlyle's "Center of Indifference." Taking the idea even further, as Leopardi does in some of his *Zibaldone* entries and *Pensieri, noia* is the state in which life-energy or desire pulsates for engagement but there is no goal or journey to occupy it. Put another way, it is desire, having no object, eating away at its own psychic container—a kind of mental or spiritual ulceration. Add to these ideas the fact that Leopardi eventually came to consider the experience of *noia* not only as a curse but as the paradoxical badge of a person's sensitivity and capacity to be regenerated and exalted, and one begins to appreciate his meanings. (While compelled to find rough equivalents in the translations of the poems, I have usually left the Italian word undisturbed in the prose.) As to the cause of man's fall from the natural Eden, Leopardi is quite ambiguous. Refusing to blame the devil or cite the abhorrent idea of original sin, he is left to shadowy references to the passage of time and the pursuit of truth. While this myth of a decline may be philosophically untidy, Leopardi does no worse than other thinkers on the problem of evil. Besides, the myth is imaginatively productive, suggesting as it does a parallel between the life of the race and that of each human who falls from childhood.

There is, of course, a large fly in the Rousseauvian broth: Leopardi could not explain through this scheme the recorded misery of the ancients, and the more he read and pondered Theophrastus, Pindar, Sophocles, the writers of *Job* and *Esslesiastes,* and other tragic ancient authors, the more the pressure mounted on him to discard Rousseau. In mid-career, therefore, and certainly by the time he wrote most of the *Operette Morali* in 1824, Leopardi began to stress what is often called his "cosmic" pessimism. In this view, the inevitable suffering of man has not developed historically but has always been. The "unhappy truth" is that man's undeserved pain, unfulfillable longing, and monumental insignificance are not anomalies caused by his alienation from nature but features built into his existence by nature herself. Nature is conceived as an abstract force whose surface beauty masks a core sometimes indifferent, usually hostile, always inscrutable. As the Icelander of the dialogue puts it, she is the "executioner" of her own children. Since being means pain, emptiness, and *noia*—the more sentience the more *noia*—it would have been better for man, as Leopardi and Job agree, had he not been born. Failing that, the existence of the zoophyte[22] is preferable. If one is condemned to life as a human, then one might as well prefer to be great rather than puny, reasons the soul in one of Leopardi's dialogues; to which nature responds with an amen: "Live then, and be great and unhappy."[23] At this rock-bottom of Leopardi's despair, there are only a few explicit avenues of temporary escape for humans: the conscious pursuit of illusions and diversions and the occasional burst of beauty afforded by love or the aesthetic experience. The ruling principle, however, is *male.* If in Italian the word means more than "evil"—the ideas of hurt and wrongness may also be implied—that is little compensation for suffering man in Leopardi's system.

Leopardi expresses this full-fledged cosmic pessimism in the *Operette Morali,* the works which (Carducci noted) Dante would have described as "eating away layer by layer at the heart and mind producing them. . . ."[24] Although there are still holdovers of attraction toward the ancient state, it is significant that in the *Operette Morali* Leopardi places characters over a wide spectrum of real or mythic time and space so as to generalize their woe. There are real historical persons (Plotinus, Columbus, Copernicus, Tasso, Parini), figures from traditional mythology (Prometheus, Momus, Atlas), and more or less mythic personae of his own creation who exist timelessly (the Icelander, Nature). In any case, it is these *Operette,* on the surface so disenchanted, which came to identify Leopardi as an unwavering pessimist to be grouped, and sometimes dismissed, along with Schopenhauer, Hartmann, and the Buddha.

If Leopardi's vision consisted only of the negative lessons of his cosmic pessimism there would be little further to say about him or to experience through him. One who courts or studies nonbeing can only repeat himself and wait. But Leopardi does not end there and we cannot; his works have redemptive and energetic values which invite attention.

Sporadically through Leopardi's writings and then emphatically after 1828–29, a different explicit attitude emerges toward nature, man, and civilization. Call this posture what we will—titanism, heroism, humanism, existentialism—the fact is that Leopardi gradually clarified a stubborn positive belief in man's ability to move with relative grace in a world where the odds are against him. As far back as the June 23, 1823, letter to his Belgian friend Jacoppsen, Leopardi mused that men might be happier if they could be loving, enthusiastic, and virtuous, important words to him. If to love virtue and each other ardently is to indulge in illusions, so be it: the trick of life then is to agree on our shared illusions (Wallace Stevens was to call them the "supreme fiction") and to pursue them. Here, as Whitfield observes, is the motif which will grow pronounced in works like the *Dialogue of Plotinus and Porphyry* and swell majestically in Leopardi's late poetic testament to man, *La ginestra,* or *Broom.* Leopardi's final and humanistic position, which is clear even though he did not live to articulate it completely, rests on our distinguishing limitations from capabilities, creative illusions from destructive ones, wishes from realities, friends from foes. In his thinking, nature is the chief enemy. Although she brings us forth, we are to her as children to a mindlessly destructive stepmother; or, to change the image, we are as expendable as the broom-plant is to Vesuvius, on whose desert slopes it briefly lives. Leopardi argues—in a sweeping attack on nineteenth-century idealisms—that we should reject the false myth-makers and illusion-weavers: those who would teach us that we are perfectible either in this world or another; that through religion or socio-scientific engineering, or some combination, we can achieve, regain, or create paradise. In the satirical and awesomely entitled *Paralipomeni della Batracomiomachia* (his "additions" to the pseudo-Homeric *War of the Mice and the Crabs*), Leopardi strongly attacks the idea that man has fallen from anything; there never was a glorious primitive state *(pace* Rousseau). As Leopardi says in a startling metaphor, the city did not precede the citizens, the citizens came before the city.

This concept of existential citizenry is the heart of Leopardi's humanism. If we are to live with dignity on the volcano's edge with no aid from without, we must become ever more civilized. This means recognizing that *we* are all we have, that against our common doom we must pit the force of fraternal love. We can do this because despite our weakness, vulnerability, and lamentable tendencies toward self-love and self-deception, humans are flexible and can learn through necessity and habituation (the Lockean attack on innate ideas served Leopardi till the end). Leopardi suggests something even more important, if quite sacrilegious—that despite our smallness relative to the vast impersonal cosmos, we are potentially more decent and civil than anything else in that cosmos. Some aspects of this position look back to Lucretius, others to *Candide,* although the garden Leopardi urges us to cultivate is even more modest, dry, and besieged than Voltaire's. Furthermore, the reader may see anticipations here of the Sartre who could write that "life begins on the other side of despair" and the Camus who could recreate the toil of Sisyphus for us.

As important to Leopardi as the nature of existence was the nature of poetry,[25] and not surprisingly there are connections between his reflections on both subjects. The young Leopardi tended to see art the way Aristotle and most neoclassical writers had, in terms of imitating the objective experiences and truths *there* in nature. The older Leopardi was much more romantically oriented in stressing the creativity of the individual human imagination. In short, nature or the outer world cedes some power and authority to man and the subjective faculties. One element that remains constant is Leopardi's stubborn attempt to root the aesthetic experience within the material dimension.

Leopardi's early view of poetry is linked essentially to his schematic interpretation of the ancient state's superiority over the modern. The imagination of the ancient poet, Homer being the supreme example, was intimately activated by a benign nature. His goal was to imitate nature directly, to capture beauty and sublimity, the proffered illusions, clearly, simply, and with a kind of natural ease or negligence (*sprezzatura*). The ancient could be truly imaginative because he was closer to nature, the source of imagination, and he was not as intellectually prone "to murder to dissect" as the modern poet is. The modern, distanced from nature and living in an age of "truth," science, and prose, substitutes the sentimental for the imaginative; the pathetic for the sublime; the analysis of self for the presentation of nature; emotion about things for the things themselves; the willed for the inevitable. If the modern occasionally rises to imaginative heights, it is usually through evoking childhood, the state wherein his vision approximates the ancient's. Common to poets of any era is the imaginative craving for the infinite despite the tendency of the intellect to shrink perception and deny the infinite. Influenced by Longinus and such English theoreticians as Burke and Akenside, Leopardi dwells lovingly on the subject of how certain words and things can electrify the imagination to contemplate the sublime and seemingly raise us above the sphere of earth and reason.

This ancient-modern aesthetic is not unique, must of it resting on neoclassical doctrine and on the ideas of earlier writers who had exalted the naive and the primitive (e.g., Vico, Rousseau, Schiller). As Leopardi matured, however, his aesthetic ideas shifted like his general philosophy and took on a more romantic and personal character. It is striking that just as he came to distrust the intentions and validity of objective nature and to put a greater faith in man's active creating and controlling of illusions, so in his criticism there grew a greater respect for the most subjective of poetic forms—the lyric—and for the creative, not imitative, power of the imagination. René Wellek points out that in the privacy of his *Zibaldone,* Leopardi eventually urged "more radically than anybody else in contemporary Europe" the cause of the lyric, which he came to consider the "summit" of literary expression.[26] Simultaneously, he grew to deprecate the more objective genres like the drama and epic; indeed his comments on the epic sound much like Poe's attacks on the essential prosiness of *Paradise Lost*. The essence of the lyric poem for Leopardi is the initial emotional-imaginative surge or impulse *(impeto),* which when processed in tranquility through the poet's memory could result in good poetry. As for the imagination, it does not merely record or combine, but rather it invents or makes *(fabbrica);* and the imagination's product not only can stir our sense of beauty but can also lift us morally, no matter how dark the substance. Here Poe is left to one side, and Leopardi draws closer to Shelley and Wordsworth.

Even though the imagination can ennoble and *seem* to carry us beyond, Leopardi is usually careful to locate the source of beauty *within* the universe. Those who attempt to idealize or supernalize his attitude or diction must reckon with a pervasive caution he himself shows. For example, there is a passage from the early *Discourse of an Italian on Romantic Poetry* where Leopardi describes an unearthly experience: "I myself remember in my childhood my imagination's seizing upon the sensation of a sound so sweet it was never heard on earth." It would be easy to read this as evidence of a Shelleyan affirmation of supernal beauty—until we grow accustomed to Leopardi and recognize his belief in the illusory force of the imagination and his tell-tale inclusion of words like "sensation" in such texts. Again, in his late poem *On the Likeness of a Beautiful Woman*, Leopardi notes how humans are vile and weak but seemingly "in part of nobler birth." Some translators render the word "nobler" as "divine,"[27] but that is not what Leopardi said. Indeed, when Leopardi actually uses the word "divine" in his writing, he seems very conscious that he is using time-honored but loose and hyperbolic language, and we should be similarly conscious in order to understand him fully. Elsewhere in *On the Likeness* Leopardi explicitly cites the natural rather than supernatural derivation of beauty, its apparent rather than its real quality:

> The dazzling light which pulses from the heart
> Of timelesss nature falls
> Upon these lower sands,
> Seeming to give the index and sure hope
> Of more than human possibilities,
> Of realms more fortunate and golden worlds.

The writer who penned those lines seems clearly to be at the same time a yearning idealist *and* a careful rationalist. Reading such passages exclusively one way or the other denies to Leopardi his tensions and his agony.

Whatever the period of Leopardi's thoughts on poetry, he remains constant to certain ideas. He continually dwells on the special power in certain words to shimmer in the imagination and lure us beyond our too-definite reality. His ideas on style greatly shaped by ancient languages (especially Greek) and the habits of Greco-Roman and Italian poets, he deplores the obscurity and complexity of moderns like Goethe and applauds instead the classical virtues: clarity, naturalness, and the demand on poets to hide their art. Needless to say, Leopardi always preferred classical writers to his own contemporaries: "Everything has improved since Homer, but not poetry."[28]

Leopardi's poems are usually thought to be, especially by those who read Italian, the high point of his achievement. Indeed, the vortex of appreciation has at times threatened to swallow up the varied riches of Leopardi's other expressions. Some critics have tried to break down Leopardi's poems into exclusive types—idyllic, elegiac, heroic, philosophical, and the like. But this tendency often throws more darkness than light over the poems, and could lead as sensitive a reader as Croce to rebuke Leopardi for getting too philosophical in poems where he should have remained idyllic. What rigidly categorical readers may fail to recognize is that Leopardi himself was much more supple and iconoclastic about poetry than his admiration of the past would lead us to think. That flexibility led him to chafe increasingly against needless strictures to form and expression (including rhyme). Leopardi began by trying to make sharp distinctions between his idylls, *canzoni,* and *odi-canzoni,* but he ended by calling nearly all his poems simply *Canti.* He consciously experimented with lyric poetry, trying to expand the scope of what could be done in it. Less consciously, perhaps, he was taking part in a striking poetic development which cut across national boundaries and linked romantic poets—the evolution of what M. H. Abrams has called "the greater romantic lyric."[29] According to Abrams, who focuses on the English romantics, this new poetic form mixed lyrical nature description and internal meditation; it featured an "out-in-out process, in which mind confronts nature and their interplay constitutes the poem." In examining such poems as *Memories* and *The Village Saturday,* we can see how Abrams's acute induction applies beyond *Tintern Abbey* and the English romantics. We can also caution ourselves against *a priori* labels and admire the way in which the isolated, classically leaning Leopardi could be so attuned to the romantic frequencies of his time.

In the early patriotic *canzoni* of 1818 *(To Italy* and *On the Monument of Dante),* Leopardi showed his attraction to ancient heroic ideals and adopted the posture of the national bard trying to tongue-lash the consciousness of Italians to the level of that of their Greco-Roman forebears. Quickly, however, Leopardi found his own personal stride and by 1819-20, with the writing of *The Infinite* and *To the Moon,* he is creating subjective lyrics stamped with his own style and substance. Although the slightly later *Brutus, To Spring,* and *The Last Song of Sappho* refer on the surface to ancient myth and history, the speakers are projections of Leopardi, and the personal statements reveal his characteristic preoccupations. Except for possibly *The Infinite,* the lonely poet or persona of the early poems etches the tragic perceptions of one caught between two dimensions or times: time and self *then* as

20

against time and self *now;* the world as seen through illusion, memory, hope, and the affections compared to the world grasped by the disenchanted reason; the desire for love, life, fame, and virtue as opposed to the reality of our transience, pain, and ignominy. These themes repeat again and again in Leopardi. As Figurelli observed, "Leopardi is never the poet of immediate experience, and when he tried it he became inferior to himself. He does not chant his life, but the memory of it. . . ."[30] We could add that Leopardi must have approved of Dante's celebrated words, "No greater sorrow than to remember happy times in present misery."

One reason scholars can speak so confidently of Leopardi's later poems as a group is that they are set off by a long dry period in the middle of his career. During the 1823–28 period, Leopardi, seemingly convinced that a premature aging process had sapped his poetic abilities, devoted himself to the "truth" of existence and to the genre he then thought appropriate to it, prose. It is the period dominated by the *Operette Morali,* and although the latter have a poetry of their own— indeed in a few of them he pushed toward the prose poem[31]—the only important independent poem he produced at this time was the wistful and almost tired *To His Lady.* When the thaw came, however, it came decisively. Under the balmy influence of Pisa in the spring of 1828, Leopardi wrote *The Reawakening,* a description of the return of feeling and imagination to the dried-up mind, and *To Sylvia,* perhaps his perfect lyric. From this point on Leopardi was definitely a poet again, producing what most readers believe to be his greatest verse, for example, *Memories, Night-Song of a Wandering Shepherd of Asia,* and ultimately *Broom.* Although his earlier tragic themes persist (so that in a way one must read outside the poems to taste the complete author), the late poems show a tougher, more confident, at times heroic, cast of mind.[32] Even at the psychological low points of the later poems— which I take to be the poems of the *Aspasia* cycle inspired by the unfortunate love for Fanny Tozzetti—there is an irreducible core of flinty strength and pride. The poem *To Himself* ends with Leopardi staring down at deceiving nature as if he held her in great scorn. And in the not completely successful *Aspasia* poem, he can describe the passage through the burning rites of unreturned love and willed deception to that purified point where he can lie at ease upon the grass, "gaze at ocean, earth, and sky, and smile."

Almost inevitably, the later poems are leaner in imagery, metaphor, and diction than the earlier ones, and they have less color. Increasingly Leopardi indulges in philosophical discourse in the poems, as if he were questioning the beauty-truth, poetry-prose distinctions and moving toward a master concept of expression which would shatter the old polarities. (Perella says that the late Leopardi saw poetry "as the expression of the human spirit no longer able to wander freely in a rich illusory world and so reduced to a poetry that has more in common with 'philosophy.' "[33]) Just as noticeable in the later verse is the almost complete abandonment of classical mythology and any ornament extrinsic to Leopardi himself. Some of the later poems are extremely intimate evocations of personal history against the background of man's fate *(To Sylvia* or *The Calm after the Storm)*. Others involve mythic but not mythological figures; that is, "characters" such as the wandering shepherd and the broom-plant take on the mythic size and intensity of the Icelander of the prose piece, but all these mythic creations come from within not without. They arise not from the escape from reality but from the personal encounter with it, not from the opposition of beauty and truth but from the attempt to ground one in the other. That is why we often get the sense in Leopardi's late works of being in the presence of an ancient tragic Greek or Hebrew come again to speak in modern yet timeless terms.

Once we have sketched the explicit features of Leopardi's life, system, and art, we have still not accounted for those qualities which have sent readers away inspired rather than depressed, expanded rather than belittled. Depression comes from reading Leopardi's biography, not his work.

One of the positive appeals of Leopardi is the sheer display of and concern for morality. Many have pointed out that Leopardi was not a complete philosopher; rather, he was interested in the problem of wrong in the world and how we should act to right it, a problem which forms only part of a metaphysician's concern.[34] In a world he perceives to be dominated by mystery and pain, he searched for ways to act. The German scholar Vossler framed some of the essential Leopardian questions as these: "Why do men sympathize so much with each other while at the same time they hate each other? How is it they are sociable while each seeks his self-interest? Why are they so bold while each is so attached to life? Why is life so monotonous when once it was so varied? Why are joy, art, poetry, love, faith, and hope receding from the world? Why is happiness always more rare while everything tends toward it?"[35] Some Italian scholars have even tried to link this eudaemonistic questioning on Leopardi's part to the development of nineteenth-century Anglo-American pragmatism, the view that the justification of belief is in our action.[36]

This moral quest may seem quaint to the reader who expects moral sensibility to be based on a theistic view of the world. Such a reader must solve that problem on his own, for despite Leopardi's materialism the moral dimension is undeniably and crucially present, and it reveals itself in rhetorical as well as substantial ways. Consider what Leopardi's fundamental criticism of nature and life is. At bottom he attacks in an almost childlike way the failure of justice, virtue, and honesty. He cannot accept the idea of original sin because to him that means accepting the idea of unfair punishment for something one did not do. He will not entertain the idea of an ideal Platonic dimension because belief in such a world does not really solve the problem of hurt in this one. He will not trust in a Christian afterlife because it is too little and too late; for him, to use contemporary terms, "Justice delayed is justice denied." And he sees no reason to expect less moral behavior from nature (often seemingly invoked as a codeword for some higher force) than from men. Furthermore, the virtues Leopardi demands from actions in this life extend to *thinking* about life. Bickersteth correctly said that "scrupulous honesty both of heart and head was throughout life Leopardi's greatest moral quality."[37] While we must acknowledge the possibility of a totally corrupt person writing beautifully, nonetheless when we read Leopardi we have the inescapable sense that morality of mind and purity of style in this case do reflect each other. Leopardi is everywhere in his verbalization preoccupied with rightness. He labors to be as lucid, logical, and precise as he knows how at the moment. Except when he uses an "etcetera" to remind himself to fill in later, he is ruthlessly complete and clean in his discussion. If three elements are introduced in the premises of a paragraph or essay, those three will, almost tediously at times, reappear in the summary or conclusion. Often in his prose, Leopardi does something surprising for a poet: he apologizes for hyperbole or metaphor by inserting the words "in a sense" or "so to speak." This is partly the usage of the scholar he was, but it is also the caution of a mind that does not wish to distort, even to itself. Just as in the strictly active sphere, Leopardi demands justice and honesty—a proper relation between causes and effects, actions and results, behavior and fate—so in the sphere of words he illustrates sincerity, logic, precision, clarity, and balance. Perhaps there is only one word which can cover Leopardi's concern for verbal and ethical rightness. It is integrity.

Connected to this essential decency of Leopardi's mind, there is the central paradox that no matter how hard Leopardi works to present his disillusioned version of man's real position, his positive values shine through. Whitfield argues convincingly that "Leopardi's dismay is the gauge also of his affirmation. . . . No statement of Leopardi is greater than its opposite, and if the tragedy in which man is involved is immense for Leopardi, it is because the stature of man partakes of that immensity."[38] In the *Night-Song* he affirms the pain and *noia* of life while at the same time revealing his awed appreciation of the universe's stunning swirl. In *The Setting of the Moon*, that somber elegy on the death of man and the seeming triumph of darkness, he exhilarates us by describing the sun continuing to suffuse the world. What kind of atheist is this who takes such comfort in the stars? Even in the *Operette*, supposedly his unadorned attack on man and nature, if not more, the words "magnanimous," "virtuous," "noble" continually pop up to disclose the true value system.[39] The ideas of pain, hatred, *noia*, disillusion, and nonbeing take their ultimate meaning in terms of joy, love, vitality, wonder, and being—the desiderata of Leopardi's heart. De Sanctis, who had the pleasure when a boy studying at Naples of meeting Leopardi, described Leopardi's ambivalent impact this way:

> . . . Leopardi produces an effect opposite to the one he proposes. He does not believe in progress and he makes you crave it; he does not believe in liberty and he makes you love it. He calls love, glory, and virtue illusions, and he kindles in your breast an insatiable desire for them. And you cannot lay him down without feeling better for it; and you cannot approach him without first collecting and purifying yourself so that you will not have to blush in his presence. He is a skeptic and he makes you a believer. . . . He has so low an opinion of humanity, and his lofty, pure, and gentle spirit honors and ennobles it.[40]

The essential Leopardi does lie in the search for these qualities and in the way that search is expressed by words and art. At all moments of his career, no matter how he struggles against self-deception, no matter what his personal or philosophical torment, Leopardi shows an enduring trust in literature; in the power of well-chosen words to clarify our being and even for a time to make us whole instead of riven. That is what he is getting at in the *Zibaldone* paragraphs where he describes the exalting effect of great imaginative works, no matter how tragic. And Leopardi's spokesman in the *Dialogue of Timander and Eleander* phrases it even more explicitly:

> If any moral book could be useful, I think that poetic books could be most so. I say "poetic" in the broad sense, that is, books aimed at moving the imagination. And I mean prose works as well as verse. Now I am not impressed by that poetry which when read and meditated fails to leave in the reader's mind for half an hour a feeling noble enough to prevent him from harboring a mean thought or doing an unworthy act. But if the reader breaks

faith with his best friend one hour after the reading, I would not therefore blame that poetry—for then I would have to scorn the most beautiful, the most impassioned, the most noble poems of the world.

Despite the pervasive melancholy in Leopardi (especially in the poems) and his occasional self-pity and querulousness, many of his utterances have the feature he describes. It is a function of a style and address, for want of a better word, that is dimmed by translation and is only faintly describable in any language. Perhaps Croce came close when he said that certain Leopardi passages "express themselves with the reserve, the modesty, the chastity of one saying things he is no longer used to saying."[41] Whether the words are those of an idealist *manqué,* a supreme rationalist, a proto-existentialist, a true believer or true skeptic, are issues with which we must wrestle. Suffice to say that Leopardi reminds us of what it is to be a poet and what it is to be human.

I

YOUNG LEOPARDI (to 1822): PROMISE AND EARLY SORROW

Young Leopardi (to 1822):
Promise and Early Sorrow

———

Though Leopardi had already become a classical scholar to reckon with, the year 1817 marks the beginning of the his characteristic literary expression. It was then that he experienced the disturbing beauty of his cousin, Geltrude Cassi, a one-sided and impossible attraction which prefigured later, more damaging affairs of the heart. Even more importantly, he struck up correspondence with the liberal and patriotic ex-Benedictine, Pietro Giordani, who was to be a good friend and who sensed the promise in the youth who he felt could be a perfect writer. In the summer of the year, Leopardi began his voluminous *Zibaldone,* probably at the urging of Josef Vogel, the canon of the cathedral at nearby Loreto, who argued that every literary man should record his intellectual chaos. In the *Zibaldone* for these years, we see the log of Leopardi's mental life, from intimate observations on his mother, the attractions of suicide, and his "conversions" to more objective notes on ideas for poems, his developing system of enlightened materialism, and theories about language, art, and poetry. In the year 1821 alone, Leopardi wrote 1,853 manuscript pages in the *Zibaldone.*

Leopardi did almost no traveling in this period. Indeed, the first time he was allowed to go anywhere without supervision was in September, 1818, when he spent a few days in Macerata with the visiting Giordani. There was much from which to escape. Life in the Leopardi palazzo became more strained as Leopardi's changing ideas caused conflict with his parents and he stubbornly refused their apprehensive advice that, given his deformity, he should become a priest. As for Paolina, his beloved but homely sister, marriage was a possible escape from the family, but two successive suitors recoiled from her too eager advances and she was to remain a depressed and eccentric spinster. In July, 1819, Leopardi, having reached his majority, tried to flee Recanati, but his father's vigilance foiled him. Not till the Roman trip of 1822–23 was the young man to get a real taste of the outer world.

In these years Leopardi became a poet despite his poor eyes and generally wretched health. Fired by his frustration at the condition of Italy ("a geographical expression" to Count Metternich, the architect of Austrian occupation) and prompted by Giordani, Leopardi composed in 1818 the two *canzoni* which were to associate him with the cause of liberation—*To Italy* and *On the*

Monument of Dante. The opening lines of the first poem announce the idea and spirit uniting both:

> O native land, I see the arches, walls,
> The columns, statues, and deserted towers
> Raised by our ancestors,
> But the glory I do not see. . . .

Despite the youthful rhetoric, these sincere poems, so atypical of Leopardi's later writings, spread his name well beyond Recanati and were even quoted ·by Italian soldiers in World War I. Of much greater moment in the history of high art are the six mature poems included below, beginning with *The Infinite,* the most anthologized of Leopardi's works.

∾

1. To Pietro Giordani (Milan)

Most esteemed and dearest Signore: That I should really see and read Giordani's words, that he should be writing to me, that I may hope to have him as a mentor from now on—these are things I can barely believe. Nor would you wonder if you knew how long and how affectionately I have dwelled on this thought, for the things one desires most seem still impossible when they come to pass. I want you to believe implicitly in everything I write you now and later, even the smallest phrases, for all of them—and I promise it—will come from the heart. This I insist upon; everything else I will request.

My first letter issued more from respect than from affection, for the latter, welcome and honorable among equals, is often offensive to superiors. Now that your two dear letters have given me leave, rest assured that I will address you with all affection. You may guess that the cause of that affection is your excellence in the studies that I love. I have known you only through your writings, for here where I live, not a soul discusses literary men. But I do not know how one can admire a writer's qualities—especially when they are great and striking—without coming to like the person too. When I read Virgil, I fall in love with him. And I do so even more with the great contemporaries, who are so few, as you rightly point out. . . .

I possess an extremely great, perhaps immoderate and insolent, desire for glory, but I cannot stand it when people praise things of mine which do not please me, nor do I know why they re-issue them with more damage to me than profit to those who do so without my knowledge. . . .

As for the second book of the *Aeneid,* which I have not yet condemned, only the three men of letters you know of have seen any of it. I wrote to them from the heart, fulfilling (with some trepidation) an old and strong desire. I believed before that my book had many flaws; now I am really sure because Monti has told me so. . . . I will not write him more for fear of bothering him, but I ask you to thank him warmly for me. But it's not enough to say to a blind man, "You're going the wrong way," if you don't add, "This is the way to go." Nothing is dearer to me than learning the faults in one of my pieces, because I see the immense usefulness, and it seems to me that once one has recognized a vice one can always avoid it.

As a teacher, you say that translating is very rewarding at my age, a sure proposition which my own practice has made most clear to me. For when I read one of the classics, my mind seethes and grows confused. So then I begin to translate as best I can, and those beauties, by necessity scrutinized and mulled over one by one, fix themselves in my imagination, enrich it, and bring peace to me. Your judgment renews me and encourages me to continue.

Do not speak to me of Recanati. It is so dear to me as to suggest ideas for a dissertation on "Hatred for One's Birthplace.". . . But my country is Italy, for which I burn with love, thanking heaven for making me an Italian, for ultimately our literature, even though little cultivated, is the only legitimate daughter of the only two truly great ancient ones. . . . You can rest assured that if I live, I will do so for literature, because I cannot live for anything else, nor do I wish to.

I have chattered so much I have probably put you to sleep by now. Your letters have raised my spirits . . . [Recanati, March 21, 1817].

2. To Pietro Giordani (Milan)
    Oh how often, my dear and longed for Signor Giordani, have I prayed to heaven to let me find a man with heart, genius, and unusual erudition, and who, once found, I might hope would offer me his friendship. And truly I believed my wishes would not be granted because I hardly thought that these three qualities, so rarely found alone, could be found united. May God be praised (I say this with a full heart) for granting me what I asked and showing me the error of my doubt. . . .
    You recommend moderation in my studies with such warmth and evident concern that I wish to open my heart to you and let you know the feelings that reading your words has awakened in me, feelings which will never, never die unless the heart changes form and substance. To answer as best I can to such affection, I will tell you that my

health is not just weak but excessively so; and I will not deny that it has been a bit affected by the labors to which I subjected it the last six years. But now I have reduced them considerably: I do not study more than six hours a day, often less; I write almost nothing; I regularly read the classics of the three languages in small volumes easily carried about, so that I must always study in the mode of the Peripatetics; and—*quod maximum dictu est*—I often endure for hours and hours the torment of sitting with my hands in my lap.

Who would have dreamed Giordani would leap to the defense of Recanati? . . . The cause is too desperate for a single good advocate—or a hundred. It's all very well to say that Plutarch loved his Chaeronea and Alfieri his Asti. They loved them but did not live there. So I too shall love my birthplace when I am far away from it; meanwhile, I say I hate it because I am in it, since this poor town is guilty only of not having offered me one good thing besides my family. It is sweet and beautiful to remember the place where one has spent his childhood. Yet it is too easy to say: "Here you were born and here Providence wants you to stay." Say to a sick man, "If you try to heal yourself, you are fighting Providence," or to a poor man, "If you try to improve your lot, you are questioning Providence.". . . These maxims verge on Fatalism. "But here you are a large fish in a small pond; in a larger city it will be otherwise." This seems to me a low form of pride, one unworthy of a noble spirit. One wants to excel in virtue and genius, and who can deny that these qualities shine infinitely more in great cities than in small? . . .

"But here you could be more useful than elsewhere." In the first place, I do not like the thought of spending my life on this little group, of renouncing everything else to live and die for them in a cave. I do not think nature made me for this, nor that virtue requires of me such a fearsome sacrifice. Second, do you really believe that the Marches and southern Italy are like Romagna and northern Italy? There the word "literature" is often heard. There they have papers, academies, discussion groups, and bookshops in great number. Gentlemen read a little. Ignorance is for the masses, who wouldn't be the masses without it. But many try to study and many fancy themselves poets and philosophers; they may not really be such but they at least try. . . . Here, my dear Sir, everything is dead, everything is foolishness and stupidity. Foreigners are amazed at this silence, this universal sleep. Literature is a sound unheard of. The names of Parini, Alfieri, Monti, Tasso, and Ariosto have to be explained. There is no one who wants to be something else, not a one for whom the name of ignorant seems strange. They call each other that sincerely and know they speak the truth. Do you think a great mind would be esteemed here? As a pearl in a dung-heap. . . . Indeed, I will tell you without any boasting that our library has no equal in the province and only two inferiors. On the door it is written that this library is for citizens too and all are welcome. Now how many do you think frequent it? Never a one. . . .

In my early days, my head was full of modern principles and I scorned and loathed studying our language. All my first scribblings were translations from French; I disdained Homer, Dante, and all the classics; I would not read them; and I gloried in reading what I now detest. What made me change my tune? The grace of God, but no man certainly. Who urged me to learn the languages necessary to me? The grace of God. Who keeps me from blundering at every turn? No one. But let's suppose all of this means nothing. What is there that is beautiful in Recanati that a man would care to see or learn? Nothing. Now God has made this world of ours so lovely, men have created so many beautiful things, there are so many men who anyone but an insensate would long to see and know, and earth is rich with won-ders—and should I, at eighteen, say that I will live and die in this pit where I was born? Do you think that one can restrain these desires? That they are wrong, excessive, wild? That it is madness not to content oneself with seeing nothing, not to content oneself with Recanati?

Someone has misinformed you that the air of this town is healthy. It is most changeable, damp, salty, hard on the nerves, and because of its thinness unsuitable to some constitutions. Add to this the stubborn, black, horrendous, barbarous melancholy that wears away and de-vours me, and grows and grows whether I study or not. I well know, for I used to experience it, the sweet melancholy, sweeter than happi-ness, which gives birth to beauty. That kind of melancholy is, if I may speak so, like twilight whereas this one is densest night and horrible; it is a poison, as you say, that destroys the powers of body and soul. Now how shall I free myself from it while I do nothing but think and feed on thinking, with no distractions in the world? And how should the effect cease if the cause does not? And what do you mean by amusements? The only diversion in Recanati is studying: the only distraction is that which kills me—everything else is *noia*. . . .

You say that when one's intellect has matured to enough firmness so as to know with some surety where nature is calling it, one must necessarily begin writing prose rather than poetry. With this I must take issue. One can easily err when analyzing one's self, but I will tell you what I think has happened and is happening to me.

From the time I began to recognize a little what beauty is, only the poets aroused in me the keen desire to translate and make my own what I read; only nature and passion have led me to that rage to compose, but to compose in a forceful and elevated way, making my soul expand in all its parts and say within me: "This is poetry indeed, and I need verse, not prose, to express what I feel." And so I gave myself to poetry. Won't you allow me now to read Homer, Virgil, Dante and the other sublime poets? I do not think I could abstain, because I taste in reading them a pleasure beyond words; and very often, when I have been quiet, alone, and thinking of something entirely different, a verse of a classical author, by chance recited by a member of my family, makes me catch my breath and compels me to follow it. And when, in an hour friendly to the Muses, I have been alone in my study with my mind placid and free, and have picked up Cicero so as to try by reading him to lift my mind, I have been so distressed by the slow heaviness of that prose that I could not continue but took up Horace instead. And if you concede me these readings, can you expect me to recognize their greatness, to savor and analyze each separate beauty, without launching out after them?

Whenever I look at nature here in these truly pleasant surroundings (the only good thing my birthplace has), and in this time of year especially, I feel myself so completely transported that it would be a mortal sin to pay no heed, to let the ardor of youth go by, to wish to be a good prose-writer, and to postpone poetry a score of years—after which, first, I will not exist; second, these thoughts will have fled; or my mind will have grown colder or cooler than it is now. I need scarcely add that if nature calls one to poetry, one must ignore everything else to follow it; indeed, I think it manifest that poetry demands infinite toil and study, and that poetic art is so profound that the more one advances the more one realizes that perfection exists somewhere beyond what one had imagined. . . .

How can I, my dear Signor Giordani, beg your pardon for having written you a tome instead of a letter? I blush. . . . This is the first time I have opened my heart to you—how could I have dammed up the flood of thoughts? Another time I will be briefer, but much, much briefer . . . [Recanati, April 30, 1817].

ᕲ

3.   To Pietro Giordani (Milan)

 . . . But chiefly it is the absence of health that makes me unhappy, for I am not one of those philosophers who cares nothing for life, and beyond that, I am forced to stay far away from my beloved studies. Ah, dear Giordani, what do you think I do now? I get up late in the morning because now—oh hellish thing!—I prefer sleeping to waking. Then I immediately begin walking, and *I walk always without EVER opening my mouth or glancing at a book* until it is dinner-time. Having dined, I walk again as before, until supper. . . . Thus I live and have lived except for a few intervals the last six months. The other cause of my unhappiness is thought itself. I think you know, though I hope you haven't experienced it, how thinking can plague and torture someone who reasons somewhat differently from others, when it dominates him and he has no other relaxation but study and study itself does him more harm than good. . . . Thinking . . . will kill me if I do not alter my way of living. . . . In short, solitude is not for those who burn and consume themselves from within . . . [Recanati, August 8, 1817].

4.   A great truth it is, but one well worth contemplating. Reason is the enemy of everything great; reason is the enemy of nature; nature is great and reason is small. What I mean is that the more a man is dominated by reason, the less chance or the more difficulty he will have in being great. Few can achieve greatness (perhaps none in art or poetry) unless they are ruled by illusions. This is so because the things we deem great—a difficult undertaking, for example—lie ordinarily outside the order of things and amount to a kind of disorder. Now this disorder is condemned by reason. Example: the great enterprise of Alexander—all illusion . . . [undated, Z, 14].

5.   From my bed I hear the tower clock sound (or strike). Remembrances of those summer nights in which, as a boy left in a dark room with the shades drawn, between fear and courage I used to hear a similar clock striking . . . [undated, Z, 36].

6.   One of the great proofs of the soul's immortality is the unhappiness of man compared to the beasts, who are happy or almost so, in that the anticipation of ills (absent in animals), the passions, the discontent with the present, the impossibility of satisfying desires, and all the other sources of infelicity make us inevitably and essentially wretched

by our very nature, which produces the unhappiness and cannot be changed. This shows that our existence is not completed in this temporal space like that of the brutes . . . [undated, Z, 40].

↜

7. To Pietro Giordani (Milan)

. . . For the longest time, I firmly believed I would die in at most two or three years. But in the last eight months now, that is from about the time I entered my twentieth year . . . I have recognized and persuaded myself—with no wishful thinking or self-deceit, for these, *caro,* are unfortunately impossible with me—that there is not enough cause for me to die soon, and provided I took scrupulous care, I might live on, even if hanging on to life by my teeth. . . .

. . . In short, I have ruined myself by seven years of mad and desperate study at a time when my constitution was being shaped. And I have woefully and incurably ruined myself for the rest of my life, rendering my appearance terrible and despicable to most people, who are capable only of looking at that large aspect of man. And in this world one must converse with most people. And not just with the many, but with anyone inclined to expect that virtue have some external sign or ornament. Such persons, finding virtue nude, become depressed and by force of nature, which no wisdom can conquer, almost lack the courage to love the virtuous man who possesses no beauty outside his soul. With this and other miseries, fortune has ringed my life.

. . . But I will endure, because I was born to endure, and I will endure not only the particular loss of physical vigor but also the common loss of youth. And I will console myself with you and the thought that I have found a true friend in this life, a thing I could have only hoped for earlier . . . [Recanati, March 2, 1818].

↜

8. From the *Discourse of an Italian on Romantic Poetry*[1]

In March, 1818, Leopardi tried to enter the "war" then being waged between classicists and romanticists in Italy by penning a long essay attacking the new romantic school. Ludovico Di Breme and other romanticists were contending that Italian literature had to become modern, as that of northern Europe had done; that moderns should reject the quaint, naive mythology of the ancients in favor of a truer, more useful vision; that current writers were superior to the ancients in their ability to touch and reveal the heart; and that literature should reflect the lives and language of common men. Although Leopardi was later to share some of the assumptions of the romantics, he was at this time still very much his aristocratic father's son and a decided classicist. In his response (unfortunately unpublished till 1906), he struck at the romanticists' socio-politics as well as their aesthetics. The reader should also consult the closely related poem *To Spring,* given below.

. . . Now it is most clear that the romantics are striving to shunt poetry as much as they can away from the commerce with the senses, for which it was born and shall live as long as it is poetry, and to connect it with the intellect; to drag it from the visible to the invisible, from things to ideas; to transform it from the material, fanciful, and sensuous it once was into the metaphysical, rational, and spiritual. The Cavaliere Di Breme says that the poetic frenzy of the ancients came above all from ignorance, which caused them to marvel "stupidly" at everything, to believe they saw a miracle at every step, and thus they found subjects for poetry in every event and imagined a host of supernatural forces, ghosts, and dreams. And he adds that since modern men have examined, learned, understood, and distinguished so many things, since they are sure of so many truths . . . "the mind of man is therefore unbewitched of this kind of imagination."

[Leopardi gives many arguments in favor of the ancients, culminating,]

. . . For what the ancients were, we have all been, and what the world was for centuries, we have been for years—I mean children and sharers of that ignorance, those fears, delights, credences, and boundless workings of the fantasy. When thunder, wind, sun, stars, animals, plants, and the walls of our dwellings—when everything—seemed either our friend or enemy, with nothing indifferent, nothing insensate; when each object we saw seemed to beckon us in some way, almost as if it wished to converse; when, never alone, we interrogated the images, the walls, trees, flowers, and clouds, and we hugged to us the rocks and trees; when almost hurt we attacked, or well-treated we caressed, things incapable of hurt or benefice; when wonder—so welcome to us who often wish for belief so that we can wonder again—possessed us continually; when the colors of things, light, stars, fire, the flight of insects, bird-song, the purity of fountains, all seemed new or rare; nor did we think any event commonplace, nor did we understand the reason for anything, and thus we made it up for ourselves according to our own genius, and so too we embellished it; when tears were our daily fare and our passions were so untamed and alive they burst forth hotly and were subdued only with difficulty. What a thing our imagination was then, how often and easily it became enflamed . . .what stuff for poetry, what richness, vitality, efficacy, emotion, and delight.

I myself remember in my childhood my imagination's seizing upon the sensation of a sound so sweet it was never heard on earth. I remember gazing at shepherds and little sheep painted on my ceiling and imagining such pastoral beauties that if they could come to life for us, this would be paradise, not earth, a home not for men but gods. Without hesitation (acquit me of vanity, O readers, for what I say) I would consider myself a divine poet if I could in words bring back to life those childhood images seen, those emotions felt, and could evoke them faithfully in others.

∽

9.   My pain in hearing late at night after some holiday the night-song of passing peasants. The infinity of the past that came to my mind, remembering the Romans so fallen after so much clamor and so many events gone by, all of which I sadly compared with that profound stillness and silence of the night. And the rising up of that voice or peasant song helped me realize the meaning of that silence [undated, Z, 50-51].

∽

10.   I have never wanted to live so much as when loving, even though the rest of the world were dead for me. Love is the life and vivifying principle of nature, just as hate is the destructive and deadly principle. Things are made to love each other reciprocally, and life is born from this. From hating each other—although many hatreds are indeed natural—the opposite result derives, that is mutual destructions and even the inner corrosion and consummation of the hater [undated, Z, 59].

∽

11.   What a lovely time was that in which everything was alive to the human imagination and alive in human terms, that is lived in or formed by beings equal to us! When we knew for certain that in the lonely woods there dwelled the beautiful Hamadryads, fauns, sylvans,

38

and Pan, etc., and though you entered in and saw solitude you believed everything inhabited, fountains dwelled in by Naiads, etc. And hugging a tree to your breast, you could almost feel it tremble in your hands, believing it a woman or man like Cypress, etc.! And the same with flowers, etc., for children [undated, Z, 63-64].

$\backsim$

12.   The greatest happiness possible for a man in this world is when he lives peacefully in his calling with the quiet, certain hope of a much better future, a hope so sure and a state of life so good that his wish for this imaginary, beautiful future does not disturb him or goad him with impatience. I experienced this divine state when I was sixteen or seventeen years old for a few months at intervals—a time when I found myself quietly *occupied* in my studies with no distractions, and with the sure tranquil hope of a joyful future. I will never know this again, because this kind of hope, which *alone can make man content with the present,* can only be held by a youth of that age, or at least experience [undated, Z, 76].

$\backsim$

13. To Monaldo Leopardi (Recanati)

This was an enclosure to a letter Leopardi wrote to his brother Carlo. Both documents were written under the mistaken notion that by the time they were read Leopardi would have escaped Recanati with the help of a passport to have been secured by a friend in Macerata, Count Saverio Broglio D'Ajano. Unfortunately Count Monaldo learned of the plot and refused his son permission to travel, but he never received this letter, which Carlo wisely hid away.

Mio Signor Padre. Even though after hearing what I have done, you may think this letter not worth reading, I still hope your generosity will permit you to listen to the first and last words of a son who has always loved you and does love you, and infinitely regrets giving you pain. You know me and know my conduct until now. Perhaps if you divest yourself of subjective considerations, you would see that in all Italy, perhaps even Europe, you could not find a young man of my class, even younger and less intellectually gifted, who has shown half the prudence, abstention from juvenile pleasures, obedience and submission to his parents that I have. Although you may have a low opinion of the few talents heaven has granted to me, you cannot

entirely distrust the number of worthy, famous men who have ac-
knowledged me and share an opinion of me that you know and I need
not repeat. . . . I have seen several families in our town itself, much
less well off than ours, and I have heard of many others outside, who
noting a flicker of genius in one of their young did not hesitate to
make great sacrifices to place him in a position where he might develop
his talents. Even though many have thought that my intellect produces
more than a flicker, you nonetheless judged me unworthy a father's
sacrifice, nor did it seem to you that my present and future well-being
were worth the changing of any family plans. . . .

I knew well your plans for us, and that to secure the happiness of
something I don't really know, but which I hear called home and
family, you have demanded that Carlo and I sacrifice not material
things and security, but our own inclinations, our youth, and our very
life. . . . You knew very well the miserable life I led because of my
terrible attacks of melancholy and the continual torments generated by
my strange imagination. And you could hardly ignore the clear fact
that for these troubles and for my health, which has always been
visibly affected by them, no remedy other than powerful distractions
would suffice—all those things which can never be found in Recanati.
Nevertheless you allowed a man of my characteristics to burn himself
up for many years in killing studies or to bury himself in the most
terrible *noia* and melancholy, produced from solitude and from an
empty life, as is especially true of the last months.

It did not take me long to see that you would not be budged from
your course by any imaginable argument, and that the extraordinary
stubbornness of your character, constantly masked by a pretense of
flexibility, was such as to deny me even the vaguest ray of hope. All
this, together with my general apprehensions about mankind, con-
vinced me that though I had been denied everything I should trust
only in myself. And now that by law I am my own master, I did not
want to delay taking charge of my own fate. . . .

I detest the low-minded carefulness which freezes and binds us in
place and renders us incapable of any great action, reducing us to
animals placidly nursing the conservation of this unhappy life with no
other concern. I know people will think me crazy, as I know all great
men have been considered. And since the careers of almost all the great
have begun in despair, I am not dismayed that mine should so begin.
I would rather be unhappy than small, anguished rather than plagued
by *noia*, especially since *noia*, in me the mother of deadly melancholies,
eats at me much more than any physical discomfort. Fathers usually
overrate their children, but instead you rank us beneath others and

have never believed we might do anything important. Indeed you may recognize only that greatness which can be measured by arithmetical or geometrical calculations. . . .

I am consoled in thinking that this is the last problem I shall cause you and this will free you from the continual bother of my presence and other annoyances and those I might have caused in future.

Mio caro Signor Padre, if I may so call you, I kneel to beg that you pardon me, unhappy as I am through nature and circumstance. I wish my unhappiness had been mine alone rather than touching others, and that is what I hope for in the future. If fortune ever shines on me, my first thought will be to repay you for that which I must now use. The last favor that I ask is that if ever you remember the son who has always respected and loved you, please do not scorn or curse the memory. And if fate has not willed that you might take pride in him, do not refuse him the compassion to which even the evil are entitled [Recanati, undated but written in late July, 1819.].

∽

14. To Saverio Broglio D'Ajano (Macerata)

. . . I do not want to live in Recanati. If my father procures me the means to leave, as he has promised, I will be grateful and respectful like any good son. If not, that which should have come to pass and did not is simply postponed. . . .

My dear Count, you know the world: find me another youth anywhere who has conducted himself to the age of twenty-one as I have. Does my father believe that with a character as ardent, a heart as sensitive as mine, I have never experienced those desires and emotions that all young men on earth experience and act upon? Does he not think this has happened to me and more often and more violently than to others? . . . Does he think that if I have led till now a life so confined you would not expect it from a seventy-year-old Capuchin . . . that this proceeds from a cold nature? . . .

And if my father—who abhors every fine and unusual idea—regrets having allowed me to study and laments that heaven didn't make me a mole; if he not only refuses to concede me anything extraordinary but denies me what any father anywhere would grant to children with sparks of talent; and if he stubbornly wishes me to live and die like his ancestors—is it rebellion for a son not to submit to this iron rule? If you do not believe these are his intentions, rest assured that the matter is precisely so. And should he behave differently, believe me that he is deceiving you as he does others, few of whom completely share his

41

ideas. Do believe a young person who, though indeed young, knows profoundly the character of the persons with whom he has lived since his birth.

I know for certain that he has vowed that we will not leave as long as he is alive. Now I want him to live, but I want to live too, while I am young and not when I am old and useless to myself and others. So I will throw myself desperately into fortune's hands, and if she is against me, as will doubtlessly be the case, I will be another lost soul, the millionth example of the wickedness of humans . . . [Recanati, August 13, 1819].

∾

15. From *Recollections of Childhood and Adolescence*[2]

The following excerpts are from notes titled by editors long after Leopardi's death. Written in 1819 in a form that comes close to "automatic" writing, this prose may further indicate how assiduously the young Leopardi stored up impressions of his life for future use.

. . . Discontent in experiencing the sensations wakened in me by the landscape, etc., in being unable to probe and enjoy more deeply, to get at its depths or know how to express it, etc. Striking tenderness of some dreams of mine moving me to tears . . . and dim fancies as when I dreamt of Marie Antoinette and of a song to put in her mouth in the tragedy I then was planning, and to express those feelings I would have needed music instead of words.

My speculations on the plurality of worlds and the nothingness of us and of this earth and on the greatness and force of nature which we measure by the torrents, etc., and that I am a nothing on this globe, which is a nothing in this cosmos, and wakened by a voice calling me to dinner. . . .

Garden near the caretaker's house. I was melancholy and stood at a window overlooking the little square. Two young men, on the steps of the abandoned church, grassy, etc., sat joking under the big lantern and jostling each other. The first firefly I saw that year appeared. One of the two gets up and goes toward it. To myself I prayed for mercy for the poor thing and begged it to fly away, but he caught it and threw it to the ground and returned to the other, etc. Meanwhile the coachman's daughter, rising from dinner and going to the window to wash a plate, calls back to those inside, "Tonight it's really going to rain. What weather! Black as a hat." And soon the light vanishes from the window, and in the meantime the firefly got up, etc., or wanted to, but he noticed it and returned cursing. Another blow makes it fall, weak as it was, and he with his foot makes a bright streak in the dust, until he wipes it out. . . .

My intense desire for glory from the time I was small, manifest in everything. . . . Battles we waged in imitation of Homeric ones, in the garden with berries, stones, etc., at San Leopardo with sticks, giving each other Homeric names or those from Roman history. . . . My Latin oration recited to my dad and reflections on my hatred for the tyrant and my love and excitement in reading of his assassination, etc. Other similar performances we gave according to what we had just read. Note that I chose to be Pompey, even though being vanquished, giving to Carlo the role of Caesar, which he took with distaste.

16.   Immeasurably tired of life, standing at the edge of the pool in my garden, I looked into the water, leaned toward it tremblingly, and I thought: If I were to throw myself in, I would immediately float up, grasp the bank, and after the struggle, the escape without harm, I would experience some moments of content at being saved and of affection for this life I now so despise but which then would seem more prized. The tradition regarding the leap from the Leucadian rock might have had a similar observation at its base [undated, Z, 82].

17.   One of the many proofs of the extent that purely physical systems may influence intellectual or metaphysical systems is that of Copernicus, which to the thinker entirely revolutionizes the idea of nature and man so naturally derived from the old so-called Ptolemaic system. It reveals to us a plurality of worlds; shows man not to be unique, even as the collocation, motion, and destiny of the earth are not; throws open an immense field of meditations on the infinity of created beings that by all the laws of analogy must inhabit other globes entirely analogous to ours, and even those which—though invisible to us—must exist around the other suns (that is, the stars); moderates our concept of man and of the sublime; and opens out into new mysteries of creation, the destiny of nature, the essence of things, of our own being, the Creator's omnipotence, of the ends of the creation, etc., etc. [undated, Z, 84].

◆

18.   I was terrified at finding myself in the midst of nothingness, myself
a nothing. I felt that I was suffocating, contemplating and sensing that
all is nothing, solid nothingness [undated, Z, 85].

◆

19.   *The Infinite*

This brief work, composed sometime in 1819, is the first of Leopardi's
"idylls" and the most celebrated of his poems. The hill from which the
unearthly experience begins is that upon which Recanati perches. It was called
Mount Tabor then (the "Hill of Infinity" now), and Leopardi used to reach
the secluded setting through a gate at the rear of his father's garden.

The poem can easily be seen as a "religious contemplation,"[3] even as a
mystical description of the self being absorbed into an all-embracing tran-
scendent reality—an encounter with the numinous of the type sought out and
described by Oriental mystics. But such interpretations, though attractive,
need to be qualified in terms of Leopardi's realistic attitudes and the data in
the poem. The expansion of mind into the silence of boundless space, then
time, is the work of the imagination spurred by finite means. The very fact
that the hedge *cuts off* the vision of unknowable space releases the imagination
to create that vision; that which allows the silent eternity to arise is the sound
of actual wind and the feeling of the present season. The more than human
dimension into which the "I" dives does not exist objectively but is fashioned
by the human mind to which the poem is a tribute. *The Infinite* is, in the
words of Perella, "the triumph of the poetic imagination over a limited
reality."[4]

> This lonely hill has always been so dear
> To me, and dear the hedge which hides away
> The reaches of the sky. But sitting here
> And wondering, I fashion in my mind
> The endless spaces far beyond, the more
> Than human silences, and deepest peace;
> So that the heart is on the edge of fear.
> And when I hear the wind come blowing through
> The trees, I pit its voice against that boundless
> Silence and summon up eternity,
> And the dead seasons, and the present one,
> Alive with all its sound. And thus it is
> In this immensity my thought is drowned:
> And sweet to me the foundering in this sea.

∾

20. To Pietro Giordani (Milan)

I am so stunned by the nothingness surrounding me that I do not know how I have strength to take up my pen and answer your letter of the first. If in this moment I were to go mad, my madness would consist of sitting always with my eyes staring, my mouth open, and my hands between my knees, without laughing or crying, or even moving except for sheer necessity. I haven't the least urge to conceive a desire, not even for death—not that I fear it in any way, but because I no longer see any difference between death and this my life; where nothing comes to console me, not even pain. This is the first time that *noia* not only presses and tires me but harries and rips like the sharpest pain. And I am so terrified by the emptiness of things and the condition of human beings, that—all passion spent in my soul—I stray outside myself, deeming even my despair an utter nothing.

As for the studies you urge me so lovingly to continue, I haven't been able to think of them, the nerves in my eyes and head being so weakened that I cannot read or pay attention to whatever is read to me, or concentrate on any thought, large or small.

Mio caro, even though I am no longer aware of the terms of friendship and love, still I beg you to love me as you do, and remember me, and believe that I, as much as I can, love and will love you always, and want you to write me. *Addio* [Recanati, November 19, 1819].

∾

21.   A notable thing about the ancient poets and artisans, especially the Greeks, is that they invited the spectator or hearer to reflect beyond what was actually expressed. And the cause of this quality is nothing else than their simplicity and naturalness, by which they did not, like the moderns, probe into the minutiae of a thing, or obviously display the craft of the artist. The artist of today does not speak or describe the thing as nature presents it but instead keeps refining, explaining circumstances, atomizing and prolonging descriptions for effect—a tendency which completely reveals the idea, destroys the natural flowing and offhandedness, demonstrates craft and affectation, and reduces poetry into the poet talking instead of the thing talking. . . . A country scene, for example, etched by the ancient poet in a few strokes with-

45

out, so to speak, its horizon defined, awoke in the imagination that divine shimmering of confused ideas, glowing with an undefinable romance, that intensely dear and sweet extravagance and wonder which used to make us ecstatic in our childhood . . . [January 8, 1820, Z, 100].

∽

22. To Pietro Giordani (Piacenza)

. . . I too anxiously await the beautiful springtime as the only medicine remaining for my exhausted spirit. Before going to bed a few evenings ago, through the open window of my room I saw a clear sky and a lovely moonlight, felt the warm air, and heard dogs baying in the distance; and there awoke in me some old images, and I seemed to feel a stirring of the heart—whereupon I began shouting like a madman, asking pity from nature, whose voice I seemed to be hearing after so long a time.

And at the moment, in glancing backwards over my past condition, to which I would soon return (as I have), terror froze me, and I could not really comprehend how one can tolerate life without illusions, warm feelings, imagination, and excitement, those things which filled my days until a year ago and rendered me blessed despite my travails. Now, I am stiff and dried up like old cane, and passion no more finds a way into this poor soul, and even eternal, omnipotent love is annulled for me at my age.

Meanwhile I go on telling you these things which I would not disclose to anyone else. I am sure you will not take them for melodramas, knowing that I loathe above all cursed affectation, the corrupter of all beauty in this world, and that you are the sole person who understands me. And so, since I cannot do so with others, I discuss with you my feelings, which seem no longer useless.

This is the terrible human condition and the barbarous teaching of reason: since human pleasures and pains are mere illusions, the anguish deriving from the certainty of the nothingness of things is always the only true reality. And if we conduct our lives according to this feeling of nullity, the world would end for us and we would justly be called insane. In any case it is unarguably clear that this would be a rational madness in every respect, so that all wisdoms of the heart would be follies in fact—since everything in the world gets accomplished by the simple, continual ignoring of that universal truth, that all is nothing.

I trust these considerations would embarrass those pseudo–philosophers who console themselves with the boundless growth of reason and think that human happiness lies in the knowledge of truth, when indeed there is no truth other than nothingness; and this thought, continually adhered to as reason demands, would lead us necessarily and directly to the situation I have described: a madness according to nature, an absolute and perfect wisdom according to reason. . . [Recanati, March 6, 1820].

～

23.   Once when I was most disgusted with life, without any hope, and so bent on death that I despaired at being unable to die, I received a letter from a friend who had always encouraged me to hope and implored me toward life and assured me (he was a man of great intelligence and fame) that I would become great and a glory of Italy. In the letter he told me that he understood my afflictions so well now . . . that if God sent me death I should accept it as a good thing, and he hoped it would be soon for both our sakes and for the love he bore me. Would you believe that this letter instead of detaching me more from life re-endeared me to that which I had already abandoned? Thinking about my past hopes and of the words of comfort and high predictions once offered by my friend, which he now no longer seemed to wish to see verified, nor my anticipated greatness achieved, and seeing by chance my notes and my studies, and remembering my childhood—the thoughts, desires, the beautiful prospects and doings of adolescence—my heart was so shaken that I no longer knew how to be hopeless, and death terrified me. Not just as death itself, but as annuller of all those beautiful past expectations.

     And yet that letter had told me nothing I had not told myself already every day, and it only corroborated, not more, not less, my own thinking. I find the following causes for this effect: (1) That things which from afar seem bearable change their aspect when close. The letter and that wish for me put me into a kind of superstitious awe, as if things were closing in on me and death itself approaching; and that from which afar seemed most easy to endure—indeed the only desirable thing—appeared most painful and formidable when near. (2) I had previously considered the desire for death in stoic terms. I well knew that in fact I had no other choice, but I indeed indulged the thought of death in an imaginary way. I believed certainly that my few friends— but at least these few and especially that one—wanted me to live, would resist my desperation, and if I were to die would have been surprised and crushed, and said: "So it's all over then? O God, so many hopes, such greatness of spirit, such genius that bore no fruit! No glory, no pleasures, everything is gone as if it never were." But the thought they might say, "Praise God, he has finished suffering; I joy for him who looked forward to no other blessing; may he rest in peace"—this sudden closing of the tomb over me, this quick and total resignation of my friends to my death, however reasonable, choked me with a sense of my entire annihilation. The anticipatory and consoling preview of your death by your friends is the most terrifying thing imaginable. . . .

From these considerations one can learn how to behave in consoling a suffering person. Do not appear disbelieving of his woe, if it is real. You would not convince him and would trouble him even more in depriving him of compassion. He knows his affliction well, and in admitting it you merely go along with him. But in the depths of his heart there remains a drop of illusion. The most desperate surely retain this, one of the continuing blessings of nature. Beware of drying it up and sin in the direction of minimizing his ill and showing yourself deficient in compassion rather than by accepting that over which his imagination and reason are in conflict. Even if he exaggerates his calamity to you, you can be sure that deep in his inmost heart he believes the opposite. I say inmost, that is at depth hidden even from him. You should agree not with his words but with his heart . . . [June 26, 1820, Z, 137-40]

∾

24.   *To the Moon*

Another of Leopardi's early idylls, this poem was composed probably in the summer of 1819. The addressing of the silent moon and the idea of pain being softened by memory are elements which will recur often in Leopardi.

O lovely moon, I call up in my mind
Now that a year has turned how, full of pain,
I climbed this hill to wonder at your light.
And I beheld you hanging there above
That wood, as now, illuminating all.
But then you shimmered vaguely through the tears
Which brimmed my eyes, for life to me was hard,
And is, nor does it ever seem to change,
My charming moon. And yet, recapturing
And numbering the phases of my grief
Provides a certain balm. How sweet—when we
Are young, when memory is short and hope

Seems endless—the remembrance of things past,
Though they were sad, and though the pain endures.

ॐ

25.   In my poetic career my spirit has followed the same course as the
human spirit in general. At first imagination was my strong point, my
verses were full of images, and I always sought in my reading of
poetry to profit in terms of the imagination. I was also very sensitive
to emotions, but I knew not how to express them in poetry. I had not
really thought about things, and of philosophy I had only a glimmer
(a vague one at that), and I shared the usual illusion we have, that in
life and the world there must always be an exception in our favor. I
have always been unfortunate, but my misfortunes then were full of
life and made me despair only because I felt (not reasonably but in my
active imagination) that they deprived me of happiness, something
others enjoyed. In sum my state was thoroughly like that of the
ancients. . . .

The total transformation in me, and the passing from the ancient to
the modern condition, occurred more or less in one year, 1819, when
deprived of the use of my eyes and of the constant absorption of
reading, I began to feel my unhappiness much more darkly; to aban-
don hope; to meditate deeply about things. (In these writings, for
example, I wrote in that one year almost twice as much as I had in the
preceding year and a half, and on subjects regarding our nature, as
opposed to the generally literary thoughts of my earlier efforts.) I
began to become a philosopher instead of the poet I used to be; to feel
the certain infelicity of the world instead of just recognizing it—and
this was partly due to a lethargic physical state which all the more
distanced me from the ancients and brought me closer to modern men.

My imagination then was greatly enfeebled, and as much as the
inventive faculty actually grew larger in me (indeed seemed to be
born), it inclined chiefly toward either prose matters or sentimental
poetry. And if I set myself to writing verses, the images came with
great difficulty. Although my verses overflowed with sentiment, my
fancy was in fact nearly dried up (even apart from poetry, such as in
contemplating beautiful natural scenes, etc., as now when I remain
hard as stone). Thus it can be fairly said in all rigor that the ancients
were, above all, poets, and now none are as poetic as children or the
young, and the moderns who take this name are but philosophers.
And I, in fact, did not become sentimental until I had lost my imagi-

49

nation and had become insensitive to nature, totally dedicated to reason and truth—in sum, a philosopher [July 1, 1820, Z, 143-44].

ᔒ

26.   The sense of nothingness in all things, the inability of all pleasures to satisfy the soul, and our tendency toward an infinity we do not comprehend perhaps all come from one very simple cause, a cause more material than spiritual. The human mind (and it is the same for all living beings) always essentially desires and fastens on pleasure in its many facets, or on happiness, which correctly considered is one and the same thing. This desire and tendency has no limits because it is innate or congenital with existence itself; thus it cannot have an end in this or that finite pleasure, but ends only when life does. Hence there cannot be a pleasure which equals it either in (1) duration, for no pleasure is eternal, or (2) extent, for no pleasure is boundless; but rather the nature of things dictates that everything exist limitedly, that it be confined and circumscribed. This desire for pleasure has no limits in duration, because as I said it finishes only when existence does, and thus man would not exist if he did not experience this desire. It has no limits in extent because it is substantial in us, not as a desire for one or more pleasures, but as a desire *for pleasure*. . . .

Let us turn to a consequence. If you desire a horse, you seem to want it as a horse, a specific pleasure, but in fact you desire it as abstract, illimitable pleasure. When you finally get the horse, the pleasure you experience is necessarily restricted, and you feel a void in your soul because that desire you had has not been satisfied. If it were even possible to fulfill it by extent, it could not be satisfied by duration because, again, nature demands that nothing be eternal. . . . And so all pleasures must be mixed with displeasure, as we know by experience, for in achieving them, the soul is avidly seeking that which cannot be found—that is, an infinity of pleasure, or the fulfilling of an unlimited desire.

Let us now turn to man's inclination toward the infinite. Separately from the desire for pleasure, there exists in man an imaginative faculty, which can conceive things which are not, or see real things in an unreal way. Given the inborn tendency of man toward pleasure, it is natural that the imagination make the imagining of pleasure one of its chief occupations. With its properties, the imagination can fashion infinite, nonexistent pleasures: (1) in number, (2) in duration, (3) in extent. Infinite pleasure unfindable in reality is thus found in the imagination, from which derive hope, the illusions, etc. Therefore, it is no wonder that (1) hope is always greater than any real good, and (2) human happiness cannot consist of anything outside the imagination and the illusions. Thus, we need to acknowledge the great compassion and wisdom of nature. On the one hand she cannot strip man and other living creatures of the love of pleasure, which is an immediate consequence of (and almost the same as) self-love and the self-preservation necessary for the survival of things. On the other hand, unable to provide infinite real pleasures, she has provided us: (1) with illusions (and here she was most generous) which must be deemed arbitrary in the order of things, for she could have excluded them; and (2) with immense variety, so that a man weary or disenchanted with one pleasure can turn to another, or even if disenchanted with all pleasures, be distracted and confused by the great variety of things. . . .

And so the superiority of the ancients over the moderns in terms of happiness. The imagination, as I said, is the prime source of human happiness. The more it reigns in man, the happier he will be. We see it in children. But it cannot reign without ignorance, at least a certain ignorance like that of the ancients. Knowledge of the truth—that is, of the limits and definitions of things—restricts the imagination. . . . Furthermore, nature has determined that man should not consider the imagination what it *is*, a deceiving faculty, but rather should confuse it with the faculty of understanding or knowing; and nature makes him think his imaginative dreams are real things, and makes him animated by the imaginary as well as the true (even more by the imaginary because it has greater natural power, and nature is always superior to reason). But nowadays, educated persons, even when fertile with illusions, consider them such, and pursue them more by will than by conviction—the opposite of the ancients, of simple people, of children, and of the order of nature. . . .

And so it is clear that: (1) All good things seem most beautiful and exalted from a distance, and the unkown is more lovely than the known (an effect of the imagination determined by nature's inclination toward pleasure, an effect of the illusions that nature has wanted). (2) The soul prefers in poetry and everywhere an ethereal beauty [*il bello aereo*], ideas which are infinite. Given what we have said, the mind must naturally prefer that pleasure which it cannot embrace. . . . (3) Our minds detest everything which confines our sensations. . . . The mind imagines the unseen—that which that tree, that hedge, that tower hides from it—and goes wandering in an imaginary space. . . . Thus the pleasure I always felt as a boy (and even now) in seeing the sky through a window, a door, or between houses. . . [undated, Z, 165-71].

27.   Lord Byron in his annotations to *The Corsair* (and maybe to some other works) cites historical examples of the effects of the passions, and of those characters he describes. Bad. The reader must feel and not learn about the conformity between your description, etc., and truth and nature, and that such characters and passions in those circumstances would produce just such an effect; otherwise poetic delight vanishes, and the imitation, though treating of strange things, does not evoke wonder even if it is exact. . . . And the poetry becomes a tract, its action moving the intellect but not the heart and imagination . . . [August 24, 1820, Z, 223-24].

28. To Pietro Brighenti (Bologna)

Brighenti was a friend who practiced law, loved literature, and occasionally published books. The 1824 volume of Leopardi's poems, which caused trouble with the censors, was published through Brighenti's auspices.

Mio Carissimo. I am sorry to hear of the bad health which afflicts you. Take care of yourself and another time don't go along with your friends so easily; and if they invite you to go swimming, answer them like the English lady invited to a tiger-hunt, where she had once experienced great danger: "I've been there already.". . .
Your remarks about the nobility are well taken—they are the dead body of society. But unfortunately I do not see what we can call the live body nowadays. All the classes are infected by selfishness, the destroyer of the beautiful and fine, and a world without enthusiasms, without nobility of thoughts and deeds, is a thing more dead than alive. . . .
The villainies of women frighten me, not only for myself but because I see the misery of the world. If I were to become rich or powerful (quite impossible for I have too few vices), women would undoubtedly try to catch me. But in my condition, shunned by everyone, I have not a single merit to attract their blandishments. And besides, my spirit is so frozen and withered by constant unhappiness, and by painful recognition of the truth, that even before falling in love I have lost the faculty of loving, and an Angel of grace and beauty would not suffice to ignite me. So that, young as I am, I could function as a eunuch in some seraglio.

Addio, love me, and send me news about your health. I love and embrace you. Tell me to whom I should send the payment for the *Foscolo* [Recanati, August 28, 1820].

∾

29.   *Sunday Evening*

The Italian title of this October, 1820, idyll, *La sera del dì di festa,* means literally "the evening of the feast day." The English "feast day," however, falls well short of the intertwined meanings of the Italian: holy day, holiday, special day, any Sunday. I have therefore followed the lead of Karl Kroeber[5] in choosing just one of the meanings as a title. Leopardi's later and companion poem *The Village Saturday* offers additional warrant.

   The poem itself is a fresh treatment of the *ubi sunt* motif dear to ancient poets as well as to Leopardi's near contemporaries (he had, for example, absorbed Edward Young's *Night Thoughts* in translation). Although the idyll has attracted deep affection, it has also stirred disagreement. Is the poem a unified statement that successfully merges private and universal sorrow, or does it break down into unassimilated episodes? Giosue Carducci, himself a celebrated poet, said of the piece that "the most striking thing is the bridging from individual pain to world pain."[6] The more recent critic Giuseppe De Robertis, however, argues that Leopardi did not harmonize the "annotations" he brought to the poem and that the passage on the Romans "divides the idyll violently."[7] Those siding with Carducci might point to the ways in which Leopardi builds a unity across time and space by associating images and ideas. The sleeping girl is linked to the distant moon is linked to a vast, consuming nature. Against these superior silences, the sounds of human finiteness—the yells of Roman legions, the tunes of laborers—rise and fall. Kroeber is compelling when he says that this is "a personal poem which passes through and beyond the personal to humanistic affirmation. Because Leopardi reaches the truly humane through intense contemplation of his personal experience, his lyric has a grandeur that belies its simplicity and brevity."[8]

> Gentle the night, so clear and without wind,
> And hushed above the roofs and in the orchards
> Floats the moon, revealing from afar
> Each peaceful mountain. O my lady, now
> The paths are stilled, and from the balconies
> The night-time lanterns shimmer. You sleep,
> For cozy slumber gathers round your rooms,
> Where no care gnaws; and still you neither know
> Nor even guess how great a wound you've opened
> In my heart. You sleep. I turn to face this sky
> Which to the eye appears benign, and this

Omnipotent old Nature which fashioned me
For suffering: "To you I do deny
All hope," she said to me, "No hope for you—
Your eyes will shine with nothing more than tears."
   This was the holiday. Now from the games
You take repose. Perhaps you recollect
In dreams the men you charmed today and those
Delighting you. Not me, nor could I hope
To enter in your thoughts. Meantime, I ask
How long I have to live, and fall upon
The earth, and shake, and cry: O terrible days
In this, so green an age! Ah, from the road
I hear, not far, the isolated song
The workman sings, returning late at night
To his poor home now that the games are done.
And my heart wrenches in me at the thought
That everything the world contains goes by
And hardly leaves a trace. The festive day
Has fled, the common day comes on, and Time
Takes with it every human happening.
Where are the sounds of all those ancient men?
The shouts of our illustrious ancestors,
And the great empire of that Rome—the arms,
The clashing noise which rang throughout the earth
And ocean? All is peace and silence now,
The world is still, and of them we talk no more.
   When I was but a child, we burningly
Looked forward to the holiday, and when
It had gone by, I used to lie awake
And tossing; and late at night, a song I heard
Along the pathways slowly perishing,
Like this one failing now, would seize my heart.

⌒

30.   A house hovering in air, suspended by ropes to a star [October 1, 1820, Z, 256].

⌒

31. Although he apparently never read Wordsworth or the latter's definition of poetry as "emotion recollected in tranquility," Leopardi's analysis of poetic composition is similar.

> . . . the period of enthusiasm, heat, and agitated imagination is not right [for poetic creation]; indeed it works against it. One needs a time of intensity, but tranquil intensity, a time of real genius rather than real excitement . . . , an impression of past or future or habitual emotion rather than its actual presence—one could say its twilight rather than its bright noon. Often the best moment occurs when, the feeling or impulse being over, the mind though calm surges up again after the storm, as it were, to pleasurably recall the past sensation. That is perhaps the aptest time for conceiving an original subject or the original parts of it. We can say generally that in poetry and the fine arts, demonstrations of excitement, imagination, and sensibility are the direct fruit of the author's memory of the enthusiasm rather than of the enthusiasm itself [October 2, 1820, Z, 258-59].

↳

32. The following journal entry is perhaps as important a notation on art and its connection to philosophy, and on the redemptive function of the imagination, as Leopardi ever made. In analyzing the essential paradox he felt existing at the core of human existence and thus of great works of human imagination, Leopardi goes far toward explaining why he continued to write despite his vision of *nulla*. As Geoffrey Bickersteth said of the experience here described, "It is precisely this phenomenon which is exemplified in the poetry of Leopardi himself."[9] Though the entry is an early one, there is no reason to suppose Leopardi changed his view.

> Works of genius have this in common, that even when they vividly capture the nothingness of things, when they clearly show and make us feel the inevitable unhappiness of life, and when they express the most terrible despair, nonetheless to a great soul—though he find himself in a state of extreme duress, disillusion, nothingness, *noia,* and despair of life, or in the bitterest and *deadliest* misfortunes (caused by deep feelings or whatever)—these works always console and rekindle enthusiasm; and though they treat or represent only death, they give back to him, at least temporarily, that life which he had lost.
>
> And so that which in real life grieves and kills the soul, opens and revives the heart when it appears in imitations or other works of artistic genius (as in lyric poems, which are not properly imitations). Just as the author, in describing and strongly feeling the emptiness of

illusions still retained a great store of illusions—which he proved by so
intensely describing their emptiness—so the reader, no matter how
disenchanted *per se* and through his reading, is pulled by the author
into that very illusion hidden in the deepest recesses of that mind the
reader was experiencing. And the very recognition of the irremediable
vanity and falseness of all things great and beautiful is itself a great and
beautiful thing which fills the soul, when the recognition comes
through works of genius. And the very spectacle of nothingness pre-
sented seems to expand the soul of the reader, to exalt it, and reconcile
it to itself and to its own despair. (A tremendous thing and certainly a
source of pleasure and enthusiasm—this magisterial effect of poetry
when it works to allow the reader a higher concept of self, of his woes,
and his own depressed, annihilated spirit.)

Moreover, the feeling of nothingness is that of a dead and death-
producing thing. But if this feeling is alive, as in the case I mean, its
liveliness dominates in the reader's mind the nothingness of the thing
it makes him feel; and the soul receives life (if only briefly) from the
very power by which it feels the perpetual death of things and of itself.
Not the smallest or least painful effect of the knowledge of great
nothingness is the indifference and numbness which it almost always
inspires about that very nothingness. This indifference and insensibility
is removed by reading or contemplating such a work: it renders us
sensible to nothingness . . . [undated, Z, 259-61].

33.   The extent that even the Christian religion can be contrary to
nature, when it influences according to a simplified, rigid scheme
which is the only norm for behavior, may be seen by the following
example. I have known intimately a mother who was not at all
superstitious, but most scrupulous and demanding in her Christian
faith and practices. Not only did she refuse pity to those parents who
lost infant children, but she deeply and sincerely envied them, because
the children had soared to a safe paradise, and had freed their parents
from the bother of supporting them. Finding herself several times in
danger of losing young children, she did not pray God to let them die,
because religion does not permit that, but she did indeed rejoice; and
seeing her husband weep or grieve, she turned inwards, nursing a true
and obvious disdain. She was most solicitous in the care she gave those
poor sick children, but deep in her heart she hoped it would be useless,
and even confessed that the only fear she had in consulting with
doctors was to hear of some improvement. Seeing in the sick some

sign of approaching death, she experienced a profound joy (which she was compelled to hide only from those who would condemn it). And the day of their death, if it came, was for her an agreeable and cheerful one, nor could she comprehend how her husband could be so unwise as to be saddened.

She considered beauty true misfortune, and seeing her children ugly or deformed, she thanked God for it, not for heroic reasons but in all sincerity. She did not try in any way to help them hide their defects, but rather insisted that in light of them they should entirely renounce life in their prime of youth. If they resisted, if they sought the opposite, if they succeeded in some small way, she was displeased and she belittled as much as possible their successes (both for her plain and her handsome children). And she missed no occasion, indeed she studiously sought them out, to reproach them and make them well aware of their defects and the sure consequences, and to convince them with a fierce, pitiless veracity of their inevitable misery. The failures of her children were a true consolation to her, and she preferred to dwell with them on what she had heard to their disfavor. All this to free them from spiritual danger. And she behaved this way in everything involving begetting them, raising and educating them, and providing for their temporal happiness.

She felt infinite compassion for sinners, but very little for physical or earthly misfortunes, except when nature itself at times defeated her. The illnesses and heart-wracking deaths of young people wiped out in the flower of youth with all their lovely hopes, with great suffering for their families and others, touched her not at all. For she used to say that the time of death did not matter, only the manner. And therefore she would assiduously find out if they died a good death according to our religion or, when they were ill, if they were showing proper resignation, etc. And she spoke of these misfortunes with a marble coldness.

This woman was endowed by nature with a very sensitive character, and was reduced to this state by religion alone. What else is this but barbarism? And yet it is nothing but a mathematical working-out, an immediate and necessary consequence, of religious principles meticulously adhered to; of that religion which with good reason boasts itself the most merciful one, etc. . . . . [November 25, 1820, Z, 353-56].

34. The richest man, scattering money among a people who did not recognize or prize gold or silver, would not be honored by them unless

he had other ways to attract esteem; indeed he would be called infamous and would not attain even the necessaries. Thus it is that where genius and spirit are not valued, or cannot be, the most ingenious and spirited and great are despised and ranked low, unless they have other endowments. . . . And so things go according to the times. In every place, in every time, you must use the common currency. He who doesn't have it is poor though he may be rich in other monies [December 23, 1820, Z, 455].

35.   On those rare occasions when I have experienced some good fortune or shred of happiness, rather than announcing it outwardly, I have naturally given myself up to melancholy as far as the external world would know, even though I was content inside. I was afraid to disturb that placid, concealed contentment, afraid to change or lose it by venting it. And so I gave my joy to the custody of melancholy [December 27, 1820, Z, 460-61].

36.   Not just the cognitive faculty or that of the heart, but even the imagination is incapable of infinity or of conceiving infinitely; it can only conceive the indefinite. The latter pleases us because when the mind does not see any limits, it receives the impression of a kind of infinity and confuses the indefinite with the infinite, but it cannot really comprehend or conceive of infinity. Indeed, in our most vague and indefinite—and thus sublime and delightful—imaginings, our soul feels a certain discomfort, a certain difficulty, a certain inadequacy in desire, an impotence bent on embracing the whole measure of its imagining, its conception or idea. So that, even though these impressions may delight and satisfy the soul more than any other thing possible on earth, they do not do so entirely, and when they disappear the soul is never contented; for the soul feels and knows (or seems to) that it has not grasped and seen the idea to its fullest . . . and persuades itself that it had been within its power to do so. And therefore it experiences a certain remorse, which really is wrong since it is not at all responsible for the failure [January 4, 1821, Z, 472-73].

37.   If as children, a view, or landscape, picture, sound, etc., a tale, description, fable, poetic image or dream pleases and delights us, that pleasure or delight is always vague and indefinite. The idea it awakes in us is always indeterminate and limitless. Every comfort, every pleasure, expectation, plan, illusion, etc. (almost every idea) at that age tends always toward the infinite, and they feed and fill our soul indescribably, even by means of trivial objects.

As adults, whether the objects and pleasures are greater or the same ones that charmed us as children—like a lovely vista, landscape, picture, etc.—we will experience a pleasure but it will be in no way like the infinite, or certainly not as intensely, feelingly, lengthily, and essentially vague and undefined as before. . . . Indeed, you will note that most of the indefinite images and feelings we do experience after childhood are nothing other than a memory of childhood; they point back to it; they depend and derive from it; they are as it were an influx and consequence of it. . . . So that the present sensation does not come directly from things, is not an image of objects but of the childhood image: a remembrance, a repetition, an echoing or reflection of the old image. . . .

And observe that even pleasant dreams at our age, while they delight us considerably more than reality, nonetheless no longer represent that beauty and that pleasurable indefiniteness as so often in our childhood [January 16, 1821, Z, 514-16].

38.   Children find everything in nothing, men nothing in everything [undated, Z, 527].

39.   *Nous ne vivons que pour perdre et pour nous détacher* [quoted from Anna de Lambert's *Treatise on Old Age*]. . . . So it is. Each day we lose something, that is, one of our illusions—our only real possessions— dies or diminishes. Experience and truth strip away from us day by day some portion of our riches. One does not live except by losing. Man is born rich in all, growing up he grows poorer, and arrived at old age he finds himself with almost nothing . . . [February 10, 1821, Z, 636].

40. Perhaps there is no one of so little concern to you who when bidding you good-bye in leaving for whatever reason or place, and saying, "We will never see each other again," fails to move you, no matter what your feelings toward him. The horror and fear man has of nothingness on the one hand and *of eternity* on the other manifests itself everywhere, and that "never again" cannot be heard without a certain effect. . . . [As a child,] when I saw someone leaving, no matter how indifferent I was to him, I would consider the chances of ever seeing him again. If I thought not, I would take to watching and listening to him, and so on, to follow him with my eyes and ears as much as I could, turning over, concentrating, and developing in my mind this thought—"This is the very last time; I will not see him ever again, or maybe never again." And so the death of someone I knew, who meant little to me in life, gave me a certain pain, not so much for himself or because he now interested me, but for this concern that I mulled over deeply: "He is gone forever—forever? Yes, all about him is finished. I will never see him again, and nothing of his will have anything in common with my life." And I tried to relive, if I could, the last time I saw or heard him, etc., and I sorrowed at not having known it would be the last time, and at not having behaved according to this thought [February 11, 1821, Z, 644-45].

41. The more *self-interest* one finds in individuals, the less society can really exist. Thus if egoism becomes total, society exists in name only. For if each person thinks only of himself as the goal, cares not for the common good, and directs no thought or action toward the welfare or pleasure of others, then each person forms a separate and entire society by himself, a society as perfectly distinct as its goal is. And so the world returns to what it was in the beginning, before the origin of society—which is undone in fact and substance. Therefore, egoism has always been the plague of society. The more it has flourished, the worse the condition of society; and the more flagrant these institutions which either directly or indirectly favor egoism, such as despotism above all [February 17, 1821, Z, 670-71].

42.   Unfortunate people who are not beautiful, and especially if they are old, can be pitied, but only with difficulty lamented. So it is in tragedies, poems, romances, etc., as in life [March 6, 1821, Z, 722].

43.   Our condition today is worse than that of the animals in this way also. Surely no beast desires the end of his life; no matter how unhappy, none of them thinks of escaping unhappiness by death or would have the courage to seek it out. Nature, which retains in them all its primitive power, keeps them distanced from all that. If, however, one of them could desire to die, nothing would stand in the way of this wish. We humans are completely alienated from nature, and thus most unhappy. We desire death quite often and ardently, as the only obvious, deliberate remedy for our misery, so that we desire it often, with full recognition, and are compelled to desire and consider it as our highest good. Since this is so . . . what greater woe is there than to find ourselves blocked from dying, from pursuing that good which is not only so eminent but which also lies entirely in our own hands—blocked, I say, either by Religion or by the ineradicable, invincible, inexorable, inevitable uncertainty about our origin, our destiny, our ultimate purpose, and that which lies ahead of us after death?

I well know that nature resists suicide with all its forces, and I know that it breaks all of her laws more seriously than any other human offense. But since nature is wholly altered; since our lives have ceased being natural; since the happiness nature once ordained for us is gone forever and we are becoming incurably unhappy; since this desire for death, which (according to nature) we should not have ever even conceived, has indeed mastered us through the power of reason and despite nature—why then does this same reason prevent us from satisfying the desire, from repairing in the only way possible the damage that reason herself and she alone has done us? . . . [March 19, 1821, Z, 814-16].

44.   It is most true that clearness of expression derives chiefly from the clearness with which the writer or speaker conceives and grasps an idea in his mind. The philosopher who does not see clearly at a certain point, the historian who does not understand a fact well, etc., impress the reader as obscurely as they do themselves. But this especially

occurs when the writer will not admit to others or to himself that he does not understand the thing. For even the things we see obscurely we can arrange to impart to the reader in the same way; and we will always express ourselves clearly if we allow the reader to see the idea just as we see it, just as it lies in our mind. This is so because the effect of clarity is not, properly speaking, to make the reader conceive a clear idea of a thing in itself, but rather a clear idea of the precise state of our mind, whether it is seeing clearly or obscurely . . . [July 23, 1821, Z, 1372].

⌇

45.   Regarding sensations which please by way of indefiniteness, look to my idyll on *The Infinite* and recall the idea of a countryside sharply declining so that the sight from a certain distance cannot arrive to the valleys; and that of a row of trees, whose end is lost to the eye either by the length of the row or because this too is placed in a decline, etc. etc. etc. A building, a tower, etc. seen in such a way that it seems to rise alone above the horizon, and this [latter] not being visible, produces a most effective and sublime contrast between the finite and the indefinite, etc. etc. etc. [August 1, 1821, Z, 1430-31].

⌇

46.   The human mind is made so as to take much greater satisfaction from a small pleasure, from a small idea or impression whose limits are unknown than from a large one whose limits we see or feel. The hope of a little good is a pleasure absolutely greater than the possession of a large but already known good. . . . Science destroys the chief pleasures of our minds because it defines and shows us the boundaries of things—even though in many, many ways it has materially enlarged our ideas. I say materially, not spiritually, since, for example, the distance from the sun to earth was felt to be much greater in the human mind when it was thought to be just a few miles, and we weren't sure how many, than it is now, when we know the precise millions of miles it is.

Thus science is the enemy of greatness in ideas although it has immeasurably enlarged our opinions of nature. It has enlarged them as clear ideas, but a tiny *confused idea* is always greater than a vast one which is *clear*. The ambiguity over whether a thing actually is or is not is the source of a grandness that is destroyed by the surety that the thing really is so [August 7, 1821, Z, 1464-65].

~

47.   The past, in remembering it, is more beautiful than the present, as is the future in imagining it. Why? Because only the present has a true shape in the human mind; it is the only image of truth; and all truth is ugly [August 18, 1821, Z, 1521-22].

~

48.   "Our knowledge is but reminiscence," say the Platonists. They are wrong in their notion that the soul simply recollects what it once knew before being united to the body. But the idea can be applied to our system and Locke's. For indeed, man (and beast) knows nothing by his very nature, etc., and can know only as much as he remembers— that is, what he has learned through sense experience. We can say that memory is the only source of knowledge; that it is linked to, and almost constitutes, all our mental or physical ideas and abilities; and that without memory, humans could know or do nothing.

And just as I have said that memory is nothing other than habit, that it is born from habit (albeit very early), that it is contained in it, so conversely it can be said that memory contains all habits and is the basis of them all, i.e., all our knowledge and inclinations. . . . In short, since memory is essentially the habituation of the intellect, we can say that all the habits of a creature are almost memories experienced by the various organs as they become habituated [September 11, 1821, Z, 1675-76].

~

49.   The words "night," "nocturnal," etc., are very poetic, because since the night confuses objects, the soul can only conceive a vague, indistinct, incomplete image of her as well as what she contains. The same with "obscurity," "profound," etc. etc. [September 28, 1821, Z, 1798].

~

50. Not only the elegance, but the nobility, grandeur, and all the quali-
ties of poetic language—indeed poetic language itself—consists, be it
noted, in an indefinite or not well defined mode of speaking, or one
always less definite than that of prosaic, common speech. This is both
the result and the means of separation from the common tongue. The
precisely defined may often have a place in the language of poetry,
since we must consider language in its totality, but strictly speaking it
is not poetic *per se*. The same effect and nature can be seen in a prose
which, short of being completely poetic, may nonetheless be sublime,
elevated, magnificent, grandiloquent. Real nobility even in prose style
comes consistently from something indefinite. Such was the case with
the prose of the ancients, the Greeks and Latins. So there is not much
difference between the indefiniteness of poetic discourse and that of
certain prose, oratory, etc. . . . . [October 12, 1821, Z, 1900-1901].

51.   *Brutus*

Written in December, 1821, and entitled *Bruto minore* (Brutus the Younger) to
distinguish the protagonist from another Roman figure, this was an extremely
important poem to Leopardi. Years later, on May 24, 1832, he was to write to
his friend De Sinner, "My feelings about destiny have been and remain those
I expressed in 'Bruto minore.' " The great French critic Sainte-Beuve thought
that "here is the key to all of Leopardi's negative philosophy, the personal and
original seal of his kind of poetic sensibility."[10]

After failing in their attempt to save the Roman republic by assassinating
Caesar, Brutus and Cassius have been defeated at Philippi in Thrace. For
Leopardi, the defeat is much more than a battle lost. It signals the degradation
of the future emperors, the eventual fall of Rome, and an apocalyptic change
in the world—in the way men interpret life, death, and their own significance.
When he published the poem in a volume, Leopardi prefaced it with a long
note called "Comparison of the Last Words of Brutus and Theophrastus."[11]
According to tradition, the two ancients had at their deaths ruefully re-
nounced virtue and fame, respectively. To Leopardi, such repudiations are
common for moderns, who accept the futility of human endeavor and who
have been taught by Christianity to accept man's misery and train their sights
on the afterlife. Not so for the ancients, Leopardi argues, who humanistically

believed that the ideals of honor, virtue, and fame were not illusions but things achievable on earth; that by heroic action great souls could change the world; that their lives counted, for them and for posterity.

Thus Leopardi has his hero stand consciously at a crux in human history. The ancient ties which bound together nature, the gods, and man have loosened. The cry of the alienated Brutus is in Sainte-Beuve's words "the last sigh of all antiquity."

> Now that Italic virtue lies in one
> Vast ruin, uprooted in the Thracian dust;
> While Fate ordains for green Hesperian vales
> And for the Tiber's shores
> The stamping hoofs of the barbarian horse;
> And, from the northern wastes
> Beneath the frozen Bear,
> Calls down the Gothic sword
> To hack apart the fabled walls of Rome—
> Brutus, the battle-worn,
> Covered with brothers' blood,
> Sits lonely in the night, intent on death,
> Confronting the inexorable gods;
> And with his savage words
> He vainly strikes out at the sleeping air:

> "O senseless Virtue, your domain is one
> Of empty clouds and fields of restless ghosts
> And bitterest remorse.
> To you, you marble gods
> (If gods there really be in Phlegethon
> Or anywhere among the clouds),
> This miserable race
> From whom you ordered temples has become
> A sport, a mockery,
> And you insult us with your lying laws.
> Why does our earthly piety invite
> Celestial hate? Do you watch over, Jove,
> The wicked of the earth?
> And when the thundercloud exults and you
> Hurl down your roaring bolt,
> Is it to burn the just with sacred flame?

> "We feeble slaves of Death
> Are pressed by iron-clad Necessity

And Fate invincible, and since our pain
Can never end, console
Ourselves with our inevitable lot.
Can endless woe inure the sufferer?
Because he is hopeless does he feel less pain?
The man unused to crawling shall wage war
With you, O Fate, unending mortal war.
And though your tyrant hand weigh heavily
In victory upon his head, he shrugs
It off with scornful pride,
As deep into himself
He thrusts the bitter steel
And darkly smiles upon the gathering shades.

"The man who thus breaks into Tartarus
Offends the gods. Such bravery does not
Accord with delicate eternal hearts.
Perhaps the heavens meant our suffering,
Our passions, and our galling lives to serve
Them as their recreation.
It was not always so:
Nature, our queen and Goddess once, prescribed
For us a life of freedom in pure woods,
Not one of grief and guilt.
But now that constant evil
Has scattered the blesséd realms
And our small lives are ruled by other law—
When one strong soul rejects
His misbegotten life,
Can Nature claim his stroke is but his own?

"Animals are fortunate. They know no guilt,
Nor can they estimate their suffering.
Their final days lead calmly to an end
With no foreknowledge.
And if some pain should make
Them dash their heads against the trees, or leap
Headlong from mountain cliffs, no arcane law
Or vague imagining would foil their wish.
Of all the races heaven vivifies,
O children of Prometheus, for you
Alone is life a torment;

66

And till your mortal moment is decreed
Jove will dispute with you the shores of death.

"And you, bright moon, arising from the sea
Fed by our blood, you roam
The troubled night and fields so deadly
To the Ausonian heart.
The victor tramples on his brother's breast,
The circling hills shudder, and from the heights
Old Rome disintegrates into a ruin.
And you so placid? You who saw her birth,
The joyous early years,
The memorable honors that she won?
And just as mutely you will pour down upon
The Alps and on the shame of Italy
That same unchanging light
When the barbarian feet
Reverberate in our abandoned realm.

"Here, among green branches and bare rocks,
The birds and untamed beasts
Are wrapped within their customary sleep,
Oblivious of the wreck
And of the altered nature of the world.
And when the peasants' roofs
Grow crimson with the dawn,
One with his morning song will stir the valley,
Another sing the servile herds awake.
O fortune! O benighted race! Of all
Things in the world we are the lowliest.
The bloodstained earth and the reechoing caves
Are dumb to our despair,
Nor does our human sorrow dim the stars.

"In dying, I will not call upon the deaf
Lords of Olympus or the underworld;
Nor to the unworthy earth
Or Night do I appeal.
Nor you—O crowning beam of blackest death—
The living left behind. Shall the low crowd
Propitiate my scorning tomb with sobs?
Embellish it with words and gifts? The times

Grow ever worse. We must not leave to our
Decaying sons the honor of high minds,
The only compensation of our woe.
Let the dark bird whose wings
Move greedily above rend me, let beasts
And storms disperse my unmarked bones; and may
The wind receive my name and memory."

∾

52.

To Spring
or On the Ancient Fables

Composed in January, 1822, this work can be seen as a poetic intensification
of some of the ideas expressed in the *Discourse of an Italian on Romantic Poetry*
(see note and excerpt above). Romantic writers of Europe frequently used the
word "fable" to denote what later writers often called a "myth." While
Leopardi conceded to the romanticists that myths were not intellectually
"true," he hotly defended their use, so crucial to his system. He argued in the
essay that myths were "delightful deceptions" or "blessed illusions" necessary
to our imaginative life. Although Leopardi was increasingly to value the
disillusioning quest for truth, at this point in his life, when poetic vision was
all-important to him, he rejected the "lordship of the intellect," that faculty
which he felt compromised the imagination and its product, Beauty, and cut
us off from that primal time when we were close to nature and her gods. The
romanticists, according to Leopardi, were making a whore [*baldracca*] of the
sacred muse of poetry.

The root distinctions in this debate should seem familiar to readers of
Anglo-American literature. In his critical articles of the 1840s, Edgar Allan
Poe was to inveigh similarly against truth and the "heresy of the didactic" in
poetry; and John Keats, like Leopardi, deprecated the antipoetic effects of
"cold philosophy." The ultimate wisdom Keats ascribed to the Grecian urn—
in the poem written in May, 1819, just months after Leopardi produced his
Discourse—was after all an attempt to reconcile the very polarities sensed
simultaneously by Leopardi in another land: "Beauty is truth, truth
beauty. . . ."

As in other romantic poems recalling a lost innocence and integrity, the
activating general myth in *To Spring* is not the Christian story of the garden
of Eden, but the classical myth of the Golden Age. Leopardi knew not only
the recent primitivistic theories advanced by thinkers such as Rousseau but
also the ideas of Giambattista Vico, the eighteenth-century Italian philosopher
who had held that man develops—or atrophies—in phases, from the first age
when imagination dominates to later times when reason and science prevail,
sealing man off from his earlier poetic and primitive happiness. Leopardi was
obviously taken with the idea (as Wordsworth sometimes was) and often

noted the parallels between the phases of an individual life, of the life of the whole race, and of the natural year with its seasons.

The poem, then, is not only a lament for an age gone too soon, but also the prayer of a poet for the renewal of personal creative forces which intellect and the process of aging are already beginning to sap.

In noting the intimate link once existing between man and his cosmos, Leopardi refers to several mythic figures besides his central one, our Mother Nature. The "quivered Goddess" is, of course, Diana. Venus is both the evening "star" and the love deity. Daphne, Phyllis, and Phaeton's sisters were imprisoned in trees for various offenses. Phaeton himself was the too-proud sun-charioteer hurled into the waters of Eridanus by angry Jove. Echo was the nymph destroyed for love of a mortal, Narcissus, and doomed to a bodiless existence. The poignantly evoked musical bird or nightingale of the last two stanzas is Procne. After her husband Tereus had dishonored Procne's sister Philomela, cut her tongue out, and imprisoned her to insure her silence, Procne avenged herself and her sister by slaying her own son Itys and serving him to his unsuspecting father at a meal. To end the horror, the offended gods transformed Procne, Philomela, and Tereus into a nightingale, swallow, and hawk, respectively—although many writers and glossing editors since the Greeks have illogically identified the silent Philomela with the nightingale.

> Now that the sun remakes
> The winter-shattered sky, and warm winds stir
> The air alive, dispersing the dark clouds
> Together with their shadows;
> Since birds again confide their yielding breasts
> Unto the wind, and melting light dissolves
> The frost in woods where yearning beasts have come
> To try their new desire—
> Cannot our human minds, which grief
> Has wintered, find again
> That lovely age consumed before its time
> By tragedy and the black fire of Truth?
> Will Phoebus's bright beams not shine on us
> For all eternity?
> And more—O fragrant Spring—will you not move
> With tender warmth this heart
> Which in its flowering time
> Has known the cold, the bitterness of age?
>
> Are you alive, alive, O holy Nature?
> And can our ears, unused to hearing it,
> Still grasp the sound of your maternal voice?
> These streams were once beloved by the white nymphs,

The liquid springs their shelter and their mirror.
The intricate green woods and craggy hills
(Where now only the wind
Can play) once trembled to the secret dance
Of those immortal feet;
The shepherd boy who led his thirsty flock
Among the flitting shades
Of noon to find a flowered river bank
Could hear the silver tune of earthy Pan,
And wonderingly behold
The waters ripple as the quivered Goddess,
Invisible to him,
Descended into the warm waves to cleanse
The dust and hunting blood
Away from her white flesh and virgin arms.

Alive the grasses and the flowers were,
The forests once did live! The gentle breeze,
The clouds and the Titanic lamp watched over
The human race; the traveller could fix
His eyes upon your naked glow, O Venus,
And following you throughout the lonely night,
Imagine that you cared,
That an immortal shared his mortal way.
And if a man escaped the impure towns
Of human beings, their deadly wraths, their shame—
In the remotest woods
His arms could grip the rasping trunks of trees,
To feel the living flame
Pulse through the bloodless veins and breathing leaves,
And think that hidden trembling there in sad
Embrace, were Daphne, doleful Phyllis, or one
Of Phaeton's weeping sisters
Who inconsolably remembered how
He fell from the bright sun into his doom.

Nor then, O stubborn cliffs,
Did sounds of human sorrow go unheard,
When Echo lived among you—
Not an illusion of the tricking wind
But the unhappy spirit of a nymph,
Her lovely body shorn

70

By cruel destiny and her keen love.
Among the barren shelves
And the high caves of those deserted places,
She caught our broken cries,
Reflecting them toward the arch of heaven.
And you, sweet bird of fame,
So well acquainted with the human heart,
You still are here to sing among green shades
The reawakening year,
And to the dark and silent fields of night
You tell of ancient crimes
And shames so wicked they obscured the sun.

But now your race and ours have grown apart.
Your song no longer signifies the woe,
And the dark valley hides you—free of guilt
Yet less dear than before.
Alas! The chambers of Olympus now
Are bare, and blind the thunder wandering
The hills and the black clouds,
Dissolving with cold fear
The hearts of both the evil and the good.
We and our native earth are strangers grown;
She nurtures from afar and unaware.
Yet listen, O fair Nature:
Contemplate our grief, our fated lives,
And touch my spirit with the ancient fire—
If you do live, and if there be in heaven,
In ocean, or this sun-touched earth some thing
To watch, if not take pity on, our pain.

⌣

53.   Girls of fifteen or little more, who have not yet begun to live or
know what life is, shut themselves in a convent and embrace a way or
rule of existence whose sole and direct purpose is to cut off life. And
this is what they pursue by all means possible.

   The strictest confinement, with windows arranged so no one else
can be seen, at the expense of the air and light so vital to man, those
substances which feed his daily activities and which all nature—ani-
mals, plants, even stones—liberally enjoys. Mortifications, lost sleep,
fasts, and silences, all of which combine to undermine the health and

thus the well-being and thus the wholeness of existence, and ultimately oppose life itself. Besides absolutely excluding activity, they shut off life, for motion and activity are what distinguish the quick from the dead. Life, after all, consists of action, whereas the clear objective of monastic or hermetic life, etc., is inaction, to guard against doing, the prevention of doing.

So it is that when the nun and monk take vows, they say precisely this: I haven't yet lived and unhappiness has not yet wearied or discouraged me with life. Nature beckons me to live, just as she does all beings now and forever; not only my own nature calls, but the general nature of things, the absolute idea and structure of existence itself. Recognizing, however, that life puts us in great danger of sinning, is therefore most dangerous *in itself,* and is thus *in itself evil* (the logic absolutely follows), I resolve not to live—to act so that what nature has done be undone, the existence she gave me be rendered useless and made (as much as possible) *non-existence* . . . [February 2, Feast of the Purification of the Blessed Virgin Mary, 1822, Z, 2381-82].

∾

54.   Life is made naturally for life, and not for death. That is to say it is made for activity and for all the most vital things in the functions of the living [May 5, 1822, Z, 2415].

∾

55.   We always automatically call a person with a defect, either physical or mental, by the name of the defect itself—the deaf man, the cripple, the hunchback, the madman. Indeed these persons are rarely called except by these names, or if we call them by their proper names when they are not around, rarely do we fail to add the description. In calling or hearing them called like this, people feel superior to them, enjoy the image of the defect, sense and remind themselves in a certain way of their own superiority, and their own self-love is flattered and humored . . . [May 13, 1822, Z, 2441].

∾

56.   *The Last Song of Sappho*

Ultimo canto di Saffo, written in May, 1822, is a companion piece to *Brutus.*
Whereas the latter took his life because virtue was gone, Sappho commits
suicide because she has been denied personal beauty.

Sappho was a great poet of the 7th century B.C. whose poetry is known to
us only through a few fragments. Although Leopardi knew the homosexual
reputation of this poet of Lesbos, he ignores it, fastening instead on a tradition
mentioned by Ovid that Sappho, depressed by her ugliness and her unre-
quited love for Phaon, a handsome youth, threw herself from the Leucadian
cliff into the sea. As Leopardi says in a note, the poem "intends to represent
the sorrow of a delicate, tender, sensitive, noble and warm soul encased in an
ugly, young body. . . ." The attractions of the subject for Leopardi need no
comment. In another note Leopardi reveals something of his aesthetic when
he says he chose the topic not only because Sappho was young, homely,
brilliant, and famous, but because "the great span of time between Sappho
and us confuses the imagination and enables that indefinite beauty which
supremely favors poetry."[12]

The poem is suffused with Greek images, diction, and tone, although
Leopardi uses Roman equivalents for names. The day's messenger is Venus,
the morning "star." The car of Jove refers to the belief that thunder and
lightning were caused by the highest god, who traveled in an awesome
vehicle. The liquor of joy refers to Jove's dispensing liquids from two urns,
one containing positive, the other negative, things. Dis is the god of the
underworld (including Tartarus) who abducted Proserpina to share his dark
life. In the last Italian lines Leopardi calls Prosperpina *"la tenaria Diva"*—the
goddess of Taenarum—because that place, now Cape Matapan, on the Greek
coast was thought to be an entrance into Hades. The silent shore at the end is
that of the river Styx, where the souls of the dead crossed into the
underworld.

> You tender night and slowly setting moon
> With such pure beams. And you, day's messenger,
> Rising among the muted woods around
> This cliff—you were so dear and fair to me
> Before I knew what fate and furies were.
> The desperate heart perceives no loveliness
> In gentle scenes, although the old joy still
> Revives in me when dusty southern winds
> Whip through the liquid sky and trembling fields,
> And when we hear above our heads the car,
> The heavy thundering car of Jove, that cleaves
> The darkened air. For us it would be sweet
> To plunge with the fierce clouds from highest hill
> To deepest vale; for us the frightened herds'
> Tremendous flight; the swollen river

Whelming the dubious shore,
The raging waves and their triumphant roar.

How beautiful your mantle, holy sky,
And you are fair, O dewy earth. Alas!
The gods and hostile destiny reserved
No place for grieving Sappho in a world
Of such unbounded beauty. In this realm
Of proud and charming forms, I am to you,
O Nature, but a low, unwelcome guest,
A poor, fond lover who commits her eyes
And begging heart to an unlistening love.
The sunny banks smile not on me, nor does
The dawn from heaven's eastern gate; the song
Of many-colored birds, the murmuring
Of beeches—none of these is meant for me.
And where in the green willow's shade, the stream
Gives up its lucid breast, the sinuous waves
Avoid my slipping feet
Yet hug the fragrant shores in their retreat.

What was my crime? What terrible excess
Enstained my birth that fortune and the gods
Should look so grim on me? Did I perhaps
In childhood, when I knew not what evil was,
Offend, so that unbending fate could strip
My youth and weave this iron destiny?
You utter, O my lips, such useless sounds:
Unknowable power moves the destined facts,
And all things are unknowable but pain.
We are forgotten children born to weep;
The reasons lie locked in the hearts of gods.
O hopes of my young years! The Father gave
To forms, to pleasing forms, enduring reign
Over our minds. In music or in poems,
In acts that men admire,
The substance cannot shine in mean attire.

Then let us die. This worthless husk cast down
To earth, the unencumbred soul shall flee
Below, and with this act repair the harsh
Mistake the blind dispenser made of me.

And you for whom I have known useless love,
And kept my trust, and felt the burning bite
Of unfulfilled desire—live happy, love,
If any human be so privileged.
Once my illusions and dear dreams of youth
Had passed, the skimping Jove withheld from me
The sweet liquor of joy. The happiest
Of all our days fly by on such swift wings,
And then disease insinuates, old age,
And shadows of cold death. Behold. Instead
Of palms I might have won and luring hopes,
Black Tartarus awaits me now. The mind
Which quested for so much goes with the bride
Of Dis who went before,
To the possessing night and silent shore.

§

57.   Like jewels in rings, ideas are enclosed in and almost bound to words. Indeed they incarnate as the soul does in the body, making one being in such a way that ideas are inseparable from words, and if they are separated they are no longer the same, they escape our intellect and conception and become unrecognizable, as would our soul if it were parted from the body [July 27, 1822, Z, 2584].

II

TO ROME AND BACK (1822–25):

FAME AND THE PROSE

OF DISENCHANTMENT

To Rome and Back (1822–25):
Fame and the Prose
of Disenchantment

On November 17, 1822, Leopardi left Recanati for a few months in Rome. There he stayed with his mother's relatives, the Antici family, who led a warmer, more disordered life than he had known at home. His fame as philologist and poet preceding him, Leopardi met the Prussian scholar-diplomats Niebuhr and Bunsen, who sought Leopardi out, were amazed at his knowledge of classics ("At last I have seen an Italian worthy of ancient Rome!" reported Niebuhr), and were to remain his friends and advocates.. To free Leopardi from financial dependence, Niebuhr tried through Cardinal Consalvi to obtain him an administrative position with the Church; but when officials insisted that Leopardi don a prelate's cape as a condition of employment, Leopardi balked. He was never to have a similar chance. Years later, in 1828, Bunsen offered Leopardi a chair in literature at Bonn, but the prospect of German winters weighing more heavily than his warm respect for German scholarship, Leopardi regretfully declined. As for Rome, Leopardi's letters show how it was not the intellectual haven he had hoped. When he is not in a frank, brotherly way recreating for Carlo the world of Roman women, he is analyzing the alienation caused by large cities or registering his distaste for Roman scholarship and customs.

For Leopardi this was a time of prose, the mode he still associated in his genre-conscious way with realism. Many of his Roman days were spent absorbing Plato (a Roman publisher had suggested he produce a scholarly Italian edition), but the vision Leopardi was mulling was anything but Platonic: he was now bent on "the truth, which I so hated and loathed before." Returning to Recanati in May, 1823, he found comfort in evening chats with Carlo, Paolina, and the youngest brother, Luigi; but for many months most of his energies went into the *Operette Morali,* the dialogues and meditations which were to appall his parents and establish his international fame (or notoriety) as an apostle of disenchantment. The sole important poem of this period is *To His Lady,* a work which shows how he was simultaneously attracted and repelled by Platonism.

58. To Carlo Leopardi (Recanati)

Carlo Mio. If you think this is your brother Giacomo who writes you, you are much mistaken, for he is dead or unconscious and in his place there is a person who can barely remember his own name. Believe me, my dear Carlo, I am beside myself, not from wonder for even if I were to see the Demon I wouldn't be surprised, and I do not get a shred of pleasure from the grand things I see because I understand they are wondrous but I do not feel it. And I assure you that their number and greatness turned to boredom after the first day. . . .

Love me, by God. I need love, love, love, fire, emotion, life: the world is not made for me and I have found the devil far uglier than he is painted. Roman women, high or low, really turn one's stomach; the men arouse anger and pity. But you, just write me and love me, and talk to me much of yourself and of the rest of my family . . . [Rome, November 25, 1822].

59. To Paolina Leopardi (Recanati)

Cara Paolina. What do you want to know of my affairs? If I like Rome, if I'm having a good time, where I've been, what life I lead? As for the first question, I no longer know what to answer, for everyone asks me the same thing a hundred times a day, and wishing to vary the response I have used up my phrase-book and thesaurus.

Speaking seriously, rest assured that the dullest Recanatese has a greater dose of good sense than the sagest and most solemn Roman. The frivolity of these animals surpasses the limits of credibility. If I wished to recount all the ridiculous topics that are the stuff of their discourses, I would need a tome. This morning (to tell you of just one), I heard a group carry on seriously and at length about the good voice of a prelate who sang mass the day before yesterday, and on the dignity of his comportment in this function. . . .

All the population of Rome would not be enough to fill the piazza of Saint Peter's. I saw the cupola, even with my shortsightedness, from five miles away while traveling, and I saw it, with its ball and cross, very distinctly, the way you see the Apennines from where you are. All the grandeur of Rome serves only to multiply distances, and the number of steps you have to climb to find someone you want. These immense buildings and hence the interminable streets are so many spaces flung out to separate men instead of spaces which contain men. I do not see the beauty in placing ordinary chess pieces on a board as long as the Piazza della Madonna. I am not quite saying that Rome seems uninhabited, but I do say that if men really needed as much space to live and walk in as they do in these palazzi, these avenues, squares, churches—then the entire globe could not contain the human race . . . [Rome, December 3, 1822].

∽

60. To Carlo Leopardi (Recanati)

. . . You will say that I don't know how to live, that for you and those like you things would be different. But listen to the facts and my arguments. Man absolutely cannot live in a great sphere because his power of rapport is limited. In a small town we can become bored, but ultimately the connections among men and things do exist, because the sphere of these relations is restricted and proportioned to human nature. In a large city, men live without the least sympathy with their surroundings because the sphere is so large that a person cannot fill it, cannot feel it around him, and hence there is no point of contact between it and him. You can guess how much greater and more terrible is the *noia* one experiences in a large city—and so indifference, that horrible human passion, or lack of it, must inevitably reign in great cities, that is, in societies which are greatly spread out. . . .

But setting aside psychological and literary matters, of which I will speak another time (having already met quite a few Roman literati), I will confine myself to the topic of women and to the good luck you may think it easy to have with them in big cities. I assure you it's just the opposite. In promenading or in church, you can't find even a hag who will look at you. I've taken many walks around Rome in the company of handsome, well-dressed young men, and we've passed close by young women, who never even lifted their eyes. And it was clearly not from modesty but from total and habitual indifference. And all the women here are like that. Indeed, it is as difficult to accost a woman in Rome as in Recanati, in fact more so because of the excessive superficiality and dissipation of these female animals, who, except for this, inspire no interest whatsoever, are most hypocritical, love nothing except wandering around and amusing themselves some-how, and (believe me) do not *surrender it* ["non *la danno*"] except with the infinite difficulties it takes everywhere else. But there are always

81

the public women, whom I find much more cautious than they used to be and are in any case so dangerous, as you know.

I'm running out of paper. I will never finish chatting with you. Everyone is in bed, and I steal these moments from sleep because they will not leave me a moment's peace during the day. Say hello to Paolina. I beg you, dear Carlo, for the love you bear me, when you write me please try to enlarge your handwriting a bit and leave more space between the lines for the sake of my poor eyes. . . . You can write freely to me within reason, for I don't show your letters or others to anyone, and in this house people are incapable of violating letters addressed to me.

This evening I met some learned Germans who have somewhat comforted me. *Addio,* I kiss you, be of good cheer now [Rome, December 6, 1822].

ॐ

61. To Monaldo Leopardi (Recanati)

. . . As for the literary men, whom you inquire about, I have met very few, and those have taken away my desire to meet others. They all affect to arrive at immortality in a carriage, like the wicked Christians to Paradise. According to them, the height of human knowledge, indeed the only true study of man, is Antiquarianism. I have not been able to meet one Roman literary man who means by literature anything other than Archeology. Philosophy, morals, politics, psychology [*scienza del cuore umano*], rhetoric, poetry, philology—all this is alien to Rome and seems like child's play compared to determining whether a hunk of copper or rock belonged to Mark Antony or Mark Agrippa. Loveliest of all, there isn't one Roman who really commands Latin and Greek, and you well know what that lack portends for the study of antiquity. They chatter and argue all day, make fun of each other in periodicals, and organize cabals and alliances. And so goes Roman literature . . . [Rome, December 9, 1822].

ॐ

62. To Carlo Leopardi (Recanati)

In an earlier letter to Carlo, dated December 16, 1822, Leopardi had included more brotherly comments on Rome, Roman churchmen, and Roman women, high and low, including a judgment guaranteed to satisfy Carlo's interest in such worldly matters: "I know nothing about the high-class *puttane,* but as for the low, I swear to you that the ugliest, meanest coquette in Recanati is worth all the best ones in Rome." Eventually, the possibility that Carlo might not be the only one to read such letters suggested itself to Leopardi.

. . . My heart's beating so fast I can't express it, because on the one hand it seems impossible that if you received my letter, you wouldn't have wanted to answer promptly; on the other, I have a terrible suspicion that my letter was intercepted by someone in the house and not given to you—which would upset me greatly because I talked to you of nothing but women and obscenities. And if my father or mother has read what I wrote you . . . it would certainly show me as hypocritical and ungrateful and put me at war with them, which I cannot afford in any way now. I pray you with all my heart to resolve my doubt as soon as possible . . . [Rome, December 26, 1822].

The fears, if interesting and revealing, were unfounded: Carlo was simply not the best correspondent.

&

63. To Paolina Leopardi (Recanati)

Cara Paolina. Your letter was most welcome, as will be all those you write me. But I'm very sorry to hear you are so troubled by your imagination. In using the term, I do not wish to suggest that the fault is yours, but that from the imagination come all our evils; in fact, there is nothing in the world truly good or bad—humanly speaking—except bodily pain. I wish I could console you and purchase your happiness at the price of my own; but since I cannot, I assure you at least that you have in me a brother who deeply loves you and always will, who feels the harrowing discomfort of your situation, who sympathizes with you, who in short is part of everything that's yours.

After saying this, I shouldn't have to repeat that human happiness is a dream, that the world is not beautiful, indeed not bearable, unless seen from afar, as you see it; that pleasure is a word, not a thing; that virtue, sensibility, and greatness of heart are not only the sole consolations for our ills, but also the only good things. And these good things—since we live in society and the world—are not enjoyed or put to profit, as the young usually believe, but become utterly lost, leaving the soul in a fearful void.

You know these things, and not only know them but believe them. Nonetheless, you need and want to experience them for yourself; and this desire makes you unhappy. This happened to me, and happens and will happen eternally to all young people, as it happens to all men and even the old. And so nature bears us along. See how far I am from blaming you! But I want you, for love of me, to make some huge effort, to profit a bit from philosophy, to try to amuse yourself as best you can—as I know from long experience can be done, even in your state as in any other.

And finally I don't want you to despair, for in a day the cause of your melancholy can vanish, and most probably will. Indeed, if nature takes its course, it is most certain. . . . The happiness and unhappiness of every person (save again for bodily pain) is absolutely equal to that of every other, no matter what their respective situations. And so, precisely speaking, the poor, the old, the weak, the ugly, and the ignorant enjoy and suffer like the rich, the young, the strong, the beautiful, and the learned. This is so because each in his place fashions his own goods and evils, and the sum of good and evil that each man can create is equal to the sum creatable by anyone else . . . [Rome, January 28, 1823].

✍

64. To Carlo Leopardi (Recanati)
    . . . On Friday, February 15, 1823, I went to visit the tomb of Tasso and I wept there. This is the first and only *pleasure* I've experienced in Rome. It is a long trip and no one takes it except to see the tomb—but wouldn't one come all the way from America to taste two minutes' worth of tears? . . . Many persons become angry when they see how Tasso's ashes are marked by a meager stone in a nook of a tiny church. As for me, I wouldn't want to find these ashes in a mausoleum. You can understand what a crowd of emotions arises from seeing the contrast between the greatness of Tasso and the humbleness of his burial. But you cannot conceive the contrast of this small, naked tomb to an eye accustomed to the infinite magnificence and the sheer size of other Roman monuments. One feels a sad, trembling consolation at the thought that this bareness is enough to interest and inspire posterity, whereas one can see Rome's proudest mausoleums with perfect indifference toward the persons to whom they were erected, whose names may be less important than those of the monuments themselves . . . [Rome, February 20, 1823].

✍

65. To Carlo Leopardi (Recanati)

   . . . In short it's almost certain that had I wished to become a prelate, you would have soon heard tell that your brother in his prelate's cape had gone off to govern a province. The great expense necessary to buy the robes could have been borrowed (easily done here once you've won the office or are assured it). I took a look around and decided I wanted none of it. The reasons, which I could tell you, are many, and I think you would agree with me. If not, rest assured that I did not take this course through irresolution and lack of courage, but because for a long time before coming here and since, I have thought that my life must be as free as possible, and that my happiness cannot consist in anything other than following my own bent . . . [Rome, March 22, 1823].

∾

66.   In comparing ancient with modern philosophy, one finds the latter superior, chiefly because the ancient philosophers all wanted to teach and to build up whereas modern philosophy usually does nothing but disenchant and tear down. . . . And this latter is the true method of philosophizing—not, as some say, because the weakness of our intellect prevents us from finding positive truth, but because in effect the knowledge of truth is nothing other than the stripping away of errors; and wise is he who knows how to see the things before his eyes without conferring qualities on them they do not have.

   Nature stands all revealed before us, naked, open. To know her well we need not lift any covering veil—we need to remove the impediments and distortions in our own eyes and intellects, fabricated and caused in us by our cerebration. And so it is (as the simple know very well) that simplicity . . . is most subtle, that children and the purest savages excel in wisdom the most learned persons . . . [May 21, 1823, Z, 2709–10].

∾

67. To A. Jacopssen (Bruges)

   Leopardi returned to Recanati at the end of April, 1823. This letter, one of the relatively few composed during a two-year stay at home, was written in French to a young Belgian whom Leopardi had met and liked at Rome.

   . . . Without a doubt, my dear friend, either one should not go on living or one should always feel, always love, always hope. Sensibility would be the most precious gift if one could put it to use, or if there were in the world something to which to direct it. I have told you that the art of not suffering is now the only one I seek to learn. This is because I have renounced any hope of living. If from the time of my first attempts I had not already been convinced that this hope was completely vain and foolish for me, I would not have followed, or even recognized, any route *except* that of enthusiasm. For some time, I felt the emptiness of existence like a real thing pressing roughly down on my soul. The nothingness of things was for me the only thing that existed. It was always present like a terrifying phantom. I saw only a desert around me, and I could not conceive how one could submit to the everyday cares of life when one knew they would never amount to anything. That thought obsessed me so much that I believed I might go insane.

Truly, my friend, the world does not recognize where its own real interests lie. I will admit that virtue—like everything else beautiful and great—is nothing but an illusion. But if it were a shared illusion, if all men believed and wanted to be good, if they were compassionate, generous, high-minded, full of enthusiasm, in a word, if everyone were sensible (for I make no distinction between sensibility and that which is called virtue), wouldn't people be happier? Wouldn't each individual find a thousand sources of strength in society? As for society, shouldn't it aim at making these illusions come true as much as possible, since man's happiness cannot consist in that which is real?

In the matter of love, all the sensual delights that vulgar minds indulge in are not worth the pleasure given by one single moment of deep, rapturous emotion. But how do we make this feeling endure, or repeat itself often in our lives? Or find a heart that answers to it? Many times I have avoided for days seeing again an object which had charmed me in a sweet dream. I knew the spell would have been destroyed in confronting reality. Meanwhile, I thought always of the object, but not according to the way it really was; I contemplated it in my imagination, just as it seemed to me in my dream. Was this madness? Am I a romancer? Judge for yourself.

It is true that the habit of reflecting, which sensitive minds always have, often destroys the capacity to act and to enjoy. Too much inner life always pushes a person toward the outer, while at the same time compromising his ability to act externally. He hugs everything to him, he wants to be forever fulfilled; meanwhile all things slip away from him, precisely because they are smaller than his capacity. He demands even of his smallest actions, words, gestures, movements, superhuman grace and perfection. And so, never content with himself or ceasing his self-examination and always underestimating his own power, he cannot accomplish what everyone else does.

What then is happiness, my friend? And if there is no such thing, what then is life? I really do not know. . . . Ultimately, the imagination alone procures man the only sort of positive good of which he is capable. It is true wisdom to seek this happiness in the ideal, as you are doing. As for me, I look wistfully back on the time when I was allowed to seek it, and I see with a kind of dread that my imagination is becoming sterile and refuses me all the comfort it gave me before . . . [Recanati, June 23, 1823].

68.　Strength, originality, richness, sublimity, and even nobility of style can to a great degree come from nature, character, and education; or as a result of the latter those stylistic habits may be acquired in short time, and once acquired they can be put into practice with no real trouble. It is different with clarity and, especially nowadays, simplicity—by which I mean the quality almost identical with naturalness and the contrary of *perceptible* affectation of any kind in material, style, and composition. Clarity and simplicity (and thus charm, which cannot exist without them, and is for the most part, and often, merely another name for them) are entirely and always the work, the gift, and the effect of art. They are the basic, indispensable, indeed *absolutely* necessary, excellences of any writing: without them all other virtues are worth nothing; with them no writing, though it possess these alone, is ever contemptible. Clarity and simplicity, which must appear most natural, spontaneous, easy, and most easily achievable—qualities which it may be said consist precisely in completely concealing art and avoiding the faintest suggestion of the artificial and labored—these very qualities are precisely those which only art can produce. They are achieved only by study, are the most difficult to acquire the habit of, the last attained, and are such that, once the habit is acquired, it cannot truly be put into practice without the greatest pains . . . [July 26, Feast of St. Anne, 1823, Z, 3047–48].

69.　Nothing better demonstrates the greatness and power of the human mind or the stature and nobility of man, than his ability to recognize, completely comprehend, and strongly feel his smallness. When in considering the plurality of worlds he feels himself an infinitesimal part of one of the infinite systems composing the universe; when he marvels at the smallness and in deeply feeling and intensely contemplating it, almost fuses himself with nothingness, and almost loses himself in the thought of the immensity of things and of the incomprehensible vastness of existence—then with this act and thought he gives the best possible proof of his nobility, of the force and tremendous capacity of his mind, which though locked up in so tiny and minimal a being has been able to see and understand things so superior to his own nature, to embrace and contain in thought this actual immensity of things and of existence.

Certainly no other thinking creature on this planet is ever able to conceive or imagine being a small thing either in itself or in respect to other things, even if it is only the two-millionth part of a man in body, not to mention spirit. And truly, the greater a being is, as man is above all terrestrial beings, the more he is capable of recognizing and feeling his very smallness. And so it is that even among men this knowledge and this feeling are in fact greater, more vital, ordinary, continual, and full when the individual is greater, nobler, and possesses more intellect and genius [August 12, Feast of St. Clare, 1823, Z, 3171–72].

70.　　. . . All primitive nations and societies, as well as the savage ones of today, regarded the miserable or unfortunate person as the enemy of the gods, either because of the vices of crimes he was guilty of, or because of envy or some other passion or whim prompting the gods to hate him in particular or his race, etc., all according to the different concepts each nation had of justice and the nature of the gods. A failed undertaking showed that the gods had opposed it either *per se* or because they hated the attempter or attempters. A man habitually failing in his enterprises was inevitably thought to have provoked the gods' wrath. A sickness, a shipwreck, or other misfortunes even more common were certain signs of divine hatred. Hence a miserable person was avoided like a guilty one; people refused him every comfort and compassion, fearing that they might become accomplices in the wrong committed and thus sharers of the punishment. [Leopardi goes on to give linguistic evidence from several modern and ancient languages of the near fusing of concepts of misfortune and moral guilt in single words, e.g., French *"malhureux, miserable"* and Italian *"sciagurato, disgraziato, misero, miserabile. . . ."*] [September 3, 1823, Z, 3342–43].

∾

71.   *To His Lady*

In his Roman stay, Leopardi read intensively in Plato, a concentration which
shows in *Alla sua donna,* written in September, 1823, shortly after returning
to Recanati. The ideas and language of the poem, and of the note written for
the 1824 Bologna edition of Leopardi's poems, resemble Shelley's in his *Hymn
to Intellectual Beauty, Alastor,* or *Epipsychidion.* In Leopardi's poem, however,
religious devotion wars with a weary skepticism—the sense of "if-ness" in
the poem; the concept of an ideal beauty inspiring our lives emerges almost as
a literary theory, more to be wished than to be believed. The last sentence of
the note (which I include below) reveals the bluff, defensive cynicism of the
sophisticate and the extent to which Leopardi tried to suppress his heart and
to rebel against a Platonic-Christian idealism promising a better world
elsewhere.

. . . The beloved lady of the poet is one of those images or phan-
toms of celestial and ineffable beauty and virtue which appears often
to us in fantasy (whether we are awake or sleeping) when we are little
more than children, and also at rare times when, as youths, we are
sleeping or in an almost ecstatic state of mind. Ultimately she is the
unfindable woman ["*la donna che non si trova*"]. The author does not
know if his lady . . . was ever born or will ever be. He does know
that she is not now living on earth and that we are not her contempor-
aries. He seeks her among the ideas of Plato, in the moon, the planets
of our solar system, and those of other stars. If this *canzone* can be
termed amorous, surely such a love as described does not arouse or
deserve jealousy: with the exception of the author, no earthly lover
would wish to make love by telescope.[1]

> O dear and distant beauty
> Inspiring me although your face is veiled,
> Save when you grip the heart
> In sleep, bright deity, or when throughout
> The fields, the sun and all
> Of nature shine with more than usual light—
> Were you the one who once
> Beatified the age that men call golden?
> Whose soft-winged spirit only brushes us
> Today, while hoarding fate
> Keeps your full presence for a future time?
>
> In this, my day on earth,
> I cannot hope to see your living face

Until, until my lone, stripped essence come
By unfamiliar paths
To the unknowable and final land.
When I had just begun
My dark, uncertain sojourn here, I thought
You too might be a traveler in this waste;
But nothing we can know
Truly resembles you, and if we find
A one whose glowing movements, face, and words
Echo your loveliness,
They but recall to us your greater grace.

Despite the harrowed life
By fate assigned to creatures here below,
If one could consecrate his love to such
An image visioned in my mind, then earth
Would be a paradise;
And I might follow once
Again the fame and virtue sanctified
In me, for love of you, when I was young.
But heaven now extends
No comfort for our daily woe—with you
Our human life would be
The one enjoyed by gods, denied to us.

In this long valley,
The farmer's weary song hangs on the air,
Where I sit pondering
How my illusions have deserted me;
And in these gentle hills,
I wistfully remember lost desires
And hopes of early days—
And then I think of you
And my heart leaps awake. If only I
Could serve, in this bleak age and thickened air,
A semblance of the high reality
I rue, then ah, I would be satisfied.

If you, my love, are one
Of those undying forms the eternal mind
Will not transform to mortal flesh, to try
Funereal sorrows of ephemeral beings;

Or if you dwell in one
Of those innumerable worlds far off
In the celestial swirl,
Lit by a sun more stunning than our own,
And if you breathe a kinder air than ours—
Then from this meagre earth,
Where years are brief and dark,
This hymn your unknown lover sings, accept.

❧

72.   . . . In referring to the absence of pleasure and displeasure, one is
referring to *noia*. . . . *Noia* always and immediately runs to fill up all
the empty spaces left behind in living souls by pleasure and displeasure.
The void—that is the passionless state of indifference—cannot exist in
such a soul, just as it could not exist in physical nature according to the
ancients. *Noia* is like the air on earth, which fills all the spaces among
other objects, and races to be where they are not, unless other objects
take their place. Or shall we say that the void itself in the human mind,
and the indifference, and the absence of every other passion is *noia*,
which is itself a passion. Now what do we mean by saying that a
living being who is neither enjoying nor suffering is necessarily expe-
riencing *noia?* We mean that he can never stop desiring happiness, that
is pleasure or enjoyment. This desire—when it is neither satisfied nor
directly thwarted by the opposite of enjoyment—is *noia*. *Noia* is the
desire for happiness reduced, as it were, to purity. This desire itself is
passion. Thus the mind of a living being can never really be passion-
less. This passion when found alone, when no other actually occupies
the mind, is what we call *noia*. So *noia* is a proof of the perpetual
existence of passion in man. If this were not so, *noia* could not really
exist, nor could it be present where the others are absent [October 17,
1823, Z, 3714–15].

❧

73.   *The Story of the Human Race*

Written in January-February, 1824, this myth was partly responsible for
Leopardi's *Operette Morali* being denied the quinquennial prize awarded by
Florence's *Accademia della Crusca*. In the Florentine edition of 1834, Leopardi
was compelled to include the following note desired by the Censor: "The

91

author proclaims that in this fable and the others that follow, he is not referring to Mosaic or gospel history, nor to any traditions and doctrines of Christianity."[2]

Despite the proclamation, this cosmogony—an explanation of the origin, nature, and destiny of man—was obviously intended to anticipate and encapsulate the definitely unorthodox "system" of the other and later *Operette Morali*. Borrowing a few elements from classical mythology, Leopardi wove them into his own explanation of man's fate. In soft-spoken terms the piece is a Promethean attack against an unjust universe and a defense of humans, who have been created to aspire and are ultimately punished for so doing. (Indeed one wonders how the Censor let slip the Melvillian assertion that "those who believe that human sorrow first arose from sin and the acts committed against the gods deceive themselves; on the contrary, the wickedness of men arose from prior calamity.") Other basic Leopardian ideas are the conflict in the mind of man between corrosive Truth and illusory, if consoling, Beauty; the exaltation of childhood as the time when we are protected from truth and our illusions make our lives more beautiful than we are ever to know again; and the idea of a redemptive spiritual love (different from if sometimes related to, sexual love), which can make almost a blessing of the curse. This last idea grows in Leopardi until it culminates in the *Dialogue of Plotinus and Porphyry* and *Broom*.

Deucalion and Pyrrha, mentioned in the work, were indeed two survivors of the universal deluge as described in one of the Greek creation myths; contrary to Leopardi's reversal, they desired life, and by throwing behind them stones from Mother Earth they renewed our species.

It is told that all the men who inhabited the earth in the beginning were created as infants everywhere at the same time, and all were fed by bees, goats, and doves, as Jove was thought to have been in the poetic fables. The earth was much smaller than now, the lands were flat, the skies were starless, no sea existed, and there was less variety and magnificence. Nonetheless, men took insatiable pleasure in regarding and contemplating earth and heaven with great wonder, considering them most lovely and not merely vast but infinite in size, grace, and majesty. And they basked in most joyful hopes, extracted incredible delights from their sensations, and as they matured contentedly they almost thought themselves happy.

Having thus spent their childhood and early adolescence most sweetly, they arrived at a riper age and began to feel some alteration. For since the hopes which they had been deferring from day to day had not been realized, they lost faith in them. And contenting themselves with what they actually possessed, with no hope for improvement, seemed no longer possible, especially since the aspect of natural things and everything in their daily lives—whether by long habit or because they themselves had lost their original vitality—pleased and delighted them so much less then before. They wandered the earth visiting the farthest regions, which they could easily do because the land was flat and not divided by seas or fraught with other difficulties. And after many years most of them learned that the earth was not so large and had definite and appreciable boundaries; moreover, except for slight differences, all the places and people of the earth were alike. Thus their dissatisfaction grew, so that with their youth scarcely behind them they became universally uneasy about their being. Step-by-step in their maturity and particularly as they grew old, their satiety converted to hatred; and some despaired so much that—without the light and spirit which earlier they had so loved—they began to take their own lives in one way or another.

It seemed dreadful to the gods that living creatures should prefer death to life, and that they should be the instruments of their own destruction—with no compulsion from necessity or circumstance. It is not easy to describe how thunderstruck they were that their gifts should be considered so mean and abominable that anyone would cast them away so emphatically. To the gods it seemed they had given the world such goodness and beauty, such rules and conditions, that this dwelling-place should have been not merely tolerated but supremely loved by every animal, and especially by men, the race created with such singular care and wondrous excellence. But at the same time, the gods were moved by no small compassion at the human wretchedness shown in these results, and they also began to fear that if these sad examples were repeated and multiplied, the human race would soon die out, against fate's mandate. They also worried that the perfection attained in man would go to waste, and the gods would be deprived of the honor tendered them by man.

Since it seemed absolutely necessary, Jove decided to improve the status of humans and provide more ways to attain felicity. The chief human complaint, he found, was that things were not as vast in size, nor infinite in beauty, perfection, and variety as they had first judged, but were instead confined, imperfect, and monotonous. Humans protested not only their old age, but their maturity and even their youth; and craving the sweetness of their first years, they fervently prayed to return to childhood and stay there all their lives. This Jove could not grant, for it was contrary to the laws of nature and to the function and purpose of man as divinely decreed and determined. Nor could he share his own infinity with finite creatures, nor make matter infinite, nor render eternal the perfection and happiness of men and things.

And so it seemed best to enlarge the boundaries of the created world and to adorn and differentiate it more. This decided, he enlarged the

93

earth on every side, and introduced the oceans. Since the waters separated one populated area from another, they changed the appearance of things, and, by interrupting men's journeys, prevented them from knowing the world's boundaries. Moreover, they struck the eye with a vivid illusion of immensity. During this time, the new waters engulfed the land of Atlantis and numberless other widespread tracts, although the memory of Atlantis especially survives, passed down through centuries. And Jove made many places low and raised hills and mountains elsewhere. He sprinkled stars in the night; refined and purified the air; increased the brilliance of light and day; intensified and varied more the colors of meadows and sky; and he mixed the generations of mankind so that the old age of some coincided with the childhood or youth of others. Having resolved to multiply the appearances of infinitude man so dearly desired (since he could not grant the reality), and wishing to feed their imaginations, through which their childhood beatitude had come, he created the Echo—a device with effects like the sea—which he concealed in caves and valleys. He filled the forests with a deep, stirring sound and made the treetops move in waves. Likewise he created the people of dreams and charged them to take on many shapes to deceive men's thoughts with the promise of unknowable, unrealizable happiness; to produce for them those vague, perplexing forms of which he himself could not create the reality, no matter how men yearned.

Through these measures, Jove buttressed and refreshed the human spirit, so that men were again convinced of life's grace and dearness and once more found delight and awe in the immense beauty of earthly things. And this good state lasted longer than the first, mostly because the age differences introduced by Jove allowed the souls grown cold and weary by their experience to draw comfort from the ardent optimism of the young. But over time, the novelty wearing thin, tedium and scorn for life returned, and men sank into such a state that they then began the ancient custom, described in histories, of convening relatives and friends to mourn the birth of a child, and when he came to die, of feasting the day with speeches of congratulation for the dead. Ultimately all mortals turned to impiety, either because they felt deserted by Jove or because it is the nature of wretchedness to harden and corrupt even the best souls, turning them away from the good and the right. Thus those who believe that human sorrow first arose from sin and the acts committed against the gods deceive themselves; on the contrary, the wickedness of men arose from prior calamity.

It was then that the gods avenged themselves against the arrogance of man by sending the flood of Deucalion. The only two of our kind who survived the universal drowning were Deucalion and Pyrrha. These two agreed that only total extinction could solve the problems of the human race; and rather than lamenting or fearing the common lot, they sat on a high cliff urgently calling on death to come. When Jove ordered them to remedy the earth's desolation, they were so sorrowful and contemptuous of life they could not endure the work of sexual generation. Instead, as the gods had instructed them, they took stones from the mountain and by casting them over their shoulders, they restored the human race. Now, however, Jove had through experience grown wary of human nature, knowing that it did not suffice them (as it did the other animals) to live and be free of bodily pain and trouble; rather they desired always the unattainable, and the less they were afflicted by real torments the more they tormented themselves with imaginary ones. He therefore resolved to use two new devices to preserve this wretched race: one was to fuse real evils into their lives; the other, to embroil them in a thousand occupations and labors, so as to distract them as much as possible from communing with their own souls, or at least from the desire for that futile, unknowable happiness of theirs.

Jove began by spreading among them a host of physical and mental and other misfortunes so as to vary the conditions and possibilities of life. He hoped to prevent satiety and augment the value of the good things by contrast with woe; and to accustom their minds to wretchedness so that the absence of absolute pleasure, so unbearable to them before, would seem tolerable. He also intended to break their ferocity by teaching them to bend the neck, accept necessity, and be more content with their fate. He knew that men oppressed by ills and calamities would be less prone than before to turn their hands against themselves because their spirits would be too cowed and weakened by suffering. Those who suffer usually hope for the best and grasp at life, believing that if they overcome their ills they will be happy—and so nature persuades them.

Shortly afterwards Jove made storms of wind and rain-cloud, armed himself with thunder and lightning, gave Neptune his trident, spun the comets into flight, and arranged the eclipses. With these and other awful signs and effects, he meant to terrify humans from time to time, knowing full well that fear and present danger would at least briefly reconcile to life not only those who were unhappy but those who absolutely abhorred it and were most likely to flee it.

Then, to cure the idleness of men, he induced in them an appetite for new foods and drinks, which required much hard toil to obtain, whereas before the flood men had contented themselves with water and the greens and fruit supplied so freely by the earth and trees. . . . He gave to different regions of the earth different weather and divided the year into four seasons. And whereas before the earth's temperature had been so uniformly benign that men had no need of clothes, they now were at pains to dress themselves so as to counter the changes and inclemencies of weather.

He ordered Mercury to found the first cities and divide the race by people, nation, and language, thus sowing war and discord among them; and to teach men song and the other arts, which because of their origin and nature were, and are still, called divine. Jove himself gave laws, conditions, and civil ordinances to the new peoples. And finally, wishing to present them an incomparable gift, he sent among them phantasms of most excellent and superhuman appearance, which became the basis of human government and authority: these were called Justice, Virtue, Glory, Patriotism, and other such names. One of these phantasms was Love, who now came to earth along with the others, for before the use of clothes, it was not true love but desire which drew one sex to another—an appetite such as brute animals have always felt and much like that attracting us to food and other things.

The fruit of this divine planning for mortal life was marvelous. Despite the labors, terrors, and sufferings—things unknown by our race before—the new dispensation surpassed in sweetness and comfort the life before the flood. And this was due in part to those wonderful phantasms, which men considered sometimes genii, sometimes gods, and which they followed and worshipped with exceeding ardor and with immense and astonishing toil for a long epoch. They were spurred on to do so by the supreme efforts of noble poets and artisans, so that many mortals did not hesitate to sacrifice their blood and even lives to one apparition or another. . . .

The decline from this relatively happy human condition was due to various causes . . . , but the total revolution of fortune and the final fall from that state we now usually call ancient came chiefly from one cause, which was this. Among the prized phantasms of the ancients, there was one called Wisdom, who, universally honored and especially pursued by many men, had done her part for the recent prosperous centuries. Frequently—in fact daily—she had promised her followers to show them Truth, who she said was a tremendous genius and her own master but who sat with the gods in heaven rather than coming to earth. She promised that she would bring Truth down through her own influence and grace and induce her to roam among men for a while. By familiarity with her, humans would achieve such excellence of knowledge, institutions, and customs that their happy life would compare with that of the gods.

But how could a pure shadow or image like Wisdom hope to keep such a promise and bring Truth to earth? Thus, after long trusting in Wisdom, men became aware of the emptiness of her promises. Yet their frequent idleness made them crave anything new. Moreover, they were spurred on by their ambition to equal the gods and their desire for the happiness which the phantasm had indicated they might attain through conversing with Truth. So they turned to Jove, demanding insistently and presumptuously that he send this noble spirit to dwell awhile on earth. They reproved him for enviously denying them the infinite benefits conferrable by Truth's presence, and they renewed their old and odious lamentations on the vileness and poverty of their condition. Because the specious apparitions, the basis of so many good things in ages past, were no longer greatly respected by most—not that men had yet discovered their illusory nature but because their minds and manners had become so degraded that the phantasms hardly influenced most men now—they blasphemed the greatest gift the gods had, and could have, given. They cried out that earth had been blessed with only minor genii, whereas the greater ones, to whom earth would gladly bow, were not allowed to tread this despised part of the cosmos.

Now many things had for a long time alienated Jove's goodwill from humans, among them their unparalleled vices and misdeeds, which had for some time surpassed in gravity and number the wicked things avenged by the flood. He was thoroughly sickened, after so many trials, with the restless, insatiable, excessive nature of humans. And he now saw that no device, condition, or place would ever suffice to make them tranquil, much less happy. For even if he consented to multiply a thousandfold the dimensions and delights of earth and the imaginative wonder of things, everything would soon pall, shrink, and seem worthless to men, who were simultaneously incapable and desirous of infinitude. But now, at last, their stupid, arrogant demands so moved the god to wrath that he mercilessly resolved to punish the human race forever, condemning it for all future ages to a misery much deeper than in the past. And so he decided not merely to send Truth among men for a brief time, as they had asked, but to give her perpetual life among them, and—removing the lovely phantasms he had sent to earth before—to make Truth forever the ruler and lord of man.

The other gods were astonished by this decision, fearing it would exalt our state too much and undermine their superiority. Jove put their minds at ease, however, by pointing out that not all the great genii were necessarily beneficial, and that the quality of Truth was such that she could not affect man as she did gods. Said Jove, "Whereas to gods she reflects their own beatitude, to men she will reveal their entire misery and keep it constantly before their eyes. She will show their wretchedness to be not due to fate, but of such a nature that no chance occurrence or conscious remedy can change or interrupt it while they live. And since most human ills are evil to the extent they are believed so by the sufferer, we can easily judge how harmful the presence of Truth among men will be. For nothing will seem truer to them than the falseness of all human blessings, and nothing more solid than the emptiness of everything except their own pain. For these reasons they will even be deprived of hope, which from the beginning sustained life more than any other solace or delight. And so, hoping for nothing, and seeing no worthy goal for their activity and labor, they will reach such great neglect and hatred of every energetic and magnanimous endeavor that it will be difficult to distinguish the living from the dead. Yet, in this state of lethargic despair, they will still be tormented by that desire for immense happiness, which is innate in their souls and which will sting and torture them more than ever before because it will be less complicated and diverted by various occupations and the impetus of activity. At the same time, they will be shorn of the comfort due to the imagination, which alone has somewhat satisfied their cravings for that impossible, incomprehensible happiness unattainable by gods or men, no matter how much they wish. And every image of infinity I carefully placed in the world to deceive and nourish them (each according to his liking) with vast, indefinite thoughts will fail them because of the new doctrines and habits Truth will teach them. And if the earth and other parts of the cosmos seemed small to them before, they shall appear insignificant as men learn more about natural mysteries."

"And finally," Jove continued, "with the other phantasms gone, destroyed by Truth, who shall fully reveal to men the nature of those illusions, human life will lose all courage and uprightness in both thought and deed. Men everywhere will lose all respect for their homelands and consider themselves, as in the beginning, citizens of earth, but not in a good sense: for they will profess a universal love toward all humans, while in reality the race will disintegrate into individual units. Hence, with no native country to love dearly and no foreign one to hate, each man will hate everyone else and love himself alone. The number and nature of the resulting disturbances would take too long to tell. Yet, despite their infelicities, men will not be brave

enough to depart this life by their own hand, for the rule of Truth will
make them cowardly as well as wretched; and in the very process of
embittering their lives will deprive them of the courage to renounce
it."

On hearing Jove's intentions, the gods felt that our fate would be
too savage and terrible for divine mercy to permit. But Jove went on
to say: "Yet they shall have some small comfort from that phantasm
they call Love, whom I am disposed to leave among them while
removing all the others. And even most powerful Truth—who will
war with Love constantly—will never succeed in exterminating it, if
occasionally vanquishing it. Thus human life will be equally divided
between the worship of the phantasm Love and the genius Truth, and
together they shall have dominion over the minds of men. . . ."

So Jove withdrew from earth all the blessed phantasms save Love,
the least noble one, and he sent Truth down to dwell and rule perpet-
ually among them. And all those lamentable results he had predicted
took place, and one more marvelous thing: before Truth's arrival on
earth, when men had no commerce with it, they had honored it with
temples and sacrifices; but now that it had come to earth with imperial
power and they saw it face to face, instead of venerating it more and
more, they became so saddened and horror-stricken by it that though
forced to obey it they refused to adore it. And while other phantasms
were loved and honored by those who respected them, Truth aroused
fierce curses and deep hatred in those over whom it exerted the greatest
power. But unable to avoid or resist its tyranny, humans lived in that
supreme misery they now endure, and will endure forever.

Yet pity, never entirely extinguished in celestial hearts, moved Jove's
will (not long ago, in fact) at the sight of so much suffering, and
especially at that endured by certain humans of high intelligence, noble
behavior, and integrity, who he noticed were more oppressed and
afflicted than others by the power and harsh domination of Truth. In
ancient days, when Justice, Virtue, and the other phantasms governed
human affairs, the gods would come to earth to visit their dominions
and would reveal their presence in various ways. This custom had
always benefited men in general or one individual among them. But
now that life was again corrupt and sunken in every form of wicked-
ness, the gods avoided for a long time any commerce with humans.
At last, Jove, taking pity on our extreme unhappiness, asked the gods
whether any of them would like to visit earth again as they had once
done, to ease the misery of man, especially those who seemed to
deserve a better fate. At this, the gods remained silent save for one,
Love, the son of the Celestial Venus—alike in name to the phantasm

named after him, but most different in nature, virtue, and words. This Love, whose compassion is greater than any other god's, offered to do what Jove requested and to descend from heaven. The council of immortals had never allowed him to leave before, even for a short time, since he was so indescribably dear to them (although occasionally a few of the ancients, tricked by different frauds and transformations of the phantasms bearing the same name, thought they had received unquestionable signs of the great Love's presence). But he never visited mortals until after Truth came to dominate them; and since then, he comes down only rarely and briefly, partly because of our general unworthiness and partly because the gods fret so when he is away.

When he does come to earth, Love chooses to dwell in the tender, kind hearts of generous, high-minded persons, and there he lives for a short time, diffusing so rare and wonderful a sweetness, such noble feelings, such virtue and strength, that they experience a thing new to the human race—not the semblance of happiness but happiness itself. Very rarely does he unite two such hearts by binding them together at the same time in mutual ardor and desire. Although those possessed by Love often pray for this, Jove seldom permits him to gratify the desire, for such a blessing too nearly resembles those possessed by the gods themselves.

In any case, being filled with his spirit is a state more fortunate than any human knew in the better times. Wherever he lights, those beautiful phantasms banished by Jove from earth congregate again, invisible to everyone else, but brought back by Love with Jove's permission. Even Truth cannot forbid it, although she is a great enemy of those phantasms and is terribly offended by their return. But the genii may not dispute the gods.

And since the fates endowed Love with eternal childhood, so, in accordance with his nature, he fulfills to some degree the great desire of men to return to their own childhood. For in the souls he chooses to inhabit, he reawakens and makes green again the infinite hopes and the dear, beautiful fancies of their tender years. Many mortals, ignorant of and incapable of the delights he brings, scorn and mock him daily, whether he is there or not, with reckless audacity. But he is deaf to their insults and would not punish them even if he heard, so gentle and large is his nature. Moreover, the immortals, content with the vengeance taken against our whole race, and with the incurable misery which afflicts us, do not heed the individual offenses of men—the fraudulent, the unjust, and the blasphemers of the gods are singly punished only by being alienated forever from this divine grace.

❧

74.   *Dialogue of a Sylph and a Gnome*

This discussion of the futile solipsism of created beings was composed in
March, 1824. The discussants derive from popular mythology: the sylph was
a playful spirit from the upper air, and the gnome was one of the underground
imps charged by Dionysus with guarding the gold and silver lodes of the
earth. Lycurgus was an ancient Spartan leader who countered his people's
extravagance by forcing them to use ponderous iron money instead of gold
or silver. Caesar, mentioned in the last line, was assassinated at the base of
Pompey's statue.

Sylph: Oh it's you, little son of Dionysus? Where are you going?
Gnome: My father has sent me to find out what the devil these rascal
          human beings are up to. He's very worried because for some
          time they haven't made any trouble, nor is there one to be
          found anywhere in his kingdom. He wonders if they are
          concocting a plot against him, and whether they have re-
          turned to the old currency of sheep instead of gold and silver;
          or whether civilized people are now content with using paper
          bills for money, as they have in the past, or glass baubles like
          the barbarians; or whether the laws of Lycurgus have been
          reinstated—which seems the least likely to him.
Sylph: "You await them in vain; they are all dead," as was said at
          the end of a tragedy where all the characters had perished.
Gnome: What are you suggesting?
Sylph: I wish to suggest that men are all dead—the race is vanished.
Gnome: Oh that indeed would be newsworthy, but I haven't seen it
          in any paper.
Sylph: You idiot, hasn't the thought crossed your mind that if men
          are dead there wouldn't be any newspapers?
Gnome: Well said. But now how will we know what's new in the
          world?
Sylph: What do you mean "new"? That the sun has risen and set?
          That it's cold or hot? That here or there it has rained or
          snowed, or the wind has gusted? For, in the absence of men,
          Fortune has thrown away her blindfold, donned her glasses,
          and hung up her wheel on a hook. She sits with crossed
          arms, gazing at the events of the world without taking a
          hand in them. There are no longer kingdoms and empires
          swelling and bursting like bubbles because they are all gone.
          There is no more war, and one year looks like another, just
          like eggs.

Gnome: But we won't even know what day it is without their printed calendars.

Sylph: We'll make do, and the moon won't lose its way without calendars.

Gnome: And the days of the week shall have no names.

Sylph: So, are you afraid that if you don't call them by name they won't come? Or maybe you think you can make the ones gone by return again if you use their names?

Gnome: And we won't be able to keep track of the years.

Sylph: That means we can pretend we're young even when we're not, and by not counting the passing time we will cause ourselves less pain; and when we're very old we won't sit around thinking of death every day.

Gnome: But how did these scoundrels happen to wipe themselves out?

Sylph: Some by making war on each other; some by sailing the oceans; some by devouring each other. Quite a few died by their own hand; others rotted away in sloth; some cracked their brains on books; and some tried a thousand types of debauchery and disorder. In short, they found every possible way to violate their natures and come to a bad end.

Gnome: In any case, I just can't conceive how a whole species could annihilate itself as you say.

Sylph: You who are such a geology teacher should know that this isn't a new thing, and that many animals who used to roam the ancient world are no longer with us, except for a few fossils. And certainly those poor creatures didn't employ the artificial means I described men as using to come to perdition.

Gnome: You may be right. But I do wish one or two of that crew would come back to life so I could see what they thought of things still going on as before even though the human race has disappeared, and though they used to think the whole world was made and maintained for them alone.

Sylph: They simply wouldn't believe that it was made and maintained for the sylphs.

Gnome: You are quite mad if you are at all serious.

Sylph: Why so? I am always very serious.

Gnome: Hey, go to, you little clown! Who doesn't know the world was made for the gnomes?

Sylph: For gnomes who are always underground? Oh that's rich! What good are the sun, the moon, the air, the sea and meadows to gnomes?

Gnome: And what do sylphs have to do with silver and the whole mass of earth beneath its first layer?

Sylph: All right, all right, why don't we forget this argument, for I firmly believe that even lizards and gnats think the whole world made just for their kind. And so everyone keeps to his unshakeable opinion, and as for me I tell you only this: That had I not been born a sylph, I don't know that I'd do.

Gnome: I feel the same about being born a gnome. But I would really like to know what humans would say about their arrogance, which led them, among other tricks, to dig deep underground and steal what belonged to us, saying it belonged to the human race, and that nature had hid it, buried it down there for a game, wishing to see if they could find it and bring it to the surface.

Sylph: Is it any wonder? When they not only persuaded themselves that everything in the world functioned only for their service, but was of no importance compared to the human race. And they considered their stirrings as revolutions of the world and their history world history; even though one could distinguish merely on earth so many other species of animals, if not real creatures, as numerous as single humans. And these animals, provided expressly for their use, were not aware of the world's revolutions.

Gnome: Did they think that even the mosquitos and fleas were created for their benefit?

Sylph: Even them, to teach them patience as they used to say.

Gnome: As if there weren't enough to try their patience without fleas!

Sylph: According to Chrysippus (as cited by Cicero) pigs were mere pieces of meat prepared by nature precisely for the pleasure and cuisine of humans, and outfitted with souls to preserve them like salt.

Gnome: I do believe that if Chrysippus had had a little salt in his brain instead of a spirit, he would never imagined such an unfortunate simile.

Sylph: And here's another interesting thought: that an infinite number of animal species were never known or seen by men, their masters, either because they lived where men never traveled or because they were so small that humans had not discovered them. And they did not become aware of many other species until their last days. The same can be said of plants and countless other things. Similarly, with their telescopes they discovered from time to time some star or planet that until then, for thousands and thousands of years, they had never known to exist in the world. And then they immediately reckoned it their property; because they imagined that the stars and planets were, in a sense, so many lantern wicks planted up there to give light to their majesties because they were so busy at night.

Gnome: So that on summer nights when they saw those little shooting lights falling through the air, they must have thought some spirit was going about snuffing the stars for their benefit.

Sylph: But now that they are gone, the earth is none less for it, the rivers do not weary of flowing, and though the sea no longer serves for navigation and commerce, it does not seem to be drying up.

Gnome: And the stars and planets do not cease to be born and to set, and they have not put on their mourning clothes.

Sylph: And the sun has not plastered its face with rust as it did, according to Virgil, at the death of Caesar—for whom I think the sun cared about as much as did Pompey's statue.

∾

75. To Giuseppe Melchiorri (Rome)

Melchiorri was a close, affectionate cousin also interested in literature. His request for some occasional verses elicited these comments on Leopardi's method of composition.

Caro Peppino. You did nothing wrong in promising [them] for me, for you must have thought I was like all the others who write verses. But in this as in everything else I am much different and much inferior. As for verses, understanding my nature may stand you in good stead on some similar occasion.

I have written in my life only a few short poems. In writing them I have always pursued the inspiration (or frenzy) of a few minutes, during which I have shaped the overall design and the parts. This accomplished, I usually wait for it to return at some other moment, and when it does (which ordinarily takes some months), I take to composing. But I work so slowly that I cannot finish a poem, even a short one, in less than two or three weeks. This is my method, and if the inspiration doesn't spring up by itself, it would be easier to get water from a rock than one line from my brain. Others can write poetry at will, but I do not possess this ability at all, and no matter how much you asked, it would be useless, not because I don't want to please you but because I can't . . . [Recanati, March 5, 1824].

76. . . . Now what is *noia?* It is not any particular pain—indeed the idea and nature of *noia* excludes the presence of any specific ill or pain—but rather it is pure life, life fully felt, experienced, known, completely present to the individual and occupying him. Hence life is simply an evil, and not living, or living less (both in extent as well as intensity) is simply a good, or less of an evil—absolutely preferable *per se* to life, etc. [March 8, 1824, Z, 4043].

77. To Pietro Brighenti (Bologna)

In this letter to his lawyer-publisher friend, Leopardi refers to the hostility of censors to the *Brutus* poem and note in the *Canzoni* of 1824 which Brighenti was trying to get published. The volume was issued after a small compromise in the note.

Dear friend. I have received your two charming letters of the 17th and 27th last. I, dear friend, have a great vice, which is that I don't ask permission of the monks when I think or when I write; thus when I afterwards want to publish, the monks don't permit me to do so. I thank you endlessly for the concern you've shown for my poems, and I'm doubly obligated—for the thing itself and also for the pain it must have cost you to have to argue with that ilk. You're quite right that theologians are a race as hardheaded as women. They would sooner draw all the teeth from their mouths than one opinion from their heads. Surely it would be better to deal with women or the devil himself than with them.

I don't see, however, how my "new" *canzoni* would offend monarchs. And if the prose undermines virtue, I say expressly to anyone who has studied his theology that I mean to speak of human virtue, and do not go near the theological ones. At the beginning of the prose piece which caused this rebuke, it is written that "humanly speaking," virtue is, etc. etc.; and at the end I touch on religion in a way that wouldn't offend anyone except a brother censor [Recanati, April 3, 1824].

∾

78.   Persons accustomed to expressing themselves to the world naturally cry out even when they are quite alone, if a fly bites them or if they overturn a vase or break it. But when those used to living with themselves and keeping everything inside, even in a large company, are smitten by an accident, they do not open their mouths to complain or ask for help [April 17, Holy Saturday, 1824, Z, 4068–69].

∾

79.   *The Wager of Prometheus*

This piece, so reminiscent of Voltaire's *Candide,* was written in April-May of 1824. The imaginary celestial city where the action begins, Hypernephelus, is Leopardi's invention, meaning "beyond the clouds." Momus, the companion of Prometheus here, was a minor god devoted to sarcasm and criticism. The first stop of their journey, Popaian, was in what is now Colombia. The second is at Agra, India, where the old practice of *suttee,* or widow immolation, is being indulged. The tragic family incident in London was echoed by Federico Fellini in his film *La Dolce Vita.*

In the year 833,275 of Jove's reign, the College of the Muses printed up and posted around the public places of the city and suburbs of Hypernephelus many announcements inviting all the major and minor gods and other citizens who had ever created some praiseworthy invention to present it, or a model or description thereof, before certain judges appointed by the college. And apologizing because its noted poverty precluded the generous treatment it would have liked, it promised as a prize to the person whose discovery was judged the most lovely or useful a crown of laurel—with the privilege of wearing it day and night, privately and publicly, in and out of the city; and of being painted, sculpted, engraved, molded, or represented in any mode or material whatsoever with that crown on his head.

Quite a few celestials competed for the prize to pass the time (something just as necessary for the inhabitants of Hypernephelus as for those of other cities). They cared not at all for the crown, which in itself was not worth a cotton cap. As for the glory, if humans, after becoming philosophers, learn to scorn it, one can guess at the opinion of the gods, who are so much wiser than men, indeed the only wise ones according to Pythagoras and Plato.

In any case, with a unique fairness till than unheard of in similar contexts, without any influences, solicitations, favors, secret promises, or other machinations, the competition was judged. The winners were three: Bacchus for the invention of wine; Minerva, for that of oil, used by the gods to anoint themselves after their daily baths; and Vulcan, for having invented an economical copper saucepan which cooks things quickly and with little flame. Now if the prize had been divided into three parts, each of the winners would have been left with a twig of laurel, but all three refused their share of the whole crown as well. Vulcan alleged that in bending, working, and sweating most of the time over the fire in his forge such an encumbrance on his head would be most uncomfortable; and besides he would run the risk of being singed or roasted if by chance some spark landing on those dry leaves made them catch fire. Minerva said that since she already had to sustain a helmet great enough (as Homer writes) to cover the armies of a hundred cities in all, she could not afford to augment this weight in any way. Bacchus did not wish to change his mitre and crown of vine leaves for that of the laurel—although he would have gladly accepted it if he had been allowed to use it as a sign outside his tavern. Since the muses refused to honor his request, the crown remained in their possession.

None of the competitors for the prize envied the three gods who had won and refused it, and none complained of the judges and judgment, save one—Prometheus, who had entered the contest by submitting a clay model used by him in forming the first humans, appending a written description attesting to the qualities and functions of the human race founded by him. His chagrin caused no small astonishment among the others, winners and losers alike, who had taken the thing as a joke. But investigating his reason, they learned that he effectively did not desire the honor so much as the privilege conferred by victory, the crown itself. Some think he intended to use the laurel to defend his head against storms, much as Tiberius, who when hearing the thunder roll immediately donned his crown, thinking himself safe from the lightning. But in the city of Hyphernephelus there is no thunder or lightning. Others more convincingly affirm that Prometheus, because of his age, was beginning to lose his hair, a misfortune he suffered, as so many do, with bad spirits, and that not having read the praises of baldness written by Synesius or not convinced by them—which is more likely—he wished to hide under the diadem, as did Caesar the dictator, the nudeness of his head.

But let us return to the story. One day while discussing the matter with Momus, Prometheus complained bitterly that wine, oil, and saucepans had won out over human beings, whom he said were the greatest works of the gods yet created on earth. And thinking that Momus (who adduced I know not what contrary arguments) was not properly convinced, he proposed they descend together to earth, visiting the five major parts and staying at random wherever they found humans dwelling, with the following purpose: to see whether or not in the five regions, or most of them, they could find clear evidence that man is the most perfect creature in the universe.

With Momus agreeing on a bet and the amount of it, they began immediately to descend toward earth, heading first toward the New World, which because of its name and because no immortal had yet set foot in it most piqued their curiosity. They landed in the northern part of the country called Popaian, not far from the river Cauca, in a place showing many signs of human habitation. There were vestiges of culture throughout the countryside: several paths, definite even though interrupted in many places and grown over; felled trees; and particularly what seemed to be graves and human bones scattered around. But even in straining their eyes and ears all around the two immortals could not hear a voice or detect the shadow of a live human. They voyaged, partly walking, partly flying, for many miles, passing mountains and rivers, but finding everywhere only the same signs and same solitude. Said Momus to Prometheus, "How could these lands showing so much evidence of past inhabitants now be deserted?" Prometheus reminded him of the tidal waves, earthquakes, storms, and heavy rains of the tropical regions, and even as they spoke they heard from the forests all around the sound of water dripping from tree branches moved by the wind. But Momus could not understand how the sea, so far and out of view, could flood this area; nor could he comprehend by what destiny earthquakes, storms, and rains could have undone all the humans of the country while sparing the jaguars, monkeys, ants, eagles, parrots, and a hundred other kinds of land and sky animals roaming the area.

At last, landing in an immense valley, they discovered a small cluster of wooden houses or huts, each roofed with palm leaves and fenced in. In front of one of these huts were many persons, some standing, others sitting, around a great earthen vessel hung over a strong fire. As they drew nearer the two immortals took the forms of humans, and Prometheus, greeting everyone courteously, turned to the one who seemed to be the chief and asked, "What are you up to?"

Savage: We're eating, as you can see.

Prometheus: What good things have you?

Savage: This little bit of meat.

Prometheus: Is its domestic or wild flesh?

Savage: Domestic I suppose, since it's that of my son.

Prometheus: Was your son a calf, like the child of Pasiphae?

Savage: Not a calf but a human like others.

Prometheus: Are you really serious? Are you eating your own flesh and blood?

Savage: Not exactly mine—his. For I begot him and went to the bother of feeding him just for this purpose.

Prometheus: For the purpose of eating him?

Savage: Why so surprised? I am also going to eat his mother pretty soon, I think, once she is no longer good at bearing children.

Momus: Just as one eats the hen after eating her eggs.

Savage: And I will eat my other women too when they become useless for child-bearing. And do you think I would keep alive these slaves you see if it were not for the occasional child they produce for me to eat? But they're getting old and I'll eat them one by one if I live long enough.[3]

Prometheus: Tell me, these slaves—are they from your nation or another?

Savage: Another.

Prometheus: Very far from here?

Savage: Extremely far, so far that they lived on the other side of a brook which separated us.

And pointing his finger at a little hut, he added, "There is where they lived, but our people destroyed their nation."[4]

At this moment it seemed to Prometheus that some of the savages were watching him with the kind of loving gaze bestowed by cats on mice; so that to avoid being consumed by his own creations, he quickly soared upwards, and Momus with him. And their terror was so great that in leaving they corrupted the barbarians' food with that sort of filth discharged by the Harpies on the Trojan dinner tables. But the savages, more hungry and less fussy than Aeneas's companions, continued their dinner.

Prometheus, sorely disillusioned with the New World, turned his course immediately toward the older one, that is to Asia, and traveling in almost an instant over the space separating the new and old Indies, they descended near Agra in a field full of countless people, gathered around a pit loaded with wood. At one edge of the pit were persons with lighted torches about to set it on fire and on the other side, up on a platform, there was a young woman, dressed in sumptuous raiment with every kind of barbaric ornament, who, dancing and yelling, demonstrated the greatest joy. Prometheus, seeing this, imagined her another Lucretia or Virginia, or a fresh emulator of the daughters of Erechtheus, or of Iphigenia, Codrus, Menecius, Curtius, or Decius, who, obeying the commands of some oracle, was willingly immolating herself for her country. Learning, however, that the reason for the woman's sacrifice was the death of her husband, he thought that she, much like Alcestis, was attempting to buy back his spirit at the cost of her own life. But learning further that she would not have ventured to burn herself if not for the custom of widows of her class so to do, that she was quite drunk, and that the dead man, instead of being reborn, was to be burned in the same fire—Prometheus turned his back quickly on the scene and made off for Europe, conversing thus with Momus as they went.

Momus: Did you ever think when you stole at such great peril the sacred fire to communicate it to men that they would use it to cook each other in pots or to burn themselves to death?

Prometheus: Certainly not. But consider, my dear Momus, that those we have seen till now are barbarians, and one must not judge humans on the basis of barbarians but according to the civilized people we travel toward at present. And I'm firmly convinced that among them we will see and hear things and words which will seem not only praiseworthy but astonishing to you.

Momus: As for me, I can't see how if humans are the most perfect race in the universe they need to be civilized into not burning themselves up and not eating their children—when indeed the other animals are all wild and nonetheless do not burn themselves on purpose, except for the phoenix, which may be mythical. Rarely do animals eat their own kind, and more rarely yet do they feast on their children, and, if so, by accident, not because they generated them for that use. And furthermore, note that of the five parts of the world, a part of only one, which itself is the smallest of the five, is endowed with the civilization you so praise, although there may be some little pockets elsewhere in the world. And you yourself will not say that this civilization is so developed that today the men of Paris or Philadelphia have generally attained all the perfection achievable by their race.

Now in order to reach their present imperfect degree of culture, how long have these people had to suffer? From their origins to the present day. And yet almost all of the inventions that were either crucial or conducive to their cultural development originated by accident rather than design—so that human civilization is more the work of fate than of nature. And where such events have not occurred we see that the people are still barbarous, even though they are as ancient as the civilized peoples.

I conclude therefore: if the barbaric humans show themselves inferior by a great measure to every other animal; if civilization, the opposite of barbarism, is possessed even today by only a tiny portion of the human race; if this portion could only attain its current civil status after innumerable centuries, and with the great aid of chance; if the foresaid civilized state is not yet perfected—if all this is true, don't you think you ought to modify your judgment about the human race? Perhaps to say that it is truly the greatest in imperfection rather than perfection? It doesn't matter that men in speaking and judging use the terms interchangeably, arguing from certain presuppositions they themselves created and hold as palpable truths. All other creatures were surely most perfect from their very beginning. Furthermore, even if it were not clear that barbaric man is less good than the other animals, I cannot persuade myself that being most imperfect in one's own nature (as man seems to be) in any way argues for superiority over all other creatures. Add that human civilization, so difficult to establish and perhaps impossible to polish, is not so stable as to avoid collapse—as has happened in effect many times with many peoples who had achieved a good part of it.

In sum, I conclude that if your brother Epimetheus had presented the judges the models from which he formed the first jackass or first frog he might have won the prize you did not achieve. I will, however, concede gladly that man is perfect if you admit that his perfection resembles that which Plotinus attributed to the world itself. You will remember he said that the world is absolutely perfect in the sense that to be perfect it must have among other things all possible evils, and in fact it does. And from this point of view I would also agree with Leibniz that the present world is the best of all possible worlds.

No doubt Prometheus had an answer ready which was clear, precise, and dialectical in meeting all these arguments, but it is equally certain that he did not give it for at that very moment they found themselves over the city of London, where they descended. Seeing a great multitude of people gathered at the door of a private house, they mingled with the crowd and entered the house. There they found a man lying stretched out on a bed with a pistol by his side and a wound in his breast. He was dead, as were the two small children lying beside him. There were in the room some persons of the house and several officials interrogating them while one official took notes.

Prometheus: Who are these unfortunates?

Servant: My master and his children.

Prometheus: Who killed them?

Servant: My master, all three.

Prometheus: You mean his children then himself?

Servant: Exactly.

Prometheus: What a terrible thing! Some great misfortune must have befallen him.

Servant: None that I know of.

Prometheus: But surely he was poor, or despised by all, or unfortunate in love, or at court.

Servant: On the contrary, he was very rich, and I think everyone admired him. Love didn't bother him, and he was a favorite at court.

Prometheus: How then was he driven to such desperation?

Servant: It was the meaninglessness of life, according to the note he left.

Prometheus: And these officers, what are they doing?

Servant: They're trying to find out whether my master was insane or not, for if he was not his property goes to the government by law. And indeed that's the only way it will turn out.

Prometheus: But tell me, didn't he have any friend or relative to whom he could have left his children instead of murdering them?

Servant: Yes he did, and among others there was a very close
             friend to whom he left his dog.[5]

Momus was about to congratulate Prometheus on the good results
of civilization and the happiness it fosters in human life; and he also
wished to remind him that no animal besides man kills himself volun-
tarily or desperately wipes out the life of his children—but Prometheus
stopped him, and without bothering to see the remaining two parts of
the world he paid him the price of the wager.

~

80.   *Dialogue of Nature and an Icelander*

Composed in May, 1824, this dialogue reveals Leopardi's changing perception
of nature.[6] Whereas at other moments he had seen nature as the kindly mother
shielding her children from the pains due to reason and civilization, or had
symbolized her as a distant, silent moon, now he gives her a devastating
voice. The questions posed by the Icelander are the classic ones asked by
children of men and men of gods: why was I born and why is there pain and
evil? The nature who answers here in cryptic, unsatisfying terms contrasts
with the holy and benign essence celebrated by Emerson and Wordsworth;
this abstraction looks forward to that darkly acknowledged by later writers,
more or less conditioned by Darwin's ideas, such as Zola and Stephen Crane.
But one of the most interesting parallels is with Melville's *Moby-Dick*. Al-
though the Icelander is passive compared with the raging Ahab and desires
escape instead of confrontation or mastery, in both works the force encoun-
tered blends beauty with terror, cruelty with indifference, and is, above all,
inscrutable. The two works share yet another feature, the problem of whether
the awesome abstraction is identical to God.

An Icelander, who had traveled through most of the world and lived
in many different lands, passing one day through the interior of Africa
and crossing the equator in an area never before penetrated by man,
had an experience like that of Vasco di Gama at the Cape of Good
Hope: when the Cape itself, guardian of the Southern seas, loomed up
before him in the form of a giant to discourage him from trying those
new waters. The Icelander saw from afar a tremendous figure, which
at first he imagined to be of stone, quite like those colossal stone
figures seen by him many years earlier at Easter Island. But approach-
ing, he found that it was the vast form of a woman seated on the earth,
her trunk erect, her back and elbow leaning on a mountain, and not a

sculpture but a live being—with a face at once beautiful and terrible and the blackest of eyes and hair. She stared at him for some time without speaking, then finally said to him:

Nature: Who are you? And what do you seek in these places where your kind has been unknown?

Icelander: I am a poor Icelander fleeing Nature, and having fled her almost all my life through a hundred parts of the world, I flee her now through this one.

·Nature: So runs the squirrel from the rattlesnake, till finally he falls all by himself into her maw. I am she whom you flee.

Icelander: Nature?

Nature: None other.

Icelander: I am sorry to the bottom of my soul, for I am sure that no greater misfortune could have happened to me.

Nature: You should have known that I would especially frequent these areas, where my power is shown more obviously than elsewhere. But whatever led you to try to escape me?

Icelander: I'll tell you. Even in the prime of youth, with little experience, I was clearly convinced of the emptiness of life and the foolishness of men, who constantly struggled with each other to acquire pleasure which did not please and possessions which did not fulfill; constantly prompting and propagating the infinite woes and evils which torment and plague them—the farther they get from happiness the more they search for it. For these reasons, abandoning all other desires, I resolved—not annoying anyone whomsoever, not trying in any way to advance my state, not competing with others for any wealth in the world—to live an obscure and tranquil life. And disenchanted with pleasure, as with something denied our species, I set myself no other goal than to distance myself from sufferings. I don't mean to suggest that I thought to abstain from bodily concerns and labor—for you know very well that work and hardship are different, as are the quiet life and the slothful. And indeed, in carrying out my plan, I knew for certain how vain it is to think that among humans one can escape harm by not harming, that even by conceding everything and being content with scraps one is assured those scraps.

In any case, I freed myself from mankind's harassment most easily, cutting myself off from their society and reducing myself to solitude, a thing which in my native island can be easily accomplished. This done, and living with almost nothing resembling pleasure, I still could not keep myself free from suffering. For the winter's length, the cold's intensity, and the summer's extreme heat, characteristics of that location, bothered me continually; and the fire by which I had to spend much time burned my eyes with smoke and parched my skin; so that neither in the house nor outside could I keep myself from perpetual discomfort. Nor could I maintain that tranquility of life to which my thoughts would often turn. The fearful storms of earth and ocean, the roars and threats of Mount Ecla, the fear of frequent fires in my wooden dwelling never ceased to bother me. Such discomforts in a monotonous life, one stripped of all other desire or hope and of almost all concern except that of peace, turn out to be considerable and much more serious than they usually seem when most of our mind is caught up with society and men's abuses.

Observing that the more I shrank away and contracted into myself so as not to vex or harm anything in the world the more these other things vexed and troubled me, I decided to change habitations and climes, to see whether anywhere in the world I could without offending, not be offended, without enjoying, not suffer. In this deliberation I was influenced by a thought which occurred to me: that perhaps you had decreed for humans only certain climates and certain locations in the world (as you had for other animals and for plants); that if men scorned and exceeded these limits prescribed by your law, it was their fault they could not prosper and lived miserably.

I have, therefore, gone throughout the world and tried most countries in search of the tranquil life, always observing my rule to harm other creatures not at all or as little as possible. But I was scorched by heat in the tropics, numbed by cold at the poles, afflicted in the temperate zones by the changeable weather, hounded by the commotion of the elements everywhere. I saw many places where not a day passes without a tempest, which is to say that you daily assault and wage full-scale war against those inhabitants, who are innocent of any injury against you. In other areas, the usual serenity of the heavens is balanced by frequent earthquakes, by the multitude and fury of volcanoes, and by the subterranean fulminations of the entire land. Winds and whirlwinds rule the locations and seasons free from other furies of the air. Sometimes I nearly had the roof cave in on my head through the weight of the snow; other times, from the surplus of rain, the crumbling earth itself vanished beneath my feet; sometimes I had to run full speed from rivers which chased me as if I had been guilty of some offense against them. Many wild beasts, unprovoked by the slightest injury, wished to devour me, many serpents to poison me, and in many places, flying insects consumed me almost to the bone.

I shall ignore the daily perils, ubiquitous and infinite in number, so much so that an ancient philosopher could find no more valid remedy against fear than the consideration that everything is indeed fearsome. Nor did sicknesses spare me, although I was, as I am now, not merely temperate but almost totally abstinent from fleshly pleasures. I can only wonder at how you have infused in us so much and so firm and insatiable a thirst for pleasure, without which our life—as though it were denied that which it naturally seeks—were an imperfect thing; and at the same time you have ordained that the indulgence of that pleasure be of all human activities the most damaging to bodily forces and health, the most woeful in its effects on every man, and the most adverse to length of life itself. Thus, although I avoided almost always and entirely every delight, I yet was unable to avoid contracting many and different illnesses. Some put me at death's door, others jeopardized the use of a limb, or threatened me with a life more perpetually miserable than the past, and all, for either days or months, attacked my body and soul with a thousand pains and hardships. And indeed, although each of us experiences when he is infirm, ills for him new and unusual (as though human life weren't wretched enough normally), you have not compensated us with any periods of overflowing, unusual well-being, which could be the cause of some delight extraordinary in its quality and scope. In the lands covered mostly by snow, I was nearly blinded, as often occurs to Laplanders in their homeland. Sun and air, so vital to us and unavoidable, hurt us continuously; the one with dampness and stiffness, the other with heat and the light itself—so that man can never without greater or lesser discomfort or damage remain exposed to either.

In sum, I do not remember passing one day of my life without some pain, whereas I cannot number those that I underwent without even so much as a shadow of enjoyment. I realize now that suffering is as fated and necessary as not enjoying; that living quietly in any way is as impossible as living actively without misery. And I am forced to conclude that you are the declared enemy of men, of the other animals, and of all your creations—that here you trap us, there you threaten us, here you assault us, there you strike us, here you smash us, there you lacerate us, and always you hurt or persecute us; and that, by law and habit, you are the executioner of your own family, your own children, and, so to speak, of your own blood and bowels. Thus I remain without any hope, having understood that men will cease persecuting anyone who runs or hides himself with a sincere desire to escape, but that for no reason you never stop chasing us until you crush us. And now I see ahead of me the sad and bitter time of old age, a real and manifest evil full of the gravest ills and torments. This is not, however, accidental, but you have ordained it by law for all the living, foreseen by each of us even in childhood and gradually growing in him from his mid-twenties on toward a woeful decline and loss, through no fault of his. In sum, scarcely a third of man's life is allotted to flowering, a few moments to maturity and perfection, all the rest to decay and the attendant troubles.

Nature: Did you imagine perhaps that the world was made for your sake? Know now that in my creations, mandates, and operations, with very few exceptions, I always had and have my mind on matters other than man's happiness or unhappiness. When I offend you in whatever way and by whatever means, I am not aware, except in the rarest instances; likewise, ordinarily, if I delight or favor you, I know it not, and I have not done those things (as you think) to delight or help you. And finally, if even I took a mind to extinguish all your kind, I would not even notice it.

Icelander: Let us suppose that a man, of his own free will, invited
me with great solicitude to one of his villas, and that I, to
please him, went there. Suppose he housed me in a room
all ruined and dilapidated, where I was constantly in dan-
ger of being mangled—a place damp, fetid, open to the
wind and rain. Rather than concern himself with enter-
taining me or giving me any comforts, suppose he offered
me hardly enough to sustain me; and, even more, allowed
his children and other family members to insult, scorn,
menace, and beat me. And imagine that to my protests he
answered, "Maybe I made this villa for you? Do I main-
tain these my children and this my people for your ser-
vice?" and "I have enough to worry about besides your
amusements and provisions." To this I would reply,
"Look here, my good friend, since you did not build this
villa for my use, you therefore had it in your power not
to invite me here. But since, of your own will, you
wanted me to live here, shouldn't you see to it as much as
possible that I live here without torment or danger—at
least?"
　　　　　Thus I argue now. I well know that you did not make
the world for the service of men. Rather, I submit you
made and ordered it expressly to torment them. Now I
ask you: did I by any chance beg you to place me in this
universe? Or did I intrude, violently and against your
wishes? But, if by your own volition, without my knowl-
edge, and in a manner that I could neither protest nor
resist, you yourself, with your own hands, put me here—
is it not your obligation then, if not to keep me happy and
contented in this your kingdom, at least to guard me from
affliction and torture here, and prevent my life from pla-
guing me? And this that I say of myself, I say of all human
kind, I say of other animals, and of every created thing.

Nature: You seem to have overlooked that the life of this universe
is a perpetual circuit of creation and destruction, bound
together in such a way that each continuously promotes
the other and the conservation of the world, and if either
force were to cease, the universe itself would dissolve.
Consequently, there would be damage if there existed on
earth one thing free from suffering.

Icelander: I hear the same doctrine argued by all the philosophers.
But since that which is destroyed suffers, and that which

destroys does not benefit, and in a short time is itself destroyed, tell me what no philosopher can tell me: who likes and who enjoys this most unhappy life of the universe, propagated by hurt and by the death of all the things which constitute it?

While they were engaged in these and similar disquisitions, it is said that there arrived two lions, so worn and weak from starvation they hardly had the energy to devour the Icelander, which they did; and having refreshed themselves a bit, they kept themselves alive for that day. But there are those who deny this happening, and tell of a fierce wind arising while the Icelander spoke, which blew him to earth and on top of him erected a superb mausoleum of sand—beneath which that gentleman, perfectly desiccated and turned into a fine mummy, was later discovered by certain voyagers, who lodged him in the museum of I know not what city in Europe.

∽

81.   *Dialogue of Frederick Ruysch and His Mummies*

This dialogue derives from August, 1824. Frederick Ruysch was a great Dutch anatomist, 1638-1731, who invented a remarkable way of preserving cadavers, some of which he kept in a small museum in his house. The lifelike corpses so fascinated Peter the Great that on his second visit he purchased the museum and had it transported to Petersburg. Leopardi, who with his view of life could hardly be uninterested in theories about death and dying, was influenced in this dialogue by a passage in the *Natural History* by the eminent eighteenth-century French naturalist, Georges de Buffon.

The "mathematical year" referred to was the *annus magnus* described by Cicero and others—a great cycle in the existence of the universe. The Epicurean belief cited by Ruysch is that both the body and soul perish at the moment of death, neither being of immortal substance.

Chorus of the Dead in the Study of Frederick Ruysch

Alone eternal in the world, O Death,
In you toward whom created things all move,
Our naked essence rests;
Happy, no, but safe from the ancient pain.
This deepest night obscures
The thinking of the mind benumbed; the dry
Spirit perceives no urge
Toward hope or toward desire;

Thus, loosed from dread and caring, it consumes
The soft, black ages with no tedium.
We lived. To us that life
Is now like the confused
Remembering of a babe
Who sweating dreamed a dream of fearsome ghosts;
But our remembering contains no fear.
What were we? What the bitter point called life?
Our former time is now
A thing occult and frightening in our minds,
As unknown death appears
In the imagination of the living.
And just as it in life
Recoiled from death, so now
Our naked nature shuns the vital flame.
Happy, no, but safe;
For destiny denies
All joys to mortals living, mortals dead.

Ruysch: *(outside the laboratory, looking through the chinks in the door):* What the devil! Who taught music to these dead people, singing like cocks in the middle of the night? I'm in a cold sweat and almost as dead as they are. I didn't think my preserving them from decay would cause their resuscitation. In any case, with all my science I still am trembling from head to foot. Curses on the devil who tempted me to bring these people into my house. I don't know what to do. If I leave them locked up, who knows but that they will break down the door, or escape through the keyhole, and fall upon me in my bed? And yet I don't like the thought of crying for help in fear of dead people. Come now, a little courage, and let's try to frighten *them* a little.

(Entering) My children, what game is it we're playing? Don't you remember that you are dead? What party is this? Maybe the Czar's visit turned your heads, and now you think yourselves exempt from the old laws? I imagine this started as a joke which has now got out of hand. If you have come back to life, I am happy for you, but I cannot afford to buy groceries for the living as I did for the dead— so please leave my house. If what they say about

vampires is true, and you are such, go look for other blood to drink; for I am not inclined to your sucking mine, even if I was most generous with the artifical kind I put in your veins. In short, if you wish to continue your silent ways as in the past, we will get along quite nicely and you will have everything you need; if not, watch out for I'll take the bar out the of the door and massacre the lot of you.

Mummy: Don't get angry now, for I promise you we will stay dead as we are without your killing us.

Ruysch: Well then, just what is this fancy you've taken to singing?

Mummy: A short while ago, precisely at midnight, that great mathematical year which the ancients write so much about ended for the first time; and accordingly this is the first time the dead may speak. And not just us, but in every graveyard, every tomb, at the bottom of the sea, under snow or sand, beneath the open sky or wherever they find themselves, all the dead sang at midnight the same little song you heard.

Ruysch: And how long will this singing or speaking last?

Mummy: The singing is already over. We are able to speak for a quarter-hour. Then we become silent until another mathematical year comes round.

Ruysch: If this be true, I don't think you'll ruin my sleep again. Do talk freely among each other, and I'll just stand by gladly listening, for curiosity's sake, and I won't bother you.

Mummy: We cannot speak except to answer someone living. After the song, any of us not conversing with the living keeps quiet.

Ruysch: I am truly sorry because I imagine it would be great pleasure to hear what you would say to each other if you could talk.

Mummy: Even if it were possible you would hear nothing because we would not have anything to say to each other.

Ruysch: A thousand questions crowd my mind. But because the time is short and leaves us no room for much choice, tell me briefly what feeling you experienced in body and mind at the point of death.

Mummy:	At the moment of death itself I was not aware of it.
Other Mummies:	Nor we.
Ruysch:	How could you be unaware ot it?
Mummy:	In the same way you are not conscious of the moment you fall asleep, no matter how intent you are on it.
Ruysch:	But falling asleep is so natural.
Mummy:	And isn't dying? Show me one man or beast or plant that does not die.
Ruysch:	I am no longer surprised that you go about singing and talking if you were not aware of dying. "So he, not noticing the stroke, continued fighting although dead," as an Italian poet says. I thought that your type would know more about this business than the living. But to become serious again, did you not feel any pain at the point of death?
Mummy:	What pain can there be if the person undergoing it is unaware?
Ruysch:	In any case, everyone is convinced that the feeling of dying is most painful.
Mummy:	Almost as if death were a feeling rather than the opposite.
Ruysch:	Those who hold the Epicurean view of the nature of the soul and those who share the common opinion about death, all—or at least the majority—agree with what I say, that is, death is by its very nature the most acute pain by far.
Mummy:	Very well then. You might ask both schools for us the following questions. If man is not able to notice the point in which his vital operations are more or less interrupted by sleep or lethargy or fainting or whatever, why should he notice that moment when the same operations cease completely, not for a short time but forever? Furthermore, how can it be that a life-like feeling can occur in death? Or indeed that death by its very nature should express itself in a live feeling? When the capacity to feel is not only weakened and fitful, but reduced to such a small thing that it is nearly nothingness, do you believe the person capable of strong feeling? Further, do you think the dying out of the faculty of sentience itself must be greatly felt? Perceive also that in near-

ing death even those dying of acute and painful
ailments sooner or later before expiring quiet down
and and become restful in such a way that we can
see that their life, reduced to little, is no longer
sufficient for the pain—so that the suffering stops
first. This is what you could say for us to whoever
thinks he will have to die of pain at the last moment.

Ruysch:
Maybe these arguments would satisfy the Epicu-
reans, but not those who think otherwise about the
soul's substance, as I have in the past and will even
more from now on, having heard the dead talk and
sing. For holding death to consist in the separation
of soul and body, we cannot understand how these
two things—conjoined and almost glued together
so as to constitute one sole person—can be separated
without the greatest violence and unspeakable
agony.

Mummy:
Tell me: Is the spirit fastened to the body by some
nerve, or some muscle or membrance, which must
of necessity be broken when the spirit departs? Or
is it a limb of the body itself which has to be
violently ripped or cut away? Don't you see that the
soul only leaves the body because it is prevented
from remaining and no longer has a place therein,
and not because of any force which tears it out or
uproots it. Tell me further: In entering the body did
it feel itself driven in or strongly tied or, as you say,
glued? Why then should it feel itself unstuck in
leaving, or, let us say, experience the most vehe-
ment sensation? Rest assured, the entrance and exit
of the soul are equally peaceful, easy, and gentle.

Ruysch:
Then just what is death, if not pain?

Mummy:
More like pleasure than anything else. Know that
dying, like falling asleep, does not occur in an in-
stant but by degrees. It is true that these degrees
vary more or less, or are greater or smaller, accord-
ing to the causes and kinds of death. In the last
degree, death brings neither pain nor pleasure, in
the same way that sleep does not. In the preceding
ones, it cannot generate pain because pain is a live
thing, and man's senses at the time—that is when
death has begun—are moribund, which is to say

extremely attenuated in force. It may well be close to pleasure because pleasure is not always a live thing; rather, perhaps most human delights consist in some sort of languor. So that the senses of man are capable of pleasure even at their extinction, given that very often languor in itself gives pleasure, especially when it frees you from suffering—for you know very well that the cessation of any pain or discomfort is a pleasure in itself. Hence the languor of death must be more welcome in that it frees man from greater suffering. As for me, although I paid little attention to what I was feeling at the hour of death, because the doctors forbade me from fatiguing my brain, I do remember that the sense I had was not unlike the pleasure men derive from the languor of sleep, just when they are falling off.

Other Mummies: We also seem to remember the same thing.

Ruysch: It may be so, even though all those with whom I have had occasion to discuss this matter concluded quite differently, but then, if I remember right, they did not argue from personal experience. Now tell me, at the time of death while you were feeling that sweetness, did you believe yourself dying and that the pleasure was death's courtesy, or did you imagine something else?

Mummy: Until I was dead, I was never convinced but that I would escape that peril; or at least up to the last point at which I could still think, I hoped for another hour or two of life—as I think happens to many when they die.

Other Mummies: That is what happened to us.

Ruysch: And so Cicero says that nobody is so decrepit that he doesn't promise himself at least one more year of life. But how did you finally become conscious that the spirit had fled the body? Tell me: How did you know you were dead? They don't answer. My children, don't you hear me? The quarter-hour must have passed. Let's feel them a bit. They are quite dead again—no danger they'll frighten me another time. Back to bed.

124

❧

82.   *Dialogue of Christopher Columbus and Pedro Gutierrez*

This dialogue between the great explorer and a shipmate was written in October, 1824.

Columbus: A beautiful night, my friend.
Gutierrez: Truly beautiful. And I think seeing it from land would be even more lovely.
Columbus: Well said. You too are weary of sailing.
Gutierrez: Not of sailing itself; but this voyage seems longer than I anticipated and I do find it a bit tedious. But you must not think I'm complaining about you, as the others are. Indeed, you can count on me to support any decision you make regarding this voyage, as in the past, with all my strength. But just for the sake of conversation, I wish you would tell me precisely and in all sincerity if you are as convinced as in the beginning of finding land in this part of the world, or if after so much time and experience to the contrary you do not begin to doubt.
Columbus: Speaking frankly, as one can with an intimate friend, I confess I have begun to doubt a bit, especially since during the voyage several signs that gave me great hopes turned out vain, as for example those birds flying over from the west a few days after we left Gomera, which I thought evidence of land close by. Similarly, some of the other conjectures and projections I entertained before we put to sea regarding the events of this voyage have failed to bear fruit day after day. Hence I am thinking that if these sure prognostications have deceived me, perhaps the central conjecture itself—the belief in land beyond this ocean—may prove empty.

    In fact, if this belief, so well grounded, proves false, on the one hand I am inclined to say that we cannot put faith in any human judgment except those based wholly on things we can actually see and touch. But on the other hand, I consider that expectation and reality often clash, indeed most of the time. And so I say to myself: how can you know that each part of the world so much resembles the others that if the eastern hemisphere is made of land and water it follows that the western one is too? How do you know it isn't occupied by one immense sea? Or instead of land or land and water by yet another element? Or if there is land and water like this other, might it not be uninhabited, even uninhabitable? Assuming that it is no less inhabited than ours is, how can you be certain the inhabitants are rational creatures as here? And if they are, need they be humans and not some other type of intellectual beings? And if they are human couldn't they be entirely different from those we know: for example, bigger, braver, more skillful, more naturally endowed with genius and spirit, and even more civilized and richer in arts and sciences?

These are the things I brood about. And in truth, nature is obviously furnished with such power, and her effects are so many and varied, that we are not merely uncertain of what she has done and is doing in those distant, unknown regions, but we should even strongly question the perhaps deceptive process of arguing from the known to the unknown. And it is quite valid to imagine that the things of the unknown world will be partly or wholly wondrous and alien to us. We have already seen with our eyes that the compass needle in these seas declines quite a bit westward—a decidely novel thing until now unheard of by sailors, and one which despite all my cerebrations I cannot account for convincingly.

I am not saying by all this that one should give ear to all those ancient myths about the marvels of the unknown world and this ocean, as for instance, the lands described in Hanno's fable which were on fire at night and full of flaming rivers flowing into the sea. Indeed, we have so far seen how baseless the amazing novelties and miracles feared by our crew have been, as when they saw all that seaweed making the sea look like a meadow blocking our path and thought we had touched the limits of the navigable ocean. I wish only to suggest in response to your question that even though my conjecture is founded on most convincing reasons—not only in my judgment but in that of many geographers, astronomers, and excellent sailors with whom I have conferred (as you know) in Spain, Italy, and Portugal—it may nonetheless prove false; because, and I repeat, we see that many conclusions deriving from the best discourses do not survive experience.

And this occurs frequently in cases where there is so little to go on.

Gutierrez: In short you are admitting that you have risked your life and those of your companions on a mere speculative opinion.

Columbus: So be it—I cannot deny it. But putting aside the fact that everyday men stake their lives on much weaker foundations than these for things of negligible worth or even without thinking of the worth, consider this. If at present you and I and others were not aboard these ships, in the midst of this sea, in this unknown solitude, in whatever uncertain, risky state you may say we are, in what other state of life would we find ourselves? What would we be doing? In what way would we pass our time? More happily maybe? Or wouldn't we be experiencing some greater travail and worry, with boredom to boot? What do we mean by a state free from uncertainty and danger? If it held satisfaction and happiness, it would be preferable to any other; if tedious and miserable, one would prefer all others. I will not remind you of the glory and usefulness that we will bring if the end of our venture conforms to our hope. Outside of any other fruit we gather from this voyage, I will have found it most profitable because for a period it freed us from boredom, made life dear to us, and made us appreciate many things we took for granted otherwise.

The ancients wrote, as you may have read or heard tell, that unhappy lovers who survived a leap into the sea from the cliff at Santa Maura (once called the Leucadian cliff) were freed by Apollo ever after from the passions of love. I don't know whether to believe in that ultimate effect, but I do know that if they escaped that danger, Apollo or no Apollo, they would have for a time prized the lives which before they despised, or at least held them more dear than before.

Every voyage is, in my estimation, a leap from the Leucadian cliff, producing the same benefits as the one mentioned, but more lasting and hence quite superior. It is commonly thought that sailors, and soldiers, who face death every moment, value life less than others. I believe, on the same evidence, that no one loves and prizes life as much as those very soldiers and sailors. Think of the good things which sailors have and pay no attention to, or even those trivial things which become most dear and precious when they are denied us! Whoever ranks having a bit of sustaining earth among the number of human goods? No one except sailors and especially us, who because of the great uncertainty of this voyage's success have no greater desire than to see a chunk of land. It is our first thought on waking, our last as we fall asleep. And if but once we were to see from afar the top of a mountain or forest or some such thing, our hearts would leap for joy, and after landing, just sampling firm ground and being able to walk here and there at will would seem for a few days blessed to us.

Gutierrez: All this is true indeed, and if your main speculation turns out as sound as your justification for having pursued it, we will not fail to enjoy this beatitude some day or another.

Columbus: As for me, even though I don't dare promise it to myself any more, nonetheless I am hoping we will enjoy it soon. For some days now the plummet has sounded bottom, and the stuff it brings up may be a good sign. At dusk, the clouds around the sun seem to me to take a different shape and color than they did before. As you can feel, the air is a little softer and warmer than it has been. The wind no longer blows as strongly, directly, and continually, but is instead uncertain, varied, as if it were broken up by some obstacle. Add to this that cane we saw floating in the water which looked cut just a short time earlier; and that little tree branch with its fresh red berries. And those flocks of birds passing over which—granted they have already fooled me—nevertheless have become so frequent and large, and more so every day, that perhaps we can trust in them, especially since we can see mixed in some birds whose forms do not seem those of seabirds.

In sum, although I do not wish to appear confident, all these signs together give me a great and good hope.

Gutierrez: May God grant that it be fulfilled this time.

෧

83.   From *In Praise of Birds*

This lyric meditation or prose poem, written in October-November 1824, is one of the relatively few *Operette Morali* which are not dialogues. Its subject invites assimilation to the many poems of the romantic period voicing appreciation or envy of birds. Historically, Aemilius was a student of Plotinus, but the thoughts he utters here are Leopardi's.

Aemilius, a solitary philosopher, sitting and reading one spring morning in the shade of his country house, was struck by the singing of birds in the fields, and little by little he abandoned his reading and gave himself over to listening and reflecting. Finally, he took up his pen and there wrote the following things:

Birds are by nature the most cheerful creatures in the world. I do not mean that they always give you pleasure when you see or hear them, but that they themselves feel joy and gladness more than any other animal. Other animals usually look serious and grave and many even appear melancholy; they seldom give signs of joy, and even these are small and brief. In most of their enjoyments and delights, they do not celebrate or show merriment. If they rejoice in green fields, broad and pleasant vistas, shining suns, and sweet crystal breezes, they usually give no outward sign—except for the hares who (Xenophon says) leap and play together in the moonlight.

Birds generally are gay in both their movements and aspect; and their power to delight us derives precisely from this, that their forms and behavior universally show the signs which in nature denote a special ability and disposition to experience joy and satisfaction. And this appearance is not a vain illusion. With every one of their contentments or delights, they sing, and the greater the delight or contentment, the greater the art and urgency of their song. Since they sing a good part of the time, we can infer that ordinarily they are in good humor and enjoying themselves. And although it has been noted that they sing better, more often, and longer when they are in love, we should not believe they are not moved to sing by other causes. For it is clear that on a lovely, calm day they sing more than on a dark, uneasy one. And in storms they grow quiet, just as they do whenever they are afraid; and the storm over, they come out again, singing and playing with each other. Similarly, they sing on waking in the morning, partly for the joy they take in the new dawn, partly for the pleasure generally felt by every animal restored and remade by sleep. They also rejoice intensely in gay greenery, in fertile valleys, and in the sparkling, pure waters of a beautiful countryside. And in this it is noticeable that what seems agreeable and lightsome for us seems so to them also. . . . Some say, and it is germane here, that the voice of the birds is softer, sweeter, and the song more modulated in our regions than in those where men are savage and primitive; and they conclude that birds, even if free, take on a bit of the civilization of those men near whom they live.

Whether this is true or not, surely it was a striking provision of nature to assign both song and flight to the same creatures, so that those who had to delight other living beings with their voices would usually be on high, where the song could radiate over a greater space and reach more listeners, and so that the air, the element made for sound, would be populated by vocal, musical creatures. Truly, the song of birds brings much comfort and delight to us—and to the other animals too, I think. And this arises chiefly, I believe, not from the sweetness of the sounds (which is great), nor from their variety or constant suitability, but from the communication of joy contained in most song and especially in that of birds. Birdsong is, so to speak, a laughter the bird expresses when he feels pleased and full of well-being.

From this we could say that, in a way, birds share the human privilege of laughter, which other animals do not. And hence some think that just as man is defined as the intellectual or rational animal, he might also be described as the laughing animal, since laughter is as peculiar to him as reason. Surely it is a wonder that man, the most burdened and wretched of all creatures, has the ability to laugh, alien to every other beast. Wonderful also is the use we make of this faculty: for we see many in some terrible tribulation or sadness of soul, or others who have lost the love of life and are sure of the vanity of every human good, or are incapable of any joy or hope—who still laugh. Indeed, the better they recognize the emptiness of human good and life's unhappiness and the less they hope and tend toward enjoyment, the more they usually incline toward laughter. For the essence, forms, and working of such laughter, as far as it relates to man's spirit, can hardly be defined or explained except by saying that laughter is a kind of temporary madness, a raving or delirium—since these men, who are never really contented or delighted with anything, cannot have a reasonable, just motive for laughing.

Furthermore, it would be interesting to find out where and when humans first had occasion to use and recognize this faculty of theirs. For there is no doubt that primitive men seem mostly serious and even melancholy, like other animals. Thus I hold that laughter not only appeared in the world after tears did, but that a good space of time elapsed before it was experienced and noted. And before that, as Virgil says, no mother smiled at her baby, nor did he recognize her with a smile. If now, at least where people lead civilized lives, humans begin laughing shortly after birth, they do so in imitation of those they see laughing. . . .

That birds should be and appear to be more joyful than other creatures is very understandable, for truly, as I have noted, they are by nature better fitted to enjoy and be happy. First, they do not seem subject to *noia*. They move around constantly. They pass from country to country and from lower to upper air with marvelous quickness and ease. They see and experience in their lives an infinity of different things. They exercise their bodies continually and enjoy a wealth of external life. All other animals, once they have tended to their needs, like to rest quiet and lazy; none, except perhaps for fish and certain flying insects, go darting about long just for amusement. A primitive man, except to provide his daily needs or unless he is chased by a storm or wild beast, hardly ever moves a step, but chiefly loves idleness and inactivity. He will consume entire days sitting lazy and silent in his rude hut or outdoors or in the clefts and caves of cliffs or rocks.

On the contrary, birds linger only a short while in any one place; they come and go continuously without any necessity; they fly for amusement; and if sometimes they have for pleasure flown many miles from their usual habitation, they return there at dusk of the same day. Even in the short time they stay in one spot, you never see them keep still: they are always turning this way and that; always wheeling, bowing, stretching, shaking themselves, and fluttering with that liveliness, agility, and swiftness of movement so indescribable. In short, from the time a bird emerges from the egg until it dies, except for short intervals of sleep, it does not rest for a moment. In light of these observations, we may tentatively affirm that the natural ordinary state of other animals, including men, is rest; that of birds, motion . . . [Aemilius goes on to say that birds have great force, vivacity and powers of happy imagination, a greater abundance of internal and external life than other animals, and their nature is closer to perfection.]

In sum, just as Anacreon wanted to transform himself into a mirror so that the maiden he loved could continually gaze on him, or into a tunic to cover her, or into an ointment to anoint her, or into water to wash over her, or into a cloth that she might wrap him to her breast, or into a pearl worn at her throat, or into a shoe that she might at least press with her foot—similarly I wish, for a while, to be changed into a bird, to experience the contentment and the joy of their life.

∽

84. To Pietro Giordani (Florence)

    . . . If it please you, write and tell me that you are well, that you still love me, that I—still a nothing in the world and less than a nothing to myself—mean to you what I did before, and this will suffice me. I study day and night for as long as my health permits. When it abandons me, I walk around my room a few months, after which I return to my studies. And so I live.

As for the kind of studies I do, they have changed just as I have changed from what I was. Everything that smacks of emotions and eloquence bores me, strikes me as foolish child's play. I seek nothing other than the truth, which I so hated and loathed before. I derive pleasure from always uncovering better and better, and touching with my hand, the misery of men and things, from being coldly horrified in contemplating this sad and terrible mystery of the life of the universe. I see quite well now that since my passions are spent, the only source of pleasure in my studies is a vain curiosity, the satisfaction of which still gives me considerable delight. . . .

I am here without a hope of escape. I would gladly try a life of pure chance, earning my bread with my pen in some large city, but I don't see a way to keep from starving the day after I left here. And so I must content myself with doing and hoping nothing . . . [Recanati, May 6, 1825].

III

THE CIRCUIT OF CITIES (1825-30): FRIENDS, LOVE, AND THE RETURN TO POETRY

The Circuit of Cities (1825-30):
Friends, Love, and the Return to Poetry

During the years 1825-30, Leopardi, harried by poor health and driven by thoughts of premature old age and onrushing death, made a round of some major Italian cities, producing as he went an astonishing sum of work. In July, 1825, he traveled to Milan at the invitation of the publisher Antonio Stella, for whom he was to assemble in the next years excellent editions of Cicero and Petrarch and anthologies of Italian prose and poetry that are still models of their kind. But disoriented in Milan, as he always was in large cities, and aided by a stipend from Stella, Leopardi left in September for Bologna, which, with Florence and Pisa, was to offer special attractions for him.

In Bologna, where he briefly sojourned on his way to Milan and later stayed for more than a year in 1825-26 and for a few weeks in 1827, Leopardi was struck by the general good nature of the inhabitants and the specific kindness of the city's literary people, who pampered and tended him despite his frequent crankiness. Nothing could quite compensate, however, for the sharp Bolognese winter of 1825-26, which often forced the sickly poet literally to burrow into a feather-filled sack for warmth. At this time, Leopardi refused his father's offer of a church benefice, which went to his younger brother Luigi instead. Furthermore, Leopardi's quiet offenses to church and state authorities killed other opportunities for financial freedom. First he failed to receive a position as Secretary to the Bologna Academy of Fine Arts because of his earlier friction with censors. Then, despite the energetic attempts of the Prussian diplomat Bunsen in Rome, the papal government informed Leopardi he could not have any position administered by the Church; the reasons given were that he fraternized with "unwise" persons and had published in the 1824 volume (yet again) "sentiments favorable to the new moral and political opinions."[1] Leopardi's scorn for despots surely had a personal as well as a theoretical base. More pleasing a development, at least for a few months in the spring-summer of 1826, was the intimacy shared with Teresa Carniani Malvezzi, a Bolognese lady with an enthusiasm for poetry and poets. Partly at the insistence of Malvezzi's husband, however, the affair cooled and died quickly. Leopardi was to have only one more romantic attachment before him; as for Teresa Malvezzi, she lived long, but she was the only one of Leopardi's three great passions who inspired no poem.

Florence, where Leopardi spent two separate six-month periods in 1827 and 1828, was ultimately more important than any city except Recanati for Leopardi's development. Although many stimuli he found there were negative, the Florentine experience exposed him to some of the leading Italian intellectuals of the time and led to deep friendships. When he arrived in the city, he was honored at a party given by the influential editor Giampietro Vieusseux on June 26, 1827, where he met among others Antonio Ranieri, the handsome Neapolitan who was to be a constant friend and nurse in the last seven years of Leopardi's life. He met also in Florence the young Piedmontese priest Vincenzo Gioberti, who later remained a faithful supporter despite geographical and ideological distance. At a soiree in September, a remarkable conjunction occurred. Alessandro Manzoni, who had just published his testament of Christian and democratic faith, *I Promessi Sposi (The Betrothed)*, met Leopardi, who had just published the *Operette Morali*. Although Manzoni was reserved and both Leopardi and Giordani (also present) were put off by what they felt to be the intemperance of Manzoni's Christian conversation, the two great romantic writers treated each other with puzzled respect. Manzoni later praised the outstanding style of Leopardi's *Operette*. Leopardi's reaction to Florentine thinkers as a group was one of impatience. The general mood of utilitarian optimism, whether based on God or science or some combination, irritated Leopardi, as his documents show. Although he himself increasingly believed in relative progress and the inexorable thrust of civilization, he rejected the assumptions that culture could progress through mass movements, that the embryonic sciences of sociology and economics held ultimate answers, or that the pursuit of the useful could make men happier. For him beauty and diversion were the keys to a limited individual contentment; and, probably ironically, he projected writing at this time an *Encyclopedia of Useless Knowledge*.

There were other cities. His body extremely sensitive to wind and cold, Leopardi sought the mild air of Pisa in the winter of 1827-28. Here, the following April, he enjoyed an unexpected resurgence of feeling that resulted in two poems: *The Reawakening*, which describes the return of imagination to the arid soul; and *To Sylvia*, which Italians widely consider his perfect lyric. The relative contentment of these Pisan days was flawed, however, by the death at twenty-four of Leopardi's brother Luigi, an event which may have even prompted Leopardi to take communion (or so he told his father). And there was Recanati, to which he returned when money ran out or when his father's imploring wore down his objections. The town was a condemnation to Leopardi, but undeniably it unlocked the doors of creativity. Thus in his long and last stay at home from November, 1828, to April, 1830, Leopardi was especially lonely—Carlo had married and made good *his* escape—and he had to endure the gibes of schoolboys about his deformity; but he managed to write four of his finest poems: three intimate poems linked to his Recanati experiences and the stunning *Night-Song of a Wandering Shepherd of Asia*. During the last months at Recanati, Leopardi learned that a large prize from Florence's *Accademia della Crusca*, which would have supported him for months, had gone to Botta's *History of Italy from 1789 to 1814* instead of to his own *Operette*—a case of turgid but inoffensive history overcoming good but pessimistic art.

In the literature of these years, subtle differences in tone and stance are worth noting. There are the frequent tenderness and warmth, as when in certain poems Leopardi is remembering; the mounting note of fraternal love and the defiance of nature or fate, as in the *Dialogue of Plotinus and Porphyry;* and the considerable playfulness of *Copernicus*. But there is another voice too, one almost unique to Leopardi and more difficult to describe than to sense. It is the sound of a man who has passed through fire and is distantly looking back or down at an earth of which he is no longer part. The voice is dignified and frequently moving even when it cuts, but it is one from which human emotion and personality have almost been squeezed out. Such is the quality of the notebook entries on gardens seen as hospitals or on the way we live for the benefit of the life-force, and of the famous *Night-Song*.

∽

85. To Carlo Leopardi (Recanati)

. . . I sigh, however, for Bologna, where I was welcomed with open arms, where I made more friends in nine days than I did in five months at Rome, where they think of nothing but living cheerfully without formalities, where strangers cannot rest for the embraces they receive, where men of talent are invited to dinner nine times a week, where Giordani assures me I would live better than anywhere else in Italy except Florence. . . . In Bologna men are wasps without stings, and believe me, with infinite wonder I have had to agree with Giordani and Brighenti (fine man) that kindheartedness really does exist there, is indeed widespread, and that the human race is different from what you and I have known . . . [Milan, July 31, 1825].

∽

86. I am, if you pardon the metaphor, a walking sepulchre, who bears inside him a dead man, a heart once extremely feeling which feels no more, etc. [Bologna, November 3, 1825, Z, 4149].

∽

87. To Paolina Leopardi (Recanati)

The "Angelina" of this letter was a former domestic in the *casa Leopardi,* who afterwards managed to coax from Leopardi a sonnet for a newly ordained priest and even got him to stand as godfather to a son she bore during this time.

. . . Some weeks ago, in walking through Bologna alone, as always, I saw written at a corner *Via Remorsella*. I recalled Angelina and the number 488 that you wrote down for me on a scrap the evening before I left. I went there and found Angelina, who hearing that I was Leopardi turned red as the rising moon. She then said that she could not have a greater comfort, that she dreams of Mamma every night, and a thousand other things. She's in fine health and looks younger and fresher than I. She lives in a good area and leads a comfortable life. She has visited me many times with her husband, whose manner and clothes make him appear a perfect *signore*. They have insisted that I dine with them, which I have promised to do. I will eat very well because he is supposed to be a fine cook, and from what Angelina tells me, they have a groaning table every day. . . .

As I told Carlo I feel much, much better. But you don't tell me anything of yourself. I don't like that. From now on don't ever write me without giving me news of you and what you're doing. *Addio, mia cara;* love me . . . [Bologna, December 9, 1825].

88. What is life? The journey of a sick cripple who walks, with a heavy burden on his back, over steep mountains and places incredibly rugged, wearisome, and difficult, in snow, ice, rain, in wind and burning sun, without ever resting night or day for a space of many days, only to arrive at a precipice or pit, and there inevitably fall [Bologna, January 17, 1826, Z, 4162-63].

89. Man (like the other animals) is not born to enjoy life, but only to perpetuate life, to communicate it to others who come after, to conserve it. Neither he himself, nor life, nor any object of this world is actually made for him, but on the contrary, he exists completely for life. Terrifying, but a true proposition and the final word of all metaphysics. Existence is not for the existing—even if it offers some good, that is pure chance. That which exists does so for the sake of existence; this is its real, manifest end. Existing things exist because they do; an existing individual is born and exists because one continues to exist, and existence conserves itself in him and after him. This all becomes

clear when we recognize that the pure, true end of nature is the conservation of the species and not the conservation or felicity of individuals, a felicity which does not really exist in the world, either for individuals or the species. From this one must necessarily arrive at last to the general, summary, supreme, and terrible conclusion above mentioned [Bologna, March 11, 1826, Z, 4169].

გ

90. . . . Not only single humans, but the human race always was and will be unhappy by necessity. Not only the human race but all the animals. Not only the animals but all the other beings in their own way. Not just individuals, but species, types, realms, globes, systems, and worlds.

Enter into a garden of plants, herbs, and flowers. Be it ever so cheerful, be it the mildest season of the year, you cannot look at any part of it without finding some suffering. All that vegetable family is in a state of *souffrance,* some members more, some less. Over there that rose is offended by the sun that gives it life; it wrinkles, languishes, withers. There that lily is cruelly sucked by a bee in its most sensitive, vital parts. The industrious, patient, good, and virtuous bees do not make their sweets without unspeakable torment to the most delicate fibers, without pitiless havoc for tender flowers. That tree is infested by an anthill, another by maggots, flies, snails, mosquitos; this one is wounded in the bark and tormented by the air and sun penetrating the wound; that one is hurting in the trunk and roots; the other has many dry leaves. . . . That plant is too warm, this one too cold; too much light; too much shade; too humid; too dry. One suffers badly and finds obstacles to its growth and extension; the other finds nothing to lean against or it exhausts itself in struggling to find it.

In the whole garden you will not find one little plant in a state of perfect health. Here a little branch is broken by the wind or by its own weight; there a zephyr goes tearing a flower, making off with a piece, a filament, a leaf, a living part of this or that plant, detached and ripped away.

Meanwhile you bruise the grass with your footsteps. You crush it, rend it, squeeze out its blood, break it, kill it. That kind and gentle maiden there goes softly snapping and smashing stalks. The gardener goes judiciously truncating, snipping sensitive limbs with fingernail and steel [Bologna, April 19, 1826]. Certainly these plants live, some because their ailments are not fatal, others because plants, like animals, can keep on living a short time longer even with mortal illnesses.

This spectacle of so much abundance in entering the garden uplifts the spirit, and so it seems to be a joyous sojourn. But truly this life is sad. Every garden is almost a vast hospital (a place much more deplorable than a cemetery), and if these beings feel or, we should say, could feel, certainly nonbeing would be much better than being [Bologna, April 22, 1826, Z, 4175-76].

91. To Carlo Leopardi (Recanati)

. . . I have taken up a relationship with a lady [Teresa Malvezzi], Florentine by birth and married into one of the chief families here, which forms a great part of my life now. She is not young but has a grace and spirit which (believe me, till now I had thought it impossible) compensate for youth and create a marvelous illusion. In the first days that I knew her, I lived in a kind of feverish delirium. We have never talked of love except in jest, but we share a tender, sensitive friendship, with a mutual interest and an abandon that is like a love without disquietude. She has the highest respect for me. If I read her something of mine, she often weeps real tears with no affectation. The praises of others mean nothing to me—hers enter my blood and remain in my soul. She loves and understands literature and philosophy very much, never lacks things to talk about, and almost every evening I am with her from the Angelus to well-past midnight, and it seems but a moment to me. We confide all our secrets to each other, we reprove each other, and we tell each other our defects.

In short, this relationship forms and will form a well-defined epoch in my life, for it has disenchanted my disenchantment. It has convinced me there are truly pleasures in the world that I believed impossible, and that I am still capable of stable illusions despite the contrary knowledge and experience so deep-rooted in me. And it has revived my heart after so many years of sleep, indeed complete death . . . [Bologna, May 30, 1826].

92. To Francesco Puccinotti (Macerata)

[Puccinotti was simply a friend who enjoyed literature.]

. . . How goes it with your lecture on Byron? Indeed, he is one of the few worthy poets of this century, and one of the warm, sensitive spirits, just like you. The Memoirs of Goethe have many new and striking things in them—like all that author's work and many other German writings. But they are written in a style so wild, obscure, and confused and they display some sentiments and ideas so bizarre, mystical, and visionary that I must admit I don't like them very much. . . .

Everyone nowadays wants to write poetry, but would much prefer reading prose. And you know well that this century is not and cannot be poetic. A poet, even a great one, attracts little attention, and even if he gains fame in his own country, it is hard for his reputation to spread to the rest of Europe because perfect poetry does not transport well into foreign languages. And, furthermore, Europe wants things more solid and real than poetry. By chasing after verses and frivolities (I'm speaking generally), we serve our tyrants well, for we reduce literature to games, instead of regarding it as the only firm base for our country's regeneration . . . [Bologna, June 5, 1826].

93.   In my system on human happiness, it seems wholly contradictory that I should so highly praise action, activity, and fullness of life, and so prefer the ancient state to the modern—while at the same time judging the happiest (or least unhappy) way of life to be that of the stupidest humans; of those animals which are less animal, that is, poorer in vitality; of savages in their lethargy and sloth. In sum, it seems inconsistent to exalt above all other states that of the most intense life and that of as much death as is compatible with animal existence.

But in truth these two things agree very nicely, they derive from the same principle, and each is equally a necesary result of it. Given the impossibility both of being happy and of ever ceasing to desire happiness above all and indeed exclusively; given the inevitable tendency of the soul's life toward an unachievable goal; given that the universal and necessary misery of all living things resides in, and comes from, this yearning alone and our inability to reach the objective; given finally that this universal unhappiness is greater for those species or individuals more sensitive to the tendency in question—it follows that the highest happiness (or lowest level of unhappiness) consists in the least possible feeling of this tendency. The species and individual animals which are least sensitive and alive by their nature are least aware of this feeling. The least involved of mental states, and hence of mental lives, are the least unhappy of human conditions. Such is that of the primitive or savage, and that is why I prefer the primitive condition to the civilized.

But once mental evolution has begun and reached a certain point, it is impossible to turn it back, impossible to stop the progress of either individuals or peoples. The persons and nations of Europe and of much of the world have had a developed mind for numberless years. Reducing them to primitivism is not possible. Meanwhile, from the evolution and vitality of their minds has come more sensitivity, thus more feeling of that yearning I mentioned, thus more misery. There remains only one remedy: *diversion*. This consists of the greatest possible amount of activity and action to occupy and fill the evolved faculties and life of the mind. In this way, the feeling of yearning will either be interrupted or almost obscured and confused, its voice suppressed, suffocated, eclipsed.

This remedy of diversion is quite far from equaling the primitive state, but since man is civilized, its effects and the conditions it produces are the best we can have . . . [Bologna, July 13, 1826, Z, 4185-87].

∽

94. To Teresa Carniani Malvezzi (Bologna)

Contessa mia. The last time I had the pleasure of seeing you, you told me clearly that our private conversations were boring you, and that you could not give me the slightest pretext for continuing my frequent visits. Do not think me offended. If I had room for any complaint, it would be that your words and actions, though quite clear, might have been even more explicit. Now, after so long a time, I would like to come see you, but I dare not without your permission. I ask it immediately, greatly desiring to repeat in person that I am, as you well know, your true and cordial friend, Giacomo Leopardi [Bologna, undated but October, 1826].

∽

95. It is natural for man—weak, wretched, subject to so many dangers, mishaps, fears—to suppose, conjecture, and imagine, even gratuitously, a sagacity and prudence, an understanding and judgment, a perspicacity and experience greater than his own in some other person, whom he then watches in any trouble, finding reassurance or fear according to whether the superior is happy or sad, upset or coura-

geous; and he rests on that authority unquestioningly. . . . This is the way children, especially those of tender age, are toward their parents. And thus was I, even after I had developed and matured, with my father. In any bad situation or state of fear, before judging the degree of my own reaction, I habitually waited to see or conjecture his and looked to his opinion or judgment on the matter. It was, neither more nor less, as if I were incapable of judging for myself; and seeing him either really or apparently calm, my mind would usually become immensely reassured, in an absolutely blind submission to his authority or faith in his providence. . . . And this quality in man is one of the reasons that he so universally and willingly accepts and clings to a belief in a provident God, that is, in a being superior to us in wisdom and intellect who disposes and directs our every experience, and in whose providence we can repose for the outcome of all our lives [December 9, 1826, Z, 4229-30].

მ

96. Time is not a thing, but rather an accident of things, and independently of the existence of things it is nothing. It is an accident of this existence, an idea of ours, a word. Time is the duration of things that are—just as 7200 tickings of a clock pendulum are one hour, but that hour is an offspring of our mind and does not exist, either in itself or as a section in time, any more than it existed before the invention of the clock. In short, the essence of time is nothing else than a way—a perspective, so to speak—for considering that we lead an existence made up of things that are, or may be, or can be supposed to be. The same with space. . . .

The conclusion is that time and space are essentially only ideas or words. And those countless great debates about time and space stirred up from the birth of metaphysics onwards by the prime philosophers of every century are simply wordgames, born of misunderstandings, little clarity in handling ideas, and inadequate analysis of our intellect. And that intellect itself is the only place where time, space, and so many other abstractions actually exist and amount to anything [Recanati, December 14, 1826, Z, 4233].

მ

97. Conjectures about man's eventual civilizing of animals in the distant future, especially certain kinds like the apes. Just as we see that civilized

humans have brought civilization to many barbarous or primitive populations no less ferocious and perhaps less clever than the apes, or some strains of them; and that, in short, civilization tends naturally to propagate itself, moves ever toward new conquests, and cannot stand still or contain itself within certain boundaries (especially physical ones), as long as there are creatures to civilize and link to the large body of civilization—to the great alliance of intelligent beings pitted against nature and against nonintelligent things.

This could serve for the *Letter to a Young Man of the Twentieth Century* [undated but between April 9-13, 1827, Z, 4279-80. The projected *Letter* was never actually written.]

ᗡ

98. To Teresa Carniani Malvezzi (Bologna)

Mia cara Contessa. Finally, I receive a book from you that shows me you have remembered me, once at least, since my departure. And the address in your handwriting assures me the book is not a posthumous one, that it comes as a gift rather than a legacy or codicil. And so the many letters that you intended to write and that you often promised me have boiled down to an address. If you had intended to begin now, after five months, please be advised that you are too late, because I leave for Bologna this week or next.

Therefore, I will say nothing about your book, in which I admire the seriousness and good sense of the preface, the purity of language and style, and the way you overcame so many difficulties. Nor will I ask for news of you—for I hope to tell you soon in person what you wish to know, and ask you what I wish to know. Meanwhile, love me and believe me [the following words are in English] *your most faithful friend, or servant, or both, or what you like* [Recanati, April 18, 1827].

If Malvezzi and Leopardi met again, it was the last time. On May 21, 1827, Leopardi wrote to his friend Antonio Papadopoli in Florence the most unchivalric and defensive remarks he ever made about a woman: "How could you ever believe that I would continue to see that *puttana* Malvezzi? May my nose fall off if from the time I learned of her gossip about me I have returned or even thought of returning—and if I don't rehearse all the bad things I can about her. The other day, encountering her, I turned my face to the wall so as not to see her." The words are those of a hurt adolescent—which, as far as experience with women goes, Leopardi still was.

ᗡ

99.   Memories of my life. Changing often my dwelling place, and staying in one place more, another less, either for months or years, I saw that I was never content, never at my center, never naturalized in a place until I had memories to attach to it, to my rooms, to the streets, to the houses I visited. These memories consisted in nothing else than being able to say: I was here this long ago; here, this many months ago, I did, saw, heard such and such—something that for the most part had no great import. But the memory, my being able to remember, made it sweet and significant to me. Clearly, I could not have this faculty and the abundance of memories attached to places where I lived if it weren't for the passing of time, and with time I could not lack it. Thus, I was always unhappy in any place in the first months, and after a time I always found myself becoming contented and affectionately tied to any place. Through remembrance it became for me almost my native spot [Florence, July 23, 1827, Z, 4286-87].

100. To Antonio Fortunato Stella (Milan)
      . . . As for Manzoni's romance (of which I have heard read only a few pages), I will tell you confidentially that persons of good taste here find it much inferior to expectations. Others generally praise it.
      Regarding the opinion of the *Operette Morali* that you communicated to me, what do you want me to say? I shall say only that it was not unexpected. I am not aware that my ideas are all negative, but that others should think so does not surprise me, for I recall the saying of Bayle—that in metaphysics and morals, *reason* cannot edify but only destroy. That my opinions are not "founded in reason but in a certain partial observation" I can only wish were true . . . [Florence, August 23, 1827].

101.   A voice or a sound which is far away, or diminishing and receding little by little, or echoing with an impression of vastness, etc., is pleasing by the indefiniteness [*vago*] of the idea, etc. Similarly, we get pleasure from thunder, a cannon explosion, and so on, heard in open country, a great valley, etc., the song of farmers, of birds, the lowing of cattle, etc. in the same circumstances [September 21, 1827, Z, 4293].

∾

102.   *Copernicus*

Leopardi often practiced a kind of satirical reduction whereby he treated weighty or apocalyptic moments lightly, thus deflating the objects of his attention. In the *Dialogue of a Sylph and a Gnome* it was the end of the world so treated. In the following little four-scene drama, written in 1827, it is the philosophical convulsion caused (or corroborated) by Copernicus's treatise on the sun-centered nature of our immediate universe—a theory which for Leopardi had more than astronomical implications. Copernicus (1473-1543), the great Polish astronomer, was a canon of the Church and did indeed dedicate his work, *De Revolutionibus Orbium Terrestrium,* to Pope Paul III.

In this piece, Leopardi uses the Greek ideas of Apollo's being the inspirer of poets as well as the driver of the sun-chariot bringing the day. Leopardi blends these old mythical ideas with scientific fact to create his own jocular myth about man's fall from ancient to modern, from poetry to philosophy (i.e., science), from the center of things to the periphery.

Scene One:

The First Hour and the Sun

First Hour: Good morning, Your Highness.

Sun: Yes—or good night rather.

First Hour: The horses are all ready to go.

Sun: That's nice.

First Hour: Venus has been out for some time now.

Sun: Good, let her come or go as she pleases.

First Hour: What do you mean to say, Your Highness?

Sun: I mean you should leave me alone.

First Hour: But, Highness, the night has already lasted so long that it can't go on any longer; and if we delay, Highness, some disorder may occur.

Sun: Order or disorder, I'm not moving.

First Hour: Oh, Your Highness, what is the matter? Do you feel ill?

Sun: No, no, I don't feel anything, beyond not wanting to move. As for you, you may go about your business.

First Hour: But how can I, the first hour of the day, proceed without you? And how can the day ever be, if Your Highness doesn't deign to come out as usual?

Sun: If you don't work the day, you can work the night; or the hours of the night can do double duty, and you and your companions can be idle. Because, do you know what? I am tired of this continual moving around to give light to

146

a few little animals living on a fistful of mud so small that even I, with my good eyes, can barely see it. And tonight I have decided not to bother myself anymore. And if humans want light they can make fires or provide for themselves in some other way.

First Hour: And what way do you think those poor little folk will find, Your Highness? And to keep their lamps going, or to get enough candles to burn the whole day long, that would be too expensive. If they had already discovered that special air which burns and which could cheaply illuminate their streets, rooms, shops, cellars, and so on—well, then the matter wouldn't be so serious. But the fact is it will take at least another three hundred years until they find that remedy; and in the meantime they will exhaust their oil, wax, pitch, and tallow, and have nothing left to burn.

Sun: Let them have fireflies and glowworms.

First Hour: And how will they make do in the cold? For without the aid they had from Your Highness, the fire from all their forests would not suffice to warm them. Further, they would starve to death because the land would not bring forth its fruits. And so, after a few years the seed of those poor little animals would be lost; for when they have groped their way for a while to and fro over the earth seeking food and warmth—finally, after swallowing their final morsel and with their last spark of fire spent, they will all perish in the dark, frozen like pieces of crystal.

Sun: What does it matter to me? Am I the wet nurse of the human race or perhaps the cook, that I have to grow and prepare their food? And why should I care if a certain few invisible little creatures, millions of miles from me, cannot see and cannot bear the cold without my light? Besides, if I have to function as a stove or fireplace to this human family, it stands to reason that the family wishing to warm itself should gather around the fireplace rather than have the fireplace move around the house. In sum, if Earth needs my presence let her take the pains to come to it; as for me, I don't need a thing from Earth that would make me seek her out.

First Hour: Your Highness means, if I understand correctly, that what you have done in the past now the Earth must do.

Sun: Yes. Now and henceforward.

147

First Hour: I am sure that Your Highness is quite right in this matter, not to mention that you can do anything you please anyhow. But nonetheless, please to consider, Your Highness, how many lovely and necessary things will be undone by establishing this new order. The day will no longer have its golden chariot, with its brave horses that wash themselves in the sea; and, overlooking other particulars, we poor hours will no more have our stations in the sky, and we will be demoted from heavenly to earthly maidens—if indeed, as I fear, we don't dissolve in smoke altogether.

But let such objections be; the point is that Earth must be persuaded to travel around, which will be difficult enough, becasue she is not used to it, and it will seem strange to her to have to run and tire herself so much, not having budged a bit from her position until now. And if Your Highness now, apparently, begins to fancy a more leisurely time of it, I fear that Earth for her part isn't any more inclined to hard work than she has been in the past.

Sun: Necessity, in this case, will spur her on, and make her bounce up and run. But in any case, the fastest and surest way is to find a poet or rather a philosopher to persuade the Earth to move or, failing that, to force her to move. Because, in the last analysis, most (if not all) of this affair lies in the hands of philosophers and poets. It was the poets in the past—for I was younger then and listened to them—who inspired me, as a sport or honorable activity, to perform this silly job of desperately scurrying, big and fat as I am, around a little grain of sand. But now that I am mature in years and have turned to philosophy, I look in all things for the useful and not the beautiful. And the sentiments of poets make me laugh, when they're not turning my stomach.

In doing anything, I want good, substantial reasons; and there's no good reason to forgo an easy, idle life for a busy one which isn't worth your work or worry. Therefore, I have decided to leave work and discomfort to others, and I myself shall lounge peacefully in my house with not a care in the world.

As I told you, this change is due not only to my ripe age but to the work of philosophers, a breed that nowadays acquires more and more power. So that if we now wish the Earth to move and to run around in my stead, a poet would be better than a philosopher from one point of view; because the poets, with one fiction or another, make people believe the things of this world have weight and value, and are pleasing and lovely, and by creating a thousand joyful hopes, they often inspire others to work—whom then the philosophers promptly deflate. On the other hand, however, since philosophers have begun to rise to the top, I doubt whether today a poet would be listened to by Earth, any more than I would listen, or if listened to he wouldn't be obeyed. Hence it would be better to turn to a philosopher, for even though philosophers are not usually fit, and even less inclined, to make others function, perhaps this extreme situation may get them to change their habit. Unless indeed Earth decides that it is in her best interest to *plunge* to perdition rather than working so hard—for which I could not fault her.

Enough. We shall see what happens. Now then, you will go down to Earth, or else send one of your friends, whichever you wish. And if she finds one of those philosophers taking his fresh air and contemplating the starry heavens, as she inevitably will because of the novelty of this long night, let her hoist him up on her back and bring him here to me. And I will try to convince him of what is necessary. Have you understood me well?

First Hour: Yes, Your Highness. You will be obeyed.

Scene Two:

Copernicus, on the terrace of his house, is looking to the eastern sky by means of a paper cylinder, because telescopes have not yet been invented.

Copernicus: This is a stunning thing. Either all the timepieces have failed or the sun has fallen behind by more than an hour. And not a gleam of light to be seen yet in the east. And on top of everything the sky is as clear and vivid as a mirror. All the stars are shining as if it's midnight. Hie thyself to Ptolemy or Holywood and see if they can explain this event. I have often heard of that night Jove spent with Amphitryon's wife. And I also remember reading in a modern Spanish book that the Peruvians recount that once upon a time there occurred in their land a night so long it seemed endless; and at its end the sun rose up from a certain lake which they call Titicaca. But until now I thought these tales sheer nonsense, and I was sure of myself, as are all reasonable men. Now that I perceive that reason and science aren't worth a fig, to speak truly, I am forced to conclude that these similar accounts may be true indeed. In fact I am ready to go to all the lakes and bogs possible to see if I can fish up the sun. But what is this noise I hear, like the wings of a great bird?

Scene Three:

The Last Hour and Copernicus

Last Hour: Copernicus, I am the Last Hour.

Copernicus: The last hour? Well, I suppose one should always be ready. If you please, just give me a little time to make up a will and get my affairs in order before dying.

Last Hour: What dying? I am not the last hour of your life, you know.

Copernicus: Oh, who are you then? The last hour of the long breviaries?

Last Hour: I do believe that's the hour you like best when you're up there in your canonical choir.

Copernicus: But how did you know I was a canon? And how do you know me or my name that you just used?

Last Hour: I asked about you in the streets below. To get to the point, I am the Last Hour of the day.

Copernicus: Ah, now I see: the First Hour is sick, and that's why we haven't seen the day yet.

Last Hour: Listen. There will be no more day, not today, tomorrow, or ever if you do not arrange it.

Copernicus: That's just fine. As if I could make the day!

Last Hour: I will tell you how, but first you must come with me immediately to the house of the Sun, my master. I will tell you more along the way, and His Highness will fill in the rest after we arrive.

Copernicus: I am quite agreeable, but the journey must be a long one if I'm not mistaken. And how can I take enough provisions to keep from starving a year or three before arriving? On top of everything, I don't believe His Highness's lands produce enough to provide me even a light lunch.

Last Hour: Forget these doubts. You won't stay long in the house of the Sun, and the voyage will take but a moment, for I am a spirit, if you please.

Copernicus: But I am a body.

Last Hour: Well said, but you mustn't worry yourself over these problems—you are not yet a metaphysician after all. Come here, climb on my back, and I'll do the rest.

Copernicus: Up we go—all set. Now we'll see where this ends up.

Scene Four:

Copernicus and the Sun

Copernicus: My illustrious Lord.

Sun: Pardon me, Copernicus, if I don't ask you to sit down; here we don't use chairs. But this won't take long. My handmaiden has already broached the business to you. Since my girl has spoken for your good qualities, I judge you perfect for the task at hand.

Copernicus: My Lord, I foresee much difficulty in this matter.

Sun: Difficulties should not dismay a man of your stature. Indeed, it is said that they lift the heart of the great-hearted. But what do you generally perceive the difficulties to be?

Copernicus: First and foremost, as great as the power of philosophy is, I'm not at all sure it's great enough to make Earth submit to running instead of sitting, to working instead of loafing—especially these days, which are not exactly heroic times.

Sun: So? If you cannot persuade her, you will force her.

Copernicus: Gladly, Your Highness, if I were a Hercules, or even a Roland, but a canon from Varmia?

Sun: How is this relevant? Don't you remember one of your ancient mathematicians who said that if he had a place beyond the Earth, that standing there he was sure he could move the earth and sky? Now you don't have to move the sky, and here you are in a spot beyond the Earth. Hence, unless you're a lesser man than that ancient, you must not doubt that you can move her, whether she wishes or not.

Copernicus: Milord, it could be done; but it would require a lever so big that neither I nor your illustrious self, with all your wealth, could pay for half its material and manufacture.

There is yet another, more serious problem, indeed a tangle of problems. Until today, Earth has occupied the highest seat in the universe, that is, the central one. And (as you know) standing there motionless and with nothing to do but gaze around, she has watched all the other heavenly bodies—the large as well as small, the brilliant and the dim—whirling continuously above, below, and around her with an energy, a haste, and a fury amazing to contemplate. And thus with everything in the universe at Earth's service, that universe seemed a veritable court, in which Earth sat as on a throne, with the other globes arranged as courtiers, guards, and servants, some listening to one minister, some to another. So that, in effect, the Earth has always thought herself empress of the world. And, we must admit, since things have been as they have, that she has hardly deceived herself; indeed, if anything, her assessment is very well-founded.

And what can I tell you about human beings, who rank themselves (as we always will) the chief and most important of earthly creatures? Each of us, even in rags and without a crust to gnaw on, has deemed himself an emperor—not merely of Constantinople or Germany or over half the earth like the Roman emperors, but an emperor of the universe, of the sun, the planets, the visible and invisible stars, and the final reason for those stars and planets, for Your Highness yourself, and for everything.

So now if we wish Earth to abandon her central station, to run, revolve, continually bother herself, to do that which in the past the other bodies did, in short to become merely one of many planets—this means that Her Earthly Majesty and Their Earthly Majesties must renounce their thrones and abandon their empires, contenting themselves with only rags and considerable miseries.

Sun: And how would you sum up this discourse, my good Don Nicholas? That you have scruples over possible treason?

Copernicus: No, Your Highness, because there is no mention of this as treason in the Codices, the Digest, the books that cover public rights, the law of the Empire, nor any laws treating people and things—as far as I remember. Rather, in essence I'm saying that this plan will not merely affect mechanical things and thus the laws of physics alone, but it will convulse the dignified hierarchy of things and of beings; it will change the destinies of creatures, and hence will cause an apocalyptic revolution in metaphysics, indeed in all that relates to the speculative area of knowledge. The result will be that men, even if capable of realizing and discussing it soberly, will find themselves changed utterly from what they were heretofore and what they imagined themselves to be.

Sun: My son, these things don't frighten me at all, for I respect metaphysics about as much as I do physics, alchemy, and necromancy, if you will. And men can content themselves with being what they are. And if this displeases them, they can rationalize backwards, upside down, and counter to all evidence, as they are very good at doing. And so they can in this way believe themselves what they wish to be—barons, dukes, emperors, or more if they wish—and this will make them feel better and save me from criticism.

Copernicus: All right then, let's forget men and Earth. Consider instead, Your Highness, what we can reasonably expect from the other planets. When they see the Earth act like them, become one of their peers, they will no longer wish to be so plain and unornamented, so sadly barren as they have been, when Earth alone has such richness. They too will want their rivers, seas, mountains, and plants, with inhabitants and animals moving among them. They will see no reason to be inferior to Earth in any way. And so here's another great revolution in the world—an infinity of new families and populations popping up everywhere like mushrooms.

Sun: Let them come as fast and as much as they wish, for my light and heat will suffice for all, with no added effort; and the world will have enough to feed, clothe, house, and generously treat it without my running into debt.

Copernicus: But let's go a little farther, Your Highness, and we encounter yet another stumbling block. When the stars see you sitting down, not just on a stool but on a throne, with this handsome court of planets around you, they will not only want the sedentary life but they will want to reign. And to reign they must have subjects and therefore planets like yours, to each his own. And their planets will need inhabitants and decorations like Earth. And I don't

153

have to tell you the state of the poor human race, already reduced to almost nothing in this galaxy alone; what will become of them when they see thousands of worlds burgeoning forth and even the most impoverished star of the Milky Way with its own?

But considering only your self-interest, I may say that until now you have been, if not first in our universe, certainly second after Earth. And you have had no true equal, given the other stars' reluctance to compare themselves with you. But in the new state you will have as many equals as there are stars with their worlds. In sum, beware that with this transformation you may compromise your dignity.

Sun: Do you not remember what your Julius Caesar said when, traveling through the Alps, he came upon a hamlet of poor barbarians—that he would rather have been first in that barbarian town than second in Rome? Similarly I would prefer being first in this world of ours than second in the whole universe. It is not, however, ambition that prompts me to change the status quo; it is only a love of peace, or if you must know, laziness. As far as being equal or not, of being first or last, I really don't care much. Unlike Cicero I prefer comfort to dignity.

Copernicus: I will do my very best, Your Highness, to achieve that comfort for you, but even if we succeed I doubt our triumph will last long. I'm almost sure that in a few years you'll be twirling round like a pulley or a millstone, while remaining in one place. And I suspect that in the end, sooner or later, you may even have to run again, not necessarily around the Earth. Maybe the very rotation you make will stimulate you to further movement. Enough. Whatever will be will be. Despite the inconveniences and all other consideration, I will serve you since you persist in your plan, with the understanding that if I fail, please think of me as unable, not unwilling.

Sun: Good, my Copernicus. Just try.

Copernicus: There's only one remaining problem.

Sun: Out with it, what?

Copernicus: That I do not wish because of this to be burned alive, like a phoenix, for if this happens I am sure I will not rise again from my ashes as that bird does, and I will nevermore see the face of Your Lordship.

Sun: Hear me, Copernicus. There once was a time, as you
know, when you philosophers had hardly been born and
when poetry ruled supreme, that I was considered a
prophet. I want you to let me prophesy for one last time,
and in memory of my ancient powers I want you to trust
me.

I tell you that some approving men who follow you
may get a scorching, or the like, but as far as I can see you
will not suffer from this enterprise. And if you want to be
very sure, accept this parting advice: dedicate the book
you write on this matter to the Pope. That way, I prom-
ise, you won't even lose your holy office.

∽

103. To Paolina Leopardi (Recanati)

. . . I told you I was going to Massa, but my Florentine friends
made me decide on Pisa, a better city and one with a climate much
acclaimed. I left Florence the morning of the 9th in a post-carriage and
arrived that evening in Pisa, a voyage of fifty miles. . . . I have been
enchanted by Pisa's weather—if it lasts, it will be a beatitude. I left
behind in Florence a temperature barely above freezing; here it was so
warm I had to throw off my cloak and other clothes.

I like the look of Pisa more than that of Florence. This *lung'Arno* is
a spectacle so lovely, wide, grand, gay, and smiling that it enamours
one. I saw nothing like it in Florence, Milan, or Rome. And indeed, I
know not whether there are many such vistas in all of Europe. And
one can walk pleasantly there even in winter, for there is always a
springtime air, so that at certain times of the day that part of town is
full of people, in carriages or on foot. You can hear ten or twenty
languages spoken, and lovely sunlight reflects off the gilded fronts of
the cafés and shops full of nice things and off the windows of palaces
and houses, all with fine architecture.

Beyond this, Pisa is a blend of big city and small town, of urban and
rural folk—a mixture so romantic that I have never seen anything like
it. To the other beauties, add the beautiful language. And then add that
I—thank God—am well; that I eat with appetite; that I have a room
which faces west over a large orchard and has such a large window
that I can see to the horizon, something you have to forget in Florence.
The people of the house are nice and the prices reasonable—a good
thing for my purse, which wasn't too happy with the Florentines. And

I don't want you to think I came here in a lordly carriage; I came in one of those little Tuscan "diligences" which cost less . . . [Pisa, November 12, 1827].

◆

104. From the *Dialogue of Plotinus and Porphyry*

No one knows why Leopardi never attempted suicide, a possibility often in the forefront of his mind and one he dramatized or vented in his works. Surely the strong ban against the act in the Catholic faith (obviously residual in him) together with his own sheer will to endure were factors. In any case, he returned in this piece, written in 1827 as one of the last *Operette Morali*, to the subject he had explored in his notebook and in his early poems *Brutus* and *The Last Song of Sappho*. The kernel of this long dialogue is in Porphyry's *Life of Plotinus*, where Porphyry relates that Plotinus, the Neo-Platonist of the third century before Christ, once dissuaded him from taking his own life. In the earlier part of the dialogue, Porphyry says that a general disgust with life and the ravages of *noia* prompt his desire. Plotinus acknowledges the justice of his friend's complaint but argues that suicide has always been thought unnatural and therefore wrong. In response, Porphyry ingeniously contends that corruptive civilization has reversed for us what is natural and unnatural, reasonable and unreasonable; and that "habit and reason have formed in us another nature" which drives us now "to seek that which is indeed the greatest good for man—death."

Although Porphyry's arguments are rationally forceful, it is Plotinus who gets the last, almost Periclean words, which appeal not to reason but to the emotions and invoke the stoic doctrine of human love so compelling to Leopardi in his last years.

. . . Let us assume that killing oneself is reasonable and that accommodating one's mind to life is unreasonable. Certainly the former course is savage and inhuman. And it cannot be more gratifying to choose to be a monster according to reason rather than a man according to nature. Furthermore, should we not consider our friends and relatives, our children, brothers, parents, wives, and household people—all those with whom we have lived so long and whom in dying we must leave forever? And will we not feel great pain in our hearts from this separation? And should we not take account of what they would feel at the loss of one so dear and familiar, as well as at the atrociousness of the thing itself?

I know well that the wise man must not be too tenderhearted; nor should he let pity and anguish so conquer him that he loses his head, falls to earth, and faints, like those vile persons who drown in excessive tears and who do things beneath the dignity of him who sees the human condition clearly and full. But this strength of soul is appropriate for those sad events dealt to us by fortune and thus inevitable. Such strength should not be abused by voluntarily depriving us forever of the presence, the words, the closeness of our cherished ones. To hold as nothing the grief of relatives, intimates, and friends, or to be unconscious of the pain rendered, is the act not of a wise man but a barbaric one—of one who cares too much for self and not at all for others. And in truth, the suicide looks only to his own interests. He casts behind him, so to speak, his people and all the human race. There is in this act of renunciation the most clear and sordid, the least beautiful and generous, self-love to be found in the world.

Finally, my Porphyry, the troubles and ills of life are indeed many and constant; but when, as presently with you, there are no unusual calamities or misfortunes, no cruel bodily pains, they can be endured—especially by a man as wise and strong as you. And life is of such little moment that one should not leap either to retain or to abandon it. Therefore, without pondering the matter too curiously, we should be open to any reason inviting us to cleave to our second option rather than the first. And if a friend begs you, why would you resist pleasing him? Now then, I warmly pray you, my Porphyry, in memory of the years of our friendship, abandon this thinking. Do not choose to be the cause of such great sorrow to your good friends, who love you with all their hearts, to me who has no one more cherished, no company more sweet. Desire instead to help us endure life rather than thoughtlessly to leave us desolate.

Let us live, my Porphyry, and together comfort each other. Let us not refuse to bear the part destiny has assigned to us of the evils of our race. Let us try to be companions and go on giving to each other succor, courage, and our hands, so as to finish as best we can the labor of this life, which doubtless will be brief. And when our death shall come, we will not lament, and in those final days our friends and companions will comfort us. And there shall be cheer in the thought that when we are gone, they will remember us often, and love us still.

∽

105. To Monaldo Leopardi (Recanati)

The following passage is one of the few times, at least in writing, that Leopardi spoke openly to his father about their relationship. Noticeably enough, the letters to Monaldo from this point on are warmer and tend to begin with *"Mio Caro Papà"* instead of the earlier, more formidable *"Carissimo Signor Padre."*

. . . You criticize the dryness of my letters, which arises from a lack of material, and is common to all my letters because my life is monotonous and nothing new happens. You wish that I might look into your heart for just one moment. To this let me make a declaration, which may from now on shed some light on my feeling for you. I say, then, in all sincerity before God, that I love you as tenderly as ever it was or is possible for a son to love his father; that I know most clearly of the love you bear me, and that I feel for you a kindness, tenderness, and gratitude as deep and warm as humanly possible; that I would gladly shed my blood for you, not only from a sense of duty but with love. . . . And if you sometimes desire from me more confidences and intimacy with you, the absence of these comes only from the habits formed in childhood, habits too old and powerful to break . . . [Pisa, December 24, 1827].

106.   One of the chief results I intend and hope for from my verses is that they may warm my old age with the heat of my youth; that I may savor them at that time and experience some relic of my past feelings, set aside as in deposit to preserve it; that I may move myself in rereading them, as I often have already, and more so than in reading others' poetry. Beyond remembrance itself, there will be the reflection on what I was and the comparing of myself with myself; and finally the pleasure of enjoying and appreciating one's own works, of contemplating the beauties and worth of one's own child—with no other satisfaction than that of having created a beautiful thing in this world, whether others think so or not [Pisa, February 15, the last Friday of Carnival, 1828, Z, 4302].

107.   *To Sylvia*

On May 2, 1828, Leopardi wrote from Pisa to his sister Paolina that "after two years, I have written some verses this April, but I mean real verses in the old way, and with the heart I once had." He was referring to *The Reawakening (Il Risorgimento)*, a poem describing the resurgence of feeling and thus, as always for Leopardi, of imagination; and to *A Silvia*, written on April 19-20, 1828. This *canzone* is usually considered one of Leopardi's very best poems, attaining verbal and musical intensity that sets it apart. Scholars have attempted to link Sylvia and the Nerina of the later *Memories* to Teresa Fattorini and Maria Belardinelli, girls of Recanati who died young. The cause seems fruitless since these girls (with names Tasso also loved) are obviously symbolic projections of the poet and his past. In response to a literalist German scholar who had argued that Nerina was an actual girl who befriended Leopardi and shared his poetry, De Sanctis put the whole problem into conclusive perspective: "And he has committed a mortal sin, because with one stroke he has killed Leopardi and Nerina for me."[2]

> Sylvia. Do you remember still
> The moments of your mortal lifetime here,
> When such a loveliness
> Shone in the elusive laughter of your eyes,
> And you, contemplative and gay, climbed toward
> The summit of your youth?
>
> The tranquil chambers held,
> The paths re-echoed, your perpetual song,
> When at your woman's tasks
> You sat, content to concentrate upon
> The future beckoning within your mind.
> It was the fragrant May,
> And thus you passed your time.
>
> I often used to leave
> The dear, belabored pages which consumed
> So much of me and of my youth, and from
> Ancestral balconies
> Would lean to hear the music of your voice,
> Your fingers humming through
> The intricacies of the weaving work.
> And I would gaze upon
> The blue surrounding sky,
> The paths and gardens golden in the sun,
> And there the far-off sea, and here the mountain.
> No human tongue can tell
> What I felt then within my brimming heart.
>
> What tendernesses then,
> What hopes, what hearts were ours, O Sylvia mine!
> How large a thing seemed life, and destiny!
> When I recall those bright anticipations,

Bitterness invades,
And I turn once again to mourn my lot.
O Nature, Nature, why
Do you not keep the promises you gave?
Why trick the children so?

Before the winter struck the summer grass,
You died, my gentle girl,
Besieged by hidden illness and possessed.
You never saw the flowering of your years.
Your heart was never melted by the praise
Of your dark hair, your shy,
Enamoured eyes. Nor did you with your friends
Conspire on holidays to talk of love.

The expectation failed
As soon for me, and fate denied my youth.
Ah how gone by, gone by,
You dear companion of my dawning time,
The hope that I lament!
Is this the world we knew? And these the joys
The love, the labors, happenings we shared?
And this the destiny
Of human beings? My poor one, when
The truth rose up, you fell,
And from afar you pointed me the way
To coldest death and the stark sepulchre.

108. The following notebook entry was probably inspired by Teresa Lucignani,
the sister-in-law of Leopardi's landlord in Pisa.

A woman of twenty or thirty has perhaps more obvious attractions
and is more likely to inspire and maintain a passion . . . but truly a
girl of sixteen or eighteen has in her face, voice, movements, bounces
a certain divine something beyond comparison. Whatever her person-
ality or taste, joyous or sad, capricious or grave, lively or shy, that
purest flower of youth, fresh and intact; that untouched maiden hope
you read in her face and gesture and you imagine exist only in and for
her; that air of innocent and complete ignorance of evil, misfortune,

suffering—in short, this very first flower of life, the sum of all these things, makes on you (although you are not enamoured and may not be really interested) an impression so keen, profound, and ineffable that you never tire of looking at that face. I know of nothing else more apt to raise the soul, transport us to another world, and give us an idea of angels, paradise, and happiness . . . [Florence, June 30, 1828, Z, 4310-11].

✍

109. To Pietro Giordani (Milan)

. . . My stomach is finally beginning to turn against the superb disdain professed here for beauty and real literature—especially since I can't get it into my head that the summit of human knowledge consists in knowing politics and statistics . . . and I humbly ask whether the happiness of the masses can be achieved without the happiness of individuals. The latter are condemned to unhappiness by nature, not by men or chance, and to ease this inevitable unhappiness, the most valuable thing is the study of the beautiful, the affections, the imaginings, and illusions. Thus the delightful seems to me more useful than the useful . . . [Florence, July 24, 1828].

✍

110. In fact, the epic poem goes against the nature of poetry: (1) it requires a plan conceived and arranged in all coldness; (2) what can a labor that takes years and years to execute have to do with poetry? Poetry comes essentially from an impulse. And the long poem is against nature in the absolute sense. It is impossible that imagination, the poetic vein and spirit, could last, suffice, and not fail in so long a work on the same theme. The weariness and straining of Virgil are manifest as well as famous in the last six books of *The Aenied,* written through sheer will rather than impulse or desire [about August 25, 1828, Z, 4356].

✍

111. Memories of my life. The happiness I experienced when composing, the best time I have ever spent in my life, and in which I would be content to stay as long as I live. The days passing without my being

aware, the hours seeming so short, and I myself marveling at how easily they went by . . . [November 30, 1828, Z, 4417-18].

◊

112. To a sensitive, imaginative man who lives constantly feeling and imagining, as I have for a long time, the world and its objects are, in a certain sense, double. He sees with his eyes a tower, a landscape; he hears with his ears the sound of a bell; and at the same time with his imagination he sees another tower, another landscape, he hears another sound. In this second kind of object resides all the beauty and pleasure of things. Life is sad (and this is the common lot) for those who see, hear, and feel only simple objects, objects from which only eyes, ears, and the other senses receive the stimulus [November 30, first Sunday of Advent, 1828, Z, 4418].

◊

113. It has been observed that great grief (like every great passion) has no external language. I would add that it has no internal one either. A man in great sorrow is not capable of encircling, of articulating to himself, any idea or emotion on the subject of his agony which can focus and exercise (so to speak) the mind in its grief. He feels a thousand emotions, sees a thousand ideas all mixed up together—or perhaps feels and sees nothing but one huge idea or emotion wherein his thinking and feeling faculties become immersed and powerless, unable to embrace it all or to divide or analyze its parts. Hence he then does not have thoughts, properly speaking, nor does he even know well the cause of his pain; he is in a kind of lethargy, and if he weeps (and I've seen this in myself) he weeps as if arbitrarily and generally, without knowing how to tell himself *for what*. Those dramatists, and the like, who in moments about great passions introduce soliloquies—following that convention which permits characters to say out loud what real people would say to themselves—know that in such circumstances man would say nothing, not even to himself . . . [November 30, 1828, Recanati, Z, 4418-19].

◊

114. Memories of my life. Having gone to Rome, the necessity of living with other men, to pour myself outwards, to act, to live externally

made me stupid, inept, and inwardly dead. I was then incapable of reconciling one life with the other—so incapable that I thought this combination impossible, and that other men who I saw were adapted to living outwardly could not be experiencing the inward life I had known, and most had never done so. Only experience disabused me of this assumption. But that period was perhàps the most mortifying, painful one of my life, for in becoming so inept internally and externally, I lost almost all my self-reliance and my hopes for success in life [December 1, 1828, Z, 4420]

∽

115. In my solitary walks through the city, the most pleasant feeling and lovely images arise in me at the sight of the room interiors I see through the open windows from below in the street. These rooms would not awaken any feelings in me if I saw them from within. Is this not an image of human life, its blessing and delights? [December 1, 1828, Recanati, Z, 4421].

∽

116. Nature is like a child: with the greatest of care she labors to produce and bring her product to perfection, but no sooner is it done than she begins to think of destroying it, or working toward its dissolution. And so it is with man, with other animals, with vegetables, with everything. And man treats her as he would a child. The ways of preservation he uses to prolong the period of existence, or a similar state, either his own or of things he needs, are nothing other than a kind of taking away from the child its handiwork as soon as it has finished lest the child immediately take to undoing it [December 2, 1828, Z, 4421].

∽

117. The Spanish language seems and will always seem ridiculous to Italians for the same reason that a monkey strikes man as ridiculous— great similarity joined to important differences. But this laughing at Spanish is surely as irrational as laughing at monkeys, and is also open to reciprocity, since it is natural that Italian, by the same token, seems absurd to Spaniards . . . [December 2, 1828, Z, 4422].

❦

118.   In reading a poetic passage, whether in verse or prose (but the most forceful impressions come from verse), one can say . . . (even in prosaic times like this) what Sterne said about a smile—that it adds a thread to the short fabric of our lives. It refreshes us, so to speak, and strengthens our vitality. But this kind of passage is most rare these days [February 1, 1829, Z, 4450].

❦

119. The opening quotation is from *The Pensées* of Rousseau, from whom Leopardi has obviously drifted.

"Man, stop seeking the author of evil; that author is you yourself. There is no other evil than that which you do or you suffer, and both come to you from yourself. General evil cannot exist except in disorder, and I see in the world's system an order which does not contradict itself. As for particular ill, it is only in the feeling of the suffering person; and man has not received this feeling from nature—he has given it to himself. Suffering has little impact on whoever, having thought a bit, indulges neither memory nor anticipation. Take away our harmful improvements, take away our errors and vices, take away man's handiwork, and all is well. . . ."

Rather, to be precise, the order that is in the world, and the realization that evil is in the order, that this order could not exist without evil makes the existence of this idea inconceivable. Animals destined as food for other species. Inborn envy and hatred of the living toward their similars. . . . Other wrongs more serious and basic in the very *system* of nature, as noted elsewhere by me, etc. We more easily conceive accidental ills than regular and ordinary ones. If there were in the world *disorders,* the ills would be *extraordinary,* accidental; we would say, "The work of nature is imperfect, like that of men." We would not say, "That is wicked.". . . But what name can we give to that cause and power which includes evil in the order of things? which bases the order on ill? Disorder would be much better—it is varied and changeable. If today there is evil, tomorrow there may be good, or even total good. But what hope is there when evil is ordinary? in an order, I say, where evil is essential? [May 17, 1829, Z, 4510-11].

❦

120. Certain ideas, certain images of things supremely vague, fantastic, chimerical, impossible delight us greatly, whether in poetry or in our own imagination, because they recall to us our most remote memories, those of childhood, during which such ideas and images and beliefs were familiar and ordinary to us. And the poets who most exhibit such concepts (so supremely poetical) are the most dear to us. If you analyze well your most poetic impression and imaginings—the ones that most exalt you and pull you outside of yourself and of the real world—you would find that they and the pleasure they cause (at least after childhood) consist totally or chiefly in remembrance [May 21, 1829, Z, 4513].

∾

121.   *Memories*

This highly autobiographical poem, *Le ricordanze,* was written in August–September, 1829, during Leopardi's last stay at Recanati. It is the poem of his which most invites comparison to Wordsworth, recalling *Tintern Abbey,* the Lucy poems, and passages from *The Prelude.* Both poets analyzed the persistence of memory and its impact on the creative imagination; they dealt with the double consciousness of childhood lived and childhood remembered; they lamented the death of the young; and they wrote in a lucid and introspective style amazingly similar at times. Comparisons go only so far, however. Even in the Lucy poems, Wordsworth did not dwell on the theme of transience as darkly or obsessively as Leopardi does here, nor did he anywhere find such bitterness in remembering his youth, evoking his native soil, and assessing his life.

Leopardi may have exaggerated his feelings about Recanati—geniuses often clash with their home environments and Leopardi eventually became bored or negative about any place where he lived for long. But much of his antipathy was warranted. In addition to the loneliness he felt in the paternal mansion, it is said that he was cruelly taunted by the boys of Recanati, who often called him to his face "the hunchback of Leopardi" and even snowballed him. On the rare occasions when he ventured outdoors, he would move quickly through the streets trying to make himself invisible. It is also true, however, that Recanati held natural and nostalgic attractions for Leopardi, and that for this poet who argued that childhood means poetry, Recanati triggered the imagination.

The poem is therefore built on paradoxes, as the repetitions of the words "bitter" and "sweet" would indicate. The themes are the attraction-repulsion toward Recanati; the blessedness of youthful deceptions; the death-in-life of the poet, the comfort in remembering, even when the past was sad; the pain in remembering, because the process itself means the thing recalled is irre-

trievable; and the lovely dead Nerina, whom the poet keeps alive through
memory and imagination.

O tender stars of the Bear, I never thought
I would return to contemplate again
Your shining light upon my father's garden,
To lean out from the window and discuss
With you this place I dwelled in as a child
And where I saw the end of all my joys.
O how the glowing of your sister stars
And you struck wild imaginings within
My mind here long ago! when on green grass
I silently would pass the evenings by,
Alert to the large sky and to the song
Of frogs sequestered in the encircling country!
The fireflies flashed, now here now there, among
The flowerbeds and bushes; the cypresses
And fragrant avenues of that dark grove
Trembled to the moving wind; and from our house
I heard the cozy sound of voices vying,
The muted stir of servants. And what immense
Reflections and sweet dreams the distant sea
Begot in me, and those far blue mountains
Which I imagined crossing one fine day—
What unknown worlds and unknown happiness
I shaped to be my life! So ignorant I was
Of my real destiny, the barrenness
And pain I would so gladly change for death.

Nor did my secret heart disclose to me
How my green age was doomed to waste away
In this barbaric native town of mine,
Among a mean and boorish folk who deem
All learning and ideas alien,
Fair game for easy laughter; a folk who shun
And hate but never rise to any envy,
Who rank me low and curse me for my airs,
Though I have not shown scorn to anyone.
And so I pass my years, secluded
And obscure. I know no life, no love,
And I grow bitter in this grudging crowd;
Forsaking manliness and mercy I become
The hater of mankind. And all the while

The cherished age of youth goes by, more dear
Than laureled fame, or the pure light of day,
Or even breath itself. I see you slip
Away without a joy to mitigate
The pain of this inhuman interval—
O sole and lovely bloom of this dry life.

The sounding hour drifts to me on the wind
From the bell tower. When I was a small child
That sound was comforting at night to me,
As I lay watching in my darkened room
For the bleak terrors, and sighing for the dawn.
In this place everything I see or hear
Starts up an image of sweet remembrance,
Sweet in itself yet with intrusive pain:
The consciousness of present time, the vain
Desire to hold that very past, though it
Was sad, the uttering of the words, "I was."
That loggia there, against the dying light,
Those painted walls with their bucolic shapes,
The sun which rose above the lonely plain—
They all informed my reveries with joy
When powerful Illusion walked with me,
Delighting me wherever I would go.
In these old rooms, the bright snow all about,
When wind was rummaging among the windows,
My festive, gaming voice would echo forth,
For then the base and bitter mystery
Of things portrayed itself to me as fair.
When cheating life lies whole before his gaze,
A boy, like any untried lover, loves
The heavenly beauty he himself creates.

O dreams, dreams, you dear deceptions
Of my young years! I always turn to you,
For though time goes, and mind and heart may change,
I do not know how to forget your spell.
Honor and glory are but phantoms—now
I understand—and good and happiness
Are mere desire. This life brings forth no fruit
But empty suffering. And though my days
Are void, and being is a desert state

And dark, I cannot truly say that Fate
Has taken much from me. But ah! When I
Remember you, my first and treasured hopes,
And then compare my current life, in which
The only vital hope is that for death,
My heart within me withers and I feel
That nothing can console me for my fate.
When welcome Death shall finally reach my side
And this misfortune of a life recede,
When earth appears to me a foreign vale,
My eyes no more anticipating time,
I shall remember you, and you shall make
Me sigh, bright image of those days, and know
The bitterness again. And you shall blend
With rue the sweetness of my dying day.

Even in the first tumult of my youth,
The age of pleasure, anguish, and desire,
I often called on death, and sitting long
Beside the fountain, contemplated how
Both hope and pain would end within those waters.
Then blind and almost killing sickness came,
Which made me mourn the loveliness of youth,
The flower of my days already fallen.
And often in my wakeful bed I lay
By flickering lanternlight and versified,
Lamenting to the silences of night
How flesh and spirit now were failing me
And to myself I sang funereal songs.

Who can remember you, green time, without
A sigh? Ineffable, compelling days
When girls first smile at the enchanted lad,
And everything around competes to beam
On him, while Envy sleeps or still is kind;
When the world (new miracle!) holds forth its hand
To him, forgives his errors, and celebrates
This fresh beginning of a life. It seems
To bow before him, hailing him a lord.
So quick the days! like lightning come and gone.
What man can say he has not known misfortune,
If the bright season of his youth has fled?

Nerina mine, do I not hear this place
Still echoing of you? Has my heart ceased
To cleave to you? Where have you disappeared,
My sweetness, whose memory alone remains?
Your native town no longer sees you here;
That window there, where you and I told tales,
Reflects only the sad light of the stars.
Where are you? where the sounding of that voice
Whose accents even from afar could make
My face turn pale. That was another time,
My gentle love. Your days are gone, and you.
Others still walk these fragrant hills, but you
Passed swiftly on. Your life was like a dream
Which you went dancing through. The light
Of youth and sure anticipations filled
Your face and eyes, till Fate put out the light
And you lay softly down. Alas, Nerina,
How the old love yet dominates my heart.
And if at times I wander where people feast
And gather round, I murmur to myself:
"Nerina mine, you no more deck yourself for feasts
Or move among the gatherings." And when
The May returns and lovers bring to maids
Their songs and sprigs, I say: "Nerina fair,
The spring will nevermore return for you,
Nor love." Each sun-filled day, each flowered bank,
Each pleasant thing I come across, I say:
"O my Nerina, you joy not in the spring,
The fields and air are not for you." You are gone,
My living pain. And your bitter memory
Shall always be companion to my dear
Imaginings, to feelings ever tender,
And all the early stirrings of the heart.

∾

122.   *The Calm after the Storm*

This work, *La quiete dopo la tempesta,* was composed at Recanati, September
17-20, 1829. In mood and art it seems to fuse with *The Village Saturday,*
written a few days later. Both poems involve sharp contrasts. In *The Calm,*
Leopardi juxtaposes the idea of unattainable positive happiness with the

negatively produced kind humans do attain through release from terror or
pain; in *The Village Saturday*, Leopardi notes once again the gap between
expectation and fulfillment. In both poems there is a contrast between heart
and head; between tender appreciation of those moments when nature and
man beautifully interact and abstract regret over the ultimate meaning of such
scenes. Most readers have agreed, however, that the intellectual protest
against the injustice of life and nature is muted in these poems as compared to
other treatments of these themes by Leopardi. As in *Memories*, Leopardi has
learned to use, and partly enjoy, his native materials, and it is the warm
evocation of village and natural life which persists long after the reading. In a
sense, the poems together constitute a soft valedictory to the Recanati from
which Leopardi so often tried to detach himself, but which had inscribed itself
into his memory and affections.

> The storm has passed us now.
> I hear the birds rejoice and the careful hen
> Repeating on the road her constant verse.
> O look! the blue breaks through above the hills,
> The countryside is bright,
> The river reappears along the valley.
> All hearts again leap up
> And everywhere the hum
> Of our habitual labor now resumes.
> His work in hand, the craftsman with a song
> Leans out to see the dewy, vivid sky;
> The women rush to be the first to draw
> Upon the fresh, clean rain;
> And the vendor with his fruit
> Takes up his usual chant. Look where the sun
> Returns to smile on hills
> And houses. Balconies and rooms unfold,
> And sounds of harness bell and creaking cart
> Announce the traveler goes on his way.
>
> And so our hearts are glad.
> What moments of our lives
> Can match the sweetness of this golden time?
> When else do men with such an urgent love
> Approach their books, return
> To work, or launch upon a new endeavor?
> And when are they less mindful of their ills?
> Our pleasure is the child of suffering,
> A curious fruit of terror that has passed,
> The fear that makes the man who loathes his life

Embrace it all the more.
And so, while their chastisement lingers on,
Men tremble wordlessly
And wanly shudder at the gathering winds,
The clouds and lightning on them centering.

O gracious Nature, these then are the gifts
And pleasures which you give to mortal men.
Surviving woe is thought a joy by us.
You scatter pains with generosity,
The instant sorrow comes,
And the inevitable surging joy
Which follows seems a gain and miracle.
Humanity, so treasured by the gods!
Consider yourself blessed
If you find space to breathe between the pains,
And death to heal the storm of being human.

❧

123.   *The Village Saturday*

Il sabato del villaggio, uncharacteristically written in one day, September 29, 1829, links to *The Calm after the Storm* (see note above), but it also relates eloquently to *Sunday Evening.*

The sun is falling as the peasant girl
Returns from the open fields,
Bearing a swathe of grass and in her hand
Her customary bunch of violets
And roses which will grace
Her hair and breast the coming holiday.
And, spinning, the old woman sits upon
The steps among her neighbors,
Their faces turned against the dying light;
And she tells tales of her green days, when she
Adorned her body for the holidays
And, slenderly robust,
Would dance the night away
Among the companions of her lovely prime.
The very air seems now to deepen, the sky
Turns darker blue. Down from the hills and roofs
Returning shadows fall

At the whitening of the moon.

Now bells declare the time
Is near, the festive day,
The hour of heart's renewal.
The shouting lads invade
The village square in troops,
Leaping now here, now there,
Making such happy chatter.
Meanwhile the whistling laborer comes back
To take his meager meal
And ruminate about his day of rest.

And then, when every other lamp is out
And other sounds are stilled—
Listen—a pounding hammer and a saw:
It is the carpenter,
Awake and hurrying by lanternlight
Inside his shuttered shop
To end his task before the morning breaks.

Of all the seven days this is the one
Most cherished, full of joy and expectation.
The passing hours will bring tomorrow soon,
And tedium and sadness,
When each shall turn inside
His mind to his habitual travail.

O playful little boy,
Your flowering time is like a day of grace,
So brightly blue,
Anticipating the great feast of life.
My child, enjoy the season.
I will not tell you more; but if the day
Seems slow in coming, do not grieve too much.

124.   *Night-Song of a Wandering Shepherd of Asia*

The *Canto notturno di un pastore errante dell'Asia* is a great poem and perhaps
the finest work of art Leopardi produced.[3] It did not come easily. Overcom-
ing constant illness, Leopardi spent much time between October, 1829, and

October, 1830—the last months he was ever to spend at Recanati—working on the poem. The grain of sand which helped produce the pearl came from reading the Russian traveler Baron de Meyerdorff's book *Voyage d' Orenbourg à Boukhara, fait en 1820*. In his notebook for October 3, 1828, Leopardi jotted down the Baron's description of the nomadic Kirghiz tribe of central Asia, some of whom "pass the night seated on a rock gazing at the moon and improvising words quite melancholy set to melodies no less so."

The structure that Leopardi built from the stimulus of those few words is essentially, if tentatively, religious. In the first place, the language reminds us of certain dark passages from the Bible, especially of the Job who could ask, "Why give light to a man of grief?" or "Why did you bring me out of the womb?" or who could say, "For me there is no calm, no peace, my torments banish rest." For that matter, the questions posed by Leopardi's shepherd to the moon recall the queries put by God to Job: "What womb brings forth ice, who pent the sea up, where is snow kept?" The language may be reminiscent because the posture is. The shepherd does not give or receive any answers. He does not break through to the surety found elsewhere in the Bible. But he does raise the questions basic to religion and myth, those timelessly asked by humans bent on clarifying the mystery of their existence, their relation to the Not-Me everywhere around them, and their destiny.

Just as striking is the way the *Night-Song* distills, objectifies, and intensifies images and ideas from Leopardi's earlier writings. The address to the moon or a flock, ideas from *Copernicus* and the *Dialogue of Nature and an Icelander*, the contrast between humans and animals, notations on *noia*, pain, and *nulla*, the motif of man's smallness against the size of the cosmos—all reappear here, but transformed. The evidence of Leopardi's personal history seems burned away, and what remains is external to him, mythic in size, purity, and intensity. The key to this effect is, I think, in the way Leopardi uses the desert and astral images he has mentioned so often earlier and heightens them into setting and symbol. Not only is the scene intrinsically staggering—we are at the point where desert meets sky and the lonely questioner is limned against it all—but we are at a stark metaphysical point. Like other romantics for whom physical things can stand for mental-spiritual states (Shelley's caves of mind, Hawthorne's forest and city, Melville's ocean), Leopardi uses landscape and skyscape psychologically to reflect his torn vision. On the one hand, there is the desert world, this earth of *noia* and purposelessness and the pull toward nonbeing; on the other, the open sky which seems full of wonder, energy, possible purpose, and the attraction of being. If we add to these symbols the suggestion that the human capable of feeling so vulnerably small is on his way to an enlarged perception of self, an idea Leopardi had been mulling for some time, we begin to recognize the importance and stature of the poem.[4]

> What are you doing there, moon in the sky?
> Tell me what, O most silent moon.
> You rise in evenings,

To muse upon the deserts; then you rest.
Are you not weary yet
Of those repetitive eternal paths?
Can you still contemplate
These valleys with an interested eye?
O how the shepherd's life resembles yours.
He rises with the dawn
To move his flock among the fields, he looks
Upon the grasses, fountains, other flocks,
And in the tired evening takes his rest—
He hopes toward nothing more.
Tell me, O moon, what worth
Is this life to the shepherd, or yours to you?
Where does this, my brief roaming, tend? And where
Your everlasting course?

A white-haired, weak old man—
Barefoot and half naked
With a ponderous load upon his back,
Through valleys, over mountains and sharp rocks,
Across deep sands and chasms,
In wind and seething storm,
In burning or in freezing weather—runs,
Runs panting on, plunging through bogs and torrents,
Falls down, gets up, and hurries, hurries on
Without a stop or rest,
His body cut and bleeding, till he arrives
There where his path and so much labor aimed—
The abyss, horrid, immense,
Wherein, in falling, he unremembers all.
Such, O virgin moon,
Is this, our mortal life.

Man is brought forth in labor.
The risk of death attends the act of birth,
And his first experience is that of pain.
From the beginning
His mother and father
Attempt to comfort him for being born;
And as he lives and grows,
They both find words and acts to raise his heart,
Sustain him and console his human state.

There is no kinder thing that parents do.
But why give to the sun
And nurse along in life
The creature who must be consoled for it?
If life is a misfortune
Why must we still endure?
Such, O perfect moon,
Is this, our mortal state.
But since you are not human, you may not care.

    Yet you, eternal, lonely pilgrim there,
So pensive above earth,
Perhaps do comprehend this earthly life,
And know what suffering means, and all our sighs;
What death may signify, this ultimate
Whitening of the face,
And vanishing from earth,
And being gone to every loved companion.
And you must see the reason for all things,
The fruit of dusk and dawn, and of this mute
And infinite procession of slow time.
Your certainly must know
For which sweet lover springtime laughs, and who
Can use the summer blaze or winter frost.
You know and can discover countless things
Remaining hidden to the simple shepherd.
Often, when I behold
Your silent face above the empty plains,
Defining in their sweep
The limits of the sky;
Or when I see you following my flock
And me as if we journeyed on together;
And when I see the stars burn in the sky—
I say within myself:
"Wherefore those many lights?
This endless air, this infinite, deep vault?
And this tremendous solitude, what does
It mean? And who am I?"
And so I go reflecting:
What splendid, measureless a home is this
For so innumerable a family!
I cannot guess the purpose or the fruit

Of so much energy,
So many movements of each heavenly thing
And each terrestrial—
All circling without end
And turning back to find their origin.
But you, undying maid, do fathom it.
And I? I surely know and sense this much:
If these eternal rounds
And my own fragile being
May satisfy the whims
Of others, for me this life is only woe.

And you, my resting flock, O blessèd you.
Who cannot know, I think, your wretchedness,
How much I envy you!
Not only that you seem so free of care,
Forgetting quickly every blow or hurt
Or moment of pure dread—
But more because when you are lying on
The shadowed grass you know no tedium,
And thus contentedly you pass away
The great part of the year.
I too sit down upon the grass in shade,
But troubled thoughts seize on my mind; they goad
And almost sting, so that while in repose
I cannot find my place or any peace.
And yet I long for nothing,
Nor until now have I found cause for tears.
I do not know the source
And limits of your pleasure, O my flock—
But you are fortunate.
And if my joy is small that is but part
Of my lament. If you
Could only speak, I would ask this of you:
"Tell me, why every beast
Finds peace along with comfort lying down,
While terrible blankness flays me when I rest?"

Perhaps if I had wings,
To soar above the clouds,
To number one by one each burning star
Or wander like the thunder peak to peak,

I would be happier, O my sweet flock,
I would be happier, O my pale moon.
Or does my mind ignore
The truth, imagining such alien fates?
Perhaps whatever state or shape there be,
In cradle or in lair,
The day of birth for creatures born is dark.

IV

FLORENCE AND NAPLES (1830-37):

THE SLOPES OF VESUVIUS

AND THE FINAL VISION

Florence and Naples (1830-37):
The Slopes of Vesuvius and the Final Vision

In March of 1830, Leopardi learned that General Pietro Colletta and other friends from Florence had collected money for him so that he might live where he pleased, at least for a time. On April 2, the grateful Leopardi wrote Colletta: "For now I will say only that your letter—coming after sixteen months of horrible night, an existence which God should spare my worst enemies—was like a ray of light to me, more blessed than the first twilight gleam in the polar regions." Thus, on April 29, 1830, his departure unattended by his sulking father, Leopardi left Recanati never to return. Except for a winter in Rome, Leopardi spent the next two years in Florence, where, despite his acrid resistance to so much current thought, he was respected. The first Florentine edition of the *Canti* was published in 1831, and shortly thereafter Leopardi learned of his election to the prestigious *Accademia della Crusca*. Less happily, Leopardi had to spend much effort in 1832 delicately dissociating himself from a grossly reactionary pamphlet published by Monaldo called *Little Dialogues on the Current Events of 1831*.

In his dedication to the Florentine *Canti,* Leopardi wrote that with this book "I bid farewell to literature and my studies." We can also observe that he had entered very few items in his notebook between 1829 and 1832, when he discontinued the *Zibaldone* altogether. Obviously he thought his death was close, but several years remained for him, during which he wrote much, made more friends, and experienced the two most emotional attachments of his life. One intimate of this period was Louis De Sinner, a young Swiss classicist who later promised to try to get Leopardi's philological manuscripts published in Germany, the country Leopardi judged the most scholarly in Europe. Leopardi saw precious little publication from this plan, and no money, but De Sinner remembered him from afar; it was he, for example, who eventually gave Sainte-Beuve the manuscripts and inspiration to write the latter's fine 1844 essay on Leopardi. More vital to Leopardi's personal life, however, was his intertwined relationship with Antonio Ranieri, whom he had met earlier in Florence, and Fanny Targioni Tozzetti. When Ranieri, an exiled Neapolitan with some pretensions to literature, was not chasing women, he found time to be the best friend Leopardi ever had. In November, 1830, the affectionate Ranieri took a room next to Leopardi's, and except for a few months he remained near or with him for the rest of the poet's life.

Ranieri seemed almost to venerate Leopardi and was willing to nurse both his constant illness and his occasional irascibility. For Leopardi it must have been good to have a friend he could count on and conversation to diffuse the long-standing loneliness. Psychologically they complemented one another: Leopardi had the genius and greatness Ranieri lacked; Ranieri had the social graces and healthy good looks Leopardi could only envy. The relative happiness found in Ranieri, however, was balanced for some time by the pain Leopardi encountered through Fanny Tozzetti, whom he knew in the 1830-33 period. Fanny, wife to a Florentine doctor, was an attractive, basically empty person who enjoyed having accomplished men adore her, even deformed poets. When it came to serious choice, however, she preferred the advances of the good-looking Ranieri to those of Leopardi ("my little hunchback"). The hurt and disenchantment caused by this affair lie more or less behind a cycle of later poems, including *Aspasia*, a thinly veiled work about Fanny's cruelly attractive effect, and *To Himself*, the most bitter residue of the incident. Despite the personal anguish, Leopardi produced in Florence the most urbane and best-loved of his *Operette*, the *Dialogue of an Almanac-Vendor and a Wayfarer*, and he began to assemble the trenchant, relatively light-spirited *Reflections*.

On September 2, 1833, partly supported by a monthly stipend finally and grudgingly conceded by the Countess Adelaide, Leopardi departed with Ranieri for Naples. There, they hoped, Leopardi might benefit from the warmer climate and the added assistance of Ranieri's sister, like Leopardi's named Paolina. At first, Leopardi was fascinated by the bustle of the city, so different from the northern ones he had known; and indeed his health during the first year there allowed him to walk about, attend the theater, and listen in wonderment to bards actually singing the epic tales of Homer and Tasso. But the Neapolitan sun could not reach what ailed Leopardi, whose respiratory system and eyes were weakening with every passing month. Only a total, devoted commitment from Antonio and Paolina—who functioned as his eyes and hands—permitted Leopardi to continue to express himself literarily. While still residing in Naples proper, Leopardi generated two long satirical works in verse: the *Paralipomeni* (see introduction) and the *Retraction to Marchese Gino Capponi,* an ironic attack on contemporary materialistic idealism. Neither of these works, which puzzled and offended some of his friends in Florence, shows Leopardi at his best—his excellences never crystallized in topical satire. More important, he wrote a fine and underrated poem, *On the Likeness of a Beautiful Woman;* and he oversaw the production of a Neapolitan edition of his complete works. That the Bourbon government should have seen fit to suppress both the *Canti* and *Operette Morali* must not have surprised Leopardi even if it tasked his failing resources.

In April, 1836, the trio of friends left the city for a villa at the foot of Vesuvius between Torre del Greco and Torre Annunziata. There, in the next few months, Leopardi created two outstanding poems, both of which breathe finality and summation—*Broom* and *The Setting of the Moon.* In August, a cholera epidemic descended on Naples. Such a threat, while frightening to

Leopardi, was gratuitous. He died from other natural causes on June 14, 1837, just shy of his thirty-ninth birthday. According to Ranieri, the last words were, "I don't see you anymore." Leopardi was buried at the church of San Vitale in Fuorigrotta, then a suburb of Naples. In 1939, the bones were transferred to the heights overlooking Mergellina, close to what is thought to be the tomb of Virgil.

∾

125. To Fanny Targioni Tozzetti (Florence)

Here is one of only two letters to Fanny. Given Leopardi's ardor, the letters are striking for their caution and reserve. It is the prose of a man who does not wish to offend and force the sure issue.

Cara Fanny. I haven't written till now so as not to annoy you, knowing how busy you are. But I don't wish you to think silence is forgetfulness, although you perhaps know that it is not easy to forget you. I think I remember your saying once that you often did not answer letters from your best friends because you were sure they wouldn't take offense from your silence as others would. Do me the honor of treating me as one of your best friends, and if you are busy and writing bothers you, do not answer me. I greatly desire news from you, but will be content to get it from Ranieri or Gozzani.

I don't think you expect any news from me. You know I abominate politics. . . . And I can talk of literary news even less, for I confess I am nearly about to forget the alphabet itself from not having read or written. My friends, who have good reason to seek glory and to try to benefit mankind, are horrified by me. But I, who do not presume to benefit anyone or aspire to glory, cannot be faulted for spending my days sprawled on a sofa without batting an eyelash. And I find sweetly reasonable the custom of the Turks and other Orientals who content themselves with sitting cross-legged all day and staring stolidly into the face of this absurd existence.

But it is very wrong of me to write these things to you, who are beautiful and privileged by nature to shine in life and triumph over human destiny. I know you too tend toward melancholy, as all fine, bright natures do and will eternally. In all sincerity, however, and despite my dark and desperate philosophy, I think melancholy doesn't suit you—that is, it isn't at all reasonable even if it's natural. At least, that is what I wish for you.

. . . *Addio, cara* Fanny, and say hello for me to the little girls. If you deign to command me, please know that for me, as for others who know you, it is a joy and glory to serve you. Your Leopardi [Rome, December 5, 1831].

~

126. To Louis De Sinner (Paris)

The following is a response to an article in a German journal in which the author connected Leopardi's private condition to his published work. The original of this letter is in French.

. . . I received the pages from the *Hesperus,* for which I thank you most dearly. You point out correctly that it is absurd to attribute to my writings a religious tendency. Whatever my misfortunes may be— which the author saw fit to detail and perhaps exaggerate a bit in this journal—I have had enough courage not to try to diminish their impact either by frivolous hopes for an imaginary and unknown future happiness or by a cowardly resignation. My feelings about destiny have been and remain those I expressed in *Brutus.* With this same courage I was led by my studies to a philosophy of despair, which I did not hesitate to embrace totally. And on the other hand it was only the cowardliness of men—who need to be persuaded of the merits of existence—that made them want to consider my philosophical opinions the result of my particular sufferings and insist on attributing to my physical condition that which is due only to my understanding.

Before dying, I wish to protest this feeble and vulgar invention and beg my readers to address themselves to destroying my observations and ideas rather than citing my maladies . . . [Florence, May 24, 1832].

~

127.   *Dialogue of an Almanac-Vendor and a Wayfarer*

This graceful and compact dialogue, one of the very last of the *Operette Morali,* was written in 1832. Though the ideas are typical, the piece shows how deft the mature Leopardi was becoming in finding an interesting objective form for his thought.

Vendor: Almanacs, new almanacs! New calendars! Do you need any almanacs, milord?
Wayfarer: Almanacs for the New Year?
Vendor: Yes, milord.

Wayfarer: Do you believe the New Year will be happy?

Vendor: O yes, Your Excellence, most certainly.

Wayfarer: Like this past year?

Vendor: More, much more.

Wayfarer: Like the one before?

Vendor: More, more, Your Excellence.

Wayfarer: But like which one? Wouldn't it be nice if the New Year were exactly like one in the past?

Vendor: Milord, no, that wouldn't please me.

Wayfarer: For how many new years have you sold almanacs?

Vendor: It's about twenty years now, milord.

Wayfarer: Which of these twenty years would you wish the coming year to be like?

Vendor: I? I wouldn't know.

Wayfarer: You don't remember any particular year that seemed happy?

Vendor: No, truthfully, milord.

Wayfarer: And yet, life is a lovely thing. True?

Vendor: That's a fact.

Wayfarer: Wouldn't you like to go back and relive those twenty years, and even all the past, starting from your birth?

Vendor: Eh, my dear sir, would God we could!

Wayfarer: But, what if you had to repeat the life you've lived, neither more nor less, with all the pleasures and pains you've passed?

Vendor: I wouldn't like that.

Wayfarer: Oh, what other life would you wish to relive? The life I've lived, or that of the Prince, or whom else? Or don't you think that I, or the Prince, or whoever, would answer precisely like you; and having to relive the life already lived, that no one would wish to turn back?

Vendor: That I believe.

Wayfarer: Not even you would turn back on these terms, not being able in any other way?

Vendor: No, milord, truly, I would not go back on these terms.

Wayfarer: Oh? What kind of life would you prefer then?

Vendor: I would want a life like this, as God would give me, with no other terms.

Wayfarer: A life of chance and knowing nothing ahead of time, just as we know nothing of the New Year?

Vendor: Right.

Wayfarer: And that's what I would want too, if I could do it all over again, and so would everybody. But this means that up to this year Fate has treated everyone badly. And clearly everyone agrees that evil has fallen on him more often or more heavily, than good; since no one—offered his earlier life, with all its good and ill—would wish to be reborn. The beautiful life is not the one we know but the one we do not know; not the past life but the one to come. With the New Year, Fortune will begin to smile on you, and me, and all the others, and we will set out on the happy life. True?

Vendor: Let's hope so.

Wayfarer: Well, then, show me the best almanac you have.

Vendor: Here it is, milord. This one sells for thirty pence.

Wayfarer: And here's your money.

Vendor: Thank you, milord, and goodbye for now. Almanacs! New almanacs! New calendars!

❧

128.   There are two truths which men will not generally believe: one is not knowing anything, the other is not being anything. Add a third, that grows largely from the second: of having nothing to hope for after death [undated but 1832, Z, 4525].

❧

129. To Adelaide Leopardi (Recanati)

Mia cara Mamma. I do not ever write you, and now I do so to disturb you with a prayer. This is most displeasing to me, but you know the reasons for this unusual request. It is now some time that I wrote to *Papà* apprising him of my circumstances. I detailed to him all the efforts I have made so far to procure a living without inconveniencing the family. I explained how and why this has become impossible. And I ended by asking him to confer on me a monthly allowance of twelve *francesconi* to skimp along with. *Papà* answered that I should write directly to you. I have been ill, and my convalescence has left my eyes so weak that until now I absolutely could not write, no matter what the necessity. Today finally, no longer able to delay, I am reduced to this action, which costs me very much, and I make to you the same prayer I made to *Papà*.

Believe me, my dear Mamma, that bothering you like this is a thousand times more painful for me than you. And furthermore, if I moved back permanently with you, I would still consume much at home, and I would be a great, continuous inconvenience with my strange way of living and my melancholy . . . [Florence, November 17, 1832].

≈

130. To Antonio Ranieri (Naples)

This is one of the emotional letters written while Ranieri, allowed now to re-enter Naples, was spending a few months solidifying his claims on an allowance from his father.

. . . My poor Ranieri! If people ridicule you because of me, it consoles me at least that they certainly ridicule me also because of you, for as far as you are concerned I have always been and shall be childlike. People always laugh at those things which, if they could not laugh, they would be compelled to admire; and like the fabled fox, they always criticize what they envy. Oh, my Ranieri! When will I get you back again? Until I have this immense joy, I shall live in fear that it will not be true. I say goodbye, my soul, with all my spirit's strength. Goodbye a thousand times. Don't ever weary of loving me [Florence, January 5, 1833].

≈

From the *Reflections*

The notebook was the source of most of the *Reflections,* or *Pensieri.* We know they were assembled just before and after the move to Naples; hence, a selection of the III items, first published posthumously, is clustered here. The American poet Wallace Stevens, twenty-six years old when he read them, warmly characterized these epigrammatic passages for us in his journal: "Have just finished Leopardi's 'Pensieri' (translated by P. Maxwell—a scholarly major-general). They are paragraphs on human nature, like Schopenhauer's psychological observations, Paschal's 'Pensees,' Rochefoucauld's 'Maximes' etc. How true they all are! I should like to have a library of such things."[1]

I have cited at the close of each item the identifying roman numeral used in Italian editions.

≈

131.   I long refused to believe the things which I will say below because not only were they foreign to my nature (and the mind always tends to judge others according to itself) but because I have always inclined toward loving, rather than hating, my fellow man. In the end experience has almost brutally convinced me, and I am sure that those readers who have had much to do with men will admit that what I am about to say is true; the others will find it exaggerated, until experience—if ever they have occasion truly to sample human society— commends it to them.

I say that the world is a league of scoundrels pitted against true men, of the vile against the good-hearted. When two or more unprincipled men meet for the first time, they easily, as if by sign language, recognize each other for what they are, and quickly concur; or if their interests are at odds, they at least incline toward and greatly respect each other. If a scoundrel has dealings with other scoundrels, he will often behave honestly and will not cheat them; if with honorable people, he will inevitably break faith, and wherever it behooves him he will seek to ruin them even though they may be strong enough to revenge themselves—because he hopes that his frauds will conquer their courage, as is almost always the case. I have often seen an extremely timid man, finding himself caught between a rogue more timid than he and a good, courageous person, side through fear with the scoundrel. Indeed, this is common because the ways of the good, brave man are predictable and simple while those of the villain are hidden and infinitely varied. Now as everyone knows, the unknown frightens us more than the known, and one can easily avoid the vendettas of the good-hearted, from which vileness and fear themselves save you. But no vileness or fear can defend you from the secret houndings, the insidious or even overt blows delivered by base enemies. Generally in everyday life true courage is little feared, partly because lacking in any pretense, it lacks that apparatus which induces fear, and thus it is often not taken seriously; but scoundrels are feared as if they were brave because their imposture often makes them appear to be so.

Scoundrels are rarely poor because, among other things, if a good man falls on hard times, no one helps him and many are pleased, but if a villain becomes poor the whole city comes to his aid. The reason is clear: it is that we are naturally touched by the misfortune of our friends and associates for it otherwise might fall on us ourselves, and if possible we gladly offer help because that is the way we would wish to be treated in similar cases. Now scoundrels, who are in the majority in this world and who are very capable, deem other scoundrels, even the ones they haven't seen, their friends and associates, and feel compelled to help them in their needs by virtue of that kind of fraternity which, as I have said, exists among them. It is for them a scandal for a known scoundrel to be seen in poverty because the world, which pays lip service to virtue, usually regards misfortune as a punishment, and one which can offend and damage all of them. Thus, to avoid this scandal they labor so effectively that there are few cases of scoundrels (save the totally obscure) who have fallen on bad times not mending their affairs in some tolerable way.

On the other hand, since good and magnanimous persons are different from the majority, they are regarded by them almost as creatures of another species, and consequently not only are they not prized as friends and associates but they are not offered social rights, and as is often seen, they are more or less intensely persecuted, depending on the meanness and malevolence of the moment and of their society. For, just as in the bodies of animals nature tends always to purge itself of those humors and elements alien to those of their bodies, so in the social body the same nature dictates that whoever greatly differs from the generality—especially if the difference is outright conflict—that person should be destroyed or expelled at any cost.

The good and generous are also most hateful because they are ordinarily sincere and call things by their right names. A fault not pardonable by the human race, who hate neither the evildoer nor the evil as much as him who calls it what it is. Hence, while the evildoer often achieves riches, honors, and power, he who points out evil is often dragged to the gallows, men being most prompt to suffer anything from heaven or other men, just so they remain protected from words [I].

132.   Death is no evil, for it frees man from all evils and takes away desire as well as the good things of life. Old age is the greatest evil, for it strips man of all pleasures, leaves him his appetites, and brings with it all pains. Nonetheless, men fear death and desire old age [VI].

133.   We know for certain that most persons we allow to educate our children have not been educated themselves. Nor do we doubt that

they cannot give what they have not received and cannot acquire in any other way [X].

~

134.   The man who achieves a thing after much labor, suffering, and waiting cannot abide others reaching it easily and quickly without that thing becoming hateful to him even though he has lost nothing by their success. This is so because the achieved good imaginatively diminishes when shared by those who have paid little or nothing for it. And so the laborer in the Bible laments the injury done him when equal pay is offered those who worked less. And the friars of certain orders habitually treat novices very sternly, lest they easily reach the state which the friars had painfully achieved [XII].

~

135.   How dear and lovely an illusion is that by which the anniversaries of an event seem to have a substantial connection to it although they really have nothing more to do with it than any other day of the year. It is as if an image from the past arose and came before us on those days, tempering the sad thought of the annihilation of that which was, soothing the pain of the loss, and making that which is passed and can never return again seem not completely lost or faded. When we find ourselves in places where things have happened, memorable in themselves or only for us, and say, "Here this happened and here this," we think ourselves in a way closer to those events than elsewhere; similarly, when we say "It's now a year, or several years, since this or that happened," the thing appears, so to speak, more present or less past than on other days. And, such imagining is so rooted in man that it is hard for him to believe that an anniversary is as distant from the thing as any other day. Thus the yearly celebration of important memories, religious and civil, public and private, the birth and death days of beloved persons, and so on, is and was common in all nations which have or had memories and records. And I have noted in asking people about this that sensitive men accustomed to solitude or to self-communion are usually extemely attentive to anniversaries, and they live, so to speak, on memories of that kind, always mulling them over and saying to themselves: "In that year, on that day like this one, this happened to me" [XIII].

∽

136. I saw once in Florence a man dragging like a beast of burden, as is the style there, a cart full of goods and carrying himself with the greatest haughtiness, shouting and ordering other people to make way; and he seemed to me an emblem of many who strut with pride and insult others for reasons not unlike that which caused his haughtiness—that is, they pull carts [XVIII].

∽

137. The following piece may have sprung from an experience with a literary enthusiast Leopardi had described in a December 22, 1831, letter to Monaldo: "I already visited Monsignor Cupis, and he me, and he offered me a thousand kindnesses, imploring me to see him often, and promising to let me hear and read hundreds of his sonnets, *canzoni,* and chapters, which I could revise or polish. This has so terrified me that, despite my liking for him and his courtesies, I have not had the courage to return. . . ."

If I had Cervantes's genius, I would write a book to purge Italy and indeed the civilized world of a vice which, given the relative mildness of our present manners, is no less cruel or barbarous than the medieval savagery Cervantes tried to purge. I speak of the vice of reading or reciting one's own compositions to others, a very ancient vice which in past centuries was bearable because rare. Today, however, when everyone composes and it is difficult to find someone who is not an author, the habit has become a scourge, a public calamity, and a new tribulation in human existence. And it is no joke but the truth to say that this makes acquaintances suspect and friendships risky; and that there is now no place or time where an innocent is free from fear of attack and being subjected on the spot, or dragged elsewhere, to the torture of hearing prose without end or verses by the thousand—not at all with the pretense of hearing one's judgment, once customarily cited as the motive for such recitations, but only and expressly to give pleasure to the author, who also gets to hear the necessary praises bestowed at the end.

In good conscience, I believe that there is hardly another example of on the one hand such extreme blindness and insensitivity due to self-love, and on the other such a capacity for self-delusion as in this matter of reciting one's own work. For each of us is conscious of the unspeakable bother it is to hear the things of others, and we have seen the persons invited to listen turn pale with fear, inventing every excuse to absent themselves, even fleeing from the author to hide as best they can. Nonetheless, with stony face, with marvelous perseverance, like a famished bear he hunts his prey throughout the city, and overtaking it, drags it to his lair. And during the recital, noting first the yawning, then the stretching and writhing and the hundred other signs of the auditor's mortal anguish, he still does not desist, but becoming fierce and rabid instead, he bellows and shouts for hours, or even days and nights entire, until he becomes hoarse and until—long after the auditor has been rendered senseless—he himself is exhausted if not sated. During that period and with his friend in carnage, he obviously basks in a joy nearly superhuman and paradisal; for we see him abandon all earthly pleasures for this one, forgetting sleep and food and vanishing from life and men's eyes. This pleasure derives from an unshakeable belief in such authors that they awaken pleasure and admiration in the hearer; otherwise they might lecture the desert instead of people. Now, as I have said, everyone knows what pleasure indeed accrues to him who hears (I say "hears," not "listens"), and the reciter can well see it; and I know furthermore that many would prefer some severe corporal punishment to this experience. Even beautiful and exalted writings become killingly boring when read by their author. On this topic, one of my philologer friends observed that if the Empress Octavia indeed fainted away while hearing Virgil read the sixth book of the *Aeneid,* most probably it was not so much at the memory of her son Marcellus contained therein as it was from her boredom at being read at.

Such is humanity. This vice I describe, so barbaric and foolish and contrary to the common sense of rational beings, is truly an ailment of the human species, for there is no nation, however refined, no era or condition free from this plague. Italians, Frenchmen, Englishmen, Germans; gray old men, wise in most things and full of worth and genius; men socially adept, accomplished in manners and prone to detect and ridicule folly—all become cruel children when it comes to reciting their pieces. As it is now so was it in the times of Horace, to whom it was already unbearable; and those of Martial, who when asked by someone why he didn't read his verses responded, "So as not to hear yours." And so it was also in the great age of Greece, when reputedly the cynic Diogenes, finding himself in a company dying of ennui while listening to a recitation, and seeing appear in the author's hands the last blank page of the book, said, "Courage, friends, I see land."

In our day, however, things have come to such a pass that the supply of hearers cannot, even with compulsion, meet the demand of authors. Hence some of my industrious acquaintances, noting this and con-

vinced that reciting one's works is a deep-felt human need, have
thought up a way to satisfy that need and turn it, as public needs are
often turned, to concrete profit. They will, in brief, open a school or
academy or an atheneum for listening, where—no matter what hour
of the day or night—they or their hired associates will listen to
whoever wishes to read, at fixed prices. The price for prose will be
one *scudo* for the first hour, two for the second, four for the third, eight
for the fourth, and so on, geometrically increasing. For poetry, double.
For any repeated passage, as sometimes occurs, a charge of one *lira* per
verse. If the listener falls asleep, one-third of the cost will be remitted
to the reader. For convulsions, fainting spells, and other minor or
major accidents occurring here or there during any lecture, the school
will be furnished with cordials and medicine, dispensed gratis. In this
way, ears, which have hitherto been unprofitable, will become valua-
ble, and a new horizon will open for industry, with an increase in the
general economy [XX].

138.   The common saying that life is a play proves itself above all in this,
that the world speaks constantly in one way and acts constantly in
another. Since all of us are actors now in this daily comedy because we
all speak the same way, and since few are spectators because the world's
empty language deceives only children and fools, it follows that this
performance has become totally inept, a senseless, boring labor.
Hence, it would be an endeavor worthy of our age finally to make life
real instead of simulated and to mediate for the first time in history the
famous discord between words and actions. Since experience shows
that facts are immutable, and since it is unfeasible that men should seek
to do the impossible, the concord might be achieved by a means both
unique and easy, if until now unattempted—to change our words so as
to call things at last by their proper names [XXIII].

139.   No one is so completely disillusioned or full of rage at the world
that he is not reconciled somewhat to it if he encounters some kind-
ness. It is the same when a man we know to be mean greets us
courteously, and seems then not so mean as before. These observations
demonstrate the weakness of man rather than vindicating mean people
or the world [XXV].

✍

140. No profession is as sterile as that of literature. Yet pretense is so valuable in the world that with its aid even literature becomes edifying. Pretense is the soul, so to speak, of the social life and is an art without which no other art or faculty, considered according to its effects on the human mind, can be perfect. Consider the fortunes of two persons, one of true value in every way, the other of false value. You will find that the latter is more fortunate than the former; indeed the false one is usually fortunate, the true one unfortunate. Pretense makes an effect even if truth be lacking, but truth without pretense can do nothing. Nor does this arise, I think, from our evil inclinations, but because bare truth is always an impoverished thing, and hence if we would delight or move men we must use illusion and heightening, and promise more and better than we can give. Nature herself is an impostor with man, and renders his life likeable and bearable chiefly by means of imagination and illusion [XXIX].

✍

141. Just as humans usually curse the present and praise the past, so most travelers while traveling are lovers of their native land, and prefer it with a kind of fierceness over those places where they find themselves. Back home, they just as fiercely rank it inferior to all other lands they have known [XXX].

✍

142. In every land, the universal vices and ills of mankind and human society are attributed to the particular locale. I have never been in a place where I have not heard say: "Here women are vain and fickle and they are poorly read and taught; here people are nosy about others' business, chatterboxes, and rumor-mongers; here money, favoritism, and vileness can accomplish anything; here envy rules supreme and friendships are shallow"—and so it goes, as if elsewhere things were different. Men are unhappy by necessity, but they resolutely think themselves so by accident [XXXI].

✍

143.   In some places half-civilized, half-barbaric—like Naples, for example— one can better observe something more or less true in all places, that is, that a man known to be poor is scarcely considered a man at all, and if a man is believed to be rich, his life is in danger. From this it follows that in such places, as is the practice, one should keep his financial status a mystery so that the public does not know whether to despise you or murder you. And you then can be what men ordinarily are, half-despised and half-respected, sometimes threatened, sometimes safe [XXXV].

∾

144.   The great remedy for calumny, as for afflictions of the spirit, is time. If people criticize our ideas or behavior, good or bad, it behooves us simply to persevere. After a short time, when the matter has become stale, the gossipers will abandon it in favor of fresher things. The more decisive and unperturbed we show ourselves in seeking our ends and ignoring the voices, the sooner will that which was damnable or strange appear reasonable and normal, for the world, which never considers wrong the man who will not give in, will at last condemn itself and absolve us. And so derives a well-known fact: the weak exist at the world's pleasure, the strong at their own [XLV].

∾

145.   A man has not really lived if he has not learned to discount as pure noise other people's offers of help, especially those which are spontaneous, serious, and repeated. He should doubt not only the offers but also the vivid, complex, and specific reasons they urge upon you and the way they reason away all difficulty. If at last you are persuaded, or simply conquered by tedium or something else, and you decide to test one of these persons, you will see him quickly lose color, change the subject, utter meaningless words, and ultimately leave you without an answer. And afterwards, you will be fortunate to see him, even if you work at it, or to get an answer if you write him about it. Men do not want to benefit others because it is a nuisance and because the needs and misfortunes of acquaintances always give everyone a certain amount of pleasure. Men do, however, want to be thought of as benefactors and they desire the gratitude of others and the superiority it confers. They thus offer what they do not wish to give, and the

more you proudly resist the more they insist, not only to humble you and make you blush, but also because they do not really fear you will accept. And so with great bravado they push on to the moment of truth, expecting only your thanks and ignoring the clear and present danger of being revealed as impostors—unless you begin to make sounds of acceptance, in which case they take flight [LII].

∽

146.   It is an axiom that, save for brief intervals, men believe deep inside those things they must believe in for their peace of mind and, as it were, for life itself; and this is so even though they may hide it from others and despite sure proof contrary to their belief. The old man, especially if he moves in society, never till the end stops believing in his very soul, in spite of much opposed evidence, that he can—by a most singular exception to natural law and in a manner mysterious even to him—still make quite an impression on women; for he would be too miserable if firmly convinced he was forever and totally excluded from that happiness which man (one way or another and more or less actively pursuing) considers the reason for being.

Although a licentious woman sees every day a thousand signs of the public's true opinion of her, she steadfastly believes she is chaste in the public eye, that only a small number of old and new confidantes (small in respect to the public) know about her, and that they keep the truth secret from the world and even each other. The scoundrel whose lowness and uncertainty may lead him to seek the opinions of others believes they interpret his actions in the best light and do not understand his true motives. Similarly, in physical things, Buffon observes that a sick man at death's door refuses to believe either doctors or friends but only his inmost hope which promises escape from the present danger.

I need not dwell on the stupendous credulity and incredulity of husbands regarding their wives—the stuff of novels, plays, satires, and eternal laughter in those nations where matrimony is an irrevocable institution. For that matter, there is nothing in the world so false or absurd that reasonable men will not hold true if the mind can find no way to believe the opposite and still stay at peace with itself. I should add that the old are less apt than the young to abandon belief in that which pleases them and clasp to them that which offends; for the young are more quick to look evil in the eye, to confront it with conscience, or to die in the attempt [LIV].

147.   La Bruyère says something very true: that it is easier for a mediocre
book to gain fame by virtue of its author's established reputation than
for an excellent book to make the reputation of an unknown author.
To this one might add that the fastest way to acquire fame is to assure
people confidently and repeatedly in every way possible that you
already have it [LX].

✌

148.   The respect an artist has for his art or a scientist for his science is
usually inversely proportional to the value he ascribes to his own
efforts [LXIII].

✌

149.   If an artist or scientist or practitioner of any discipline habitually
compares himself not with fellow practitioners but with the discipline
itself, the better he is the lower the opinion he will have of himself; for
the more he knows the profundity of his field, the more he will feel
inferior by contrast. And so almost all great men are modest because
they continually compare themselves not with others but with that
idea of perfection they have in their imagination, infinitely brighter
and greater than the average man can know, and they ponder how far
they are from capturing it. Whereas, common men easily, and some-
times with good reason, believe they have not only attained their idea
of perfection but surpassed it [LXIV].

✌

150.   In this century blacks are thought to be in race and in origin entirely
different from whites, yet nonetheless totally equal to them as far as
human rights go. In the sixteenth century blacks were thought to
spring from the same roots and to be of the same family, yet it was
held, especially by certain Spanish theologians, that on the question of
rights, they were by nature and divine volition much inferior to us.
And in both centuries blacks were and are bought and sold and made

to work in chains under the lash. So much for ethics, and for the way moral beliefs affect men's actions [LXVI].

⧼

151. Quite improperly it is said that *noia* is a common ill. It is common to be unoccupied or even idle, but not *annoiato*. *Noia* exists only for those for whom the spirit counts. The more spirit in someone the more frequent is *noia,* painful and terrible. Most persons find enough to do in whatever way and enough delight in whatever foolish thing they do; and when totally unoccupied they feel no great pain. This is why average men do not understand the *noia* of sensitive ones, and it makes them marvel and laugh to hear it complainingly described with serious words normally used regarding the major and most inevitable ills of life [LXVII].

⧼

152. *Noia* is in some ways the most sublime of human sentiments. I do not attribute to it the results that many philosophers do. But never to be able to find satisfaction in any earthly thing nor, so to speak, in the entire earth itself; to consider the inestimable breadth of space, the number and wondrous mass of worlds, and find that all is tiny and limited in light of the mind's capacity; to imagine the infinite number of worlds and the infinite universe, and feel our mind and our desire to be greater still than this very universe; and always to condemn things for their inadequacy and nothingness and to suffer lack and empti- ness—in a word *noia*—this seems to me the chief sign of greatness and nobility in human nature. Hence *noia* is little known among men of small moment, and very little or not at all among other creatures [LXVIII].

⧼

153. Toward great men, and especially those who shine with extraordi- nary virility, the world behaves like a woman. It not only admires but it loves them, because their force enamors. Often, as with women, the love for these men is greater because of and in proportion to the disdain they show, the bad treatment they give, and the fear they generate. Thus Napoleon was most loved by France and a cult object, so to speak, of his soldiers, whom he called "cannon fodder" and

treated as such. Thus many leaders who used and judged their men similarly were in life most dear to their armies, and now their legends make readers fall in love. There is a sort of brutality and extravagance in them which attracts, just as it does women to their lovers. That is why Achilles is likeable whereas the goodness of Aeneas and Godfrey, and the wisdom of these and of Ulysses, generate almost hate [LXXIV].

∽

154. When two or more persons at some private or public gathering laugh with each other perceptibly and to the exclusion of others, the latter become apprehensive and serious, many become quiet, some leave, and other bold souls move to be accepted into the laughing party. It is as if artillery bursts had suddenly come out of the darkness and everyone were put to rout, not knowing if the shells were real or not and where they might strike next. Laughter prompts respect even in strangers, attracts to it the attention of all onlookers, and gives the impression of a kind of superiority. And if, as sometimes happens, you find yourself someplace where they ignore you or treat you arrogantly or discourteously, the best thing to do is to choose from the group an appropriate person and then begin laughing openly and persistently, making it seem as much as possible that the laughter is from the heart. And if any try to laugh at you, laugh all the more and harder than they. You would have to be very unlucky indeed if the proudest and most petulant of the company and those who most turned up their noses did not, after brief resistance, either take flight or quickly sue for peace, seek out your conversation, and perhaps even offer their friendship. The power of laughter is great among men and holds great terror, and no man really feels himself immune. He who has the courage to laugh is master of the world, much as he who is ready to die [LXXVIII].

∽

155. No one becomes a man until he has tested himself, a test which by revealing him to himself and shaping his self-opinion, determines in some way his future fortune and state in life. For this great experience—until which no one is much more than a child—the ancient world provided infinite and ready materials; but today our lives are so bare of opportunity and of such quality that many men, lacking the

occasion, remain almost the babies they were at birth and die without that experience.

To the others, self-knowledge and self-possession usually come from need and misfortune or from some great, strong passion, typically love—when indeed it is a great passion, which is not so for all who love. Happen as it will, however, early in life or later, after other, minor love affairs, a man who has known a strong, impassioned love now knows something of his fellow men, among whom he has tasted intense desires and deep needs perhaps unknown to him before. He knows firsthand the nature of the passions and that one of them in burning can inflame the others. He recognizes his own nature and temperament and sounds the limits of his own forces and faculties. Now he can judge how much to hope or despair of himself, and insofar as the future is predictable, he knows his destined niche in the world. In sum, life has become new in his eyes, transformed for him from the rumored to the proven, from imagination to reality. And he feels at the center of his forces, perhaps no longer happy but, so to speak, more powerful than before, better prepared to make use of himself and others [LXXXII].

*

156. Jesus Christ was the first to point out for men that practitioner and praiser of all feigned virtues, that detractor and persecuter of all the true ones, that enemy of every intrinsic greatness in humans, that mocker of every high and sincere feeling and every sweet and heartfelt emotion, that slave of the powerful, tyrant of the weak, loather of the misery-laden—which Jesus Christ called *the world,* a usage common to all civilized tongues ever since. I do not believe that this general concept—so true, current, and applicable after Christ—was used in so special and precise a way by any philosopher before him. Perhaps before him villainy and deceit had not grown mature yet, and civilization had not reached that point where much of its very being is synonymous with corruption.

Such, as I have described above, is the civilized man, whom Christ was talking about: that is, the man that reason and genius do not reveal, that books and educators celebrate, that nature constantly proclaims fictitious, and that only life experience makes us recognize and perceive truly. And it can be noted that this general idea of the world appears in all its details in countless single individuals [LXXXIV].

∾

157.   In the pagan writers, that group of civilized men we call society or
the world was never considered or held up resolutely as the enemy of
virtue, nor as the sure corrupter of all good natures and well-disposed
minds. Although the Gospel writers and modern authors, even secular
ones, have fastened on the concept of the world as enemy of the good,
it was more or less unknown to the ancients. And this is not surprising
if we consider a fact at once clear and simple, which can serve as an
index to those who wish to compare the moral states of ancients and
moderns: that whereas modern educators fear the public, the ancient
ones sought it out; and whereas the moderns have made from domestic
obscurity, retreat, and segregation a shield for the young against the
infection of worldly customs, the ancients drew the young, even by
force, out of solitude and exposed their education and lives to the
world's eye, and the world to their eyes, deeming this more apt to
better them than to corrupt [LXXXV].

∾

158.   When a man confesses his own defects, however clear to others, it
diminishes the esteem and thus affection of even those dearest to him—
so necessary is it that everyone strongly sustain himself, and that no
matter what his state or misfortune show himself strong and secure,
setting an example to others and, as it were, compelling them by sheer
authority. For if the opinion of a man does not begin with the man
himself, it will scarcely start elsewhere; and if he does not have a most
solid base in himself, it will be difficult for him to stand upright.
  Society is like a fluid, with every molecule or globule pushing
strongly against its neighbors from below, above, and all sides, and
through them against the farthest one, and being squeezed itself in the
same way. And if this resistance or tension diminishes in any part, the
whole mass of fluid rushes furiously in that direction, and the gap is
occupied by new globules [CI].

∾

159.   The years of childhood are in everyone's memory the fabled times
of his life, just as in the memory of nations the fabled times are those
of their childhood [CII].

∾

160. Men labor when they are young and immature to appear accomplished, and when they have become so, to appear immature. Oliver Goldsmith, the author of the novel *The Vicar of Wakefield,* having reached the age of forty, subtracted from his address the title of doctor, a weighty emblem dear to him in youth and now grown distasteful [CVIII].

∾

161. Humans are almost always only as wicked as they have to be. If a man behaves uprightly, it can be judged that wickedness is not necessary for him. I have seen the tenderest, most innocent persons commit quite atrocious acts to escape some serious hurt otherwise unavoidable [CIX].

∾

162.   *To Himself*

A se stesso was written sometime in 1833 in the aftermath of Leopardi's frustrated relationship with Fanny. In another poem inspired by the passion for Fanny, *The Dominant Thought (Il pensiero dominante),* Leopardi wrote some striking lines depicting the transfiguring effect of love upon the imagination:

> What world is this! what new
> Immensity, what paradise to which
> So often your stupendous charm appears
> To lift me! Where I,
> Wandering under strange, suffusing light,
> Forget my earthly state
> And all the truth cast to oblivion.
> Such are, I think, the dreams
> Of the immortals.

The "truth cast to oblivion" in these lines is confronted in *To Himself,* which may mark Leopardi's psychological nadir. Indeed, the qualities displayed are those of an anti-poem rather than a poem in the conventional sense. Whereas Leopardi usually built his verse on the tension between intellectual and imaginative perceptions, here grim, prosaic truth has completely taken over, and significantly the piece is almost devoid of metaphor and color. Moreover, Leopardi uncharacteristically uses choppy phrases, single-word utterances, and many breaks which serve not only to underline the ugliness of the vision but to transmit the image of a man trying to catch his breath. And in the description of the world, the poet uses diction which the earlier, classically oriented Leopardi surely would have avoided. The late view of nature has taken over here; and the only redemptive note is the *"titanismo"* implied at the end, where the speaker voices his resentment of cowardly nature and suggests man's superiority to it.

> Now you may rest forever,
> My tired heart. The last illusion is dead
> That I believed eternal. Dead. I can
> So clearly see—not only hope is gone
> But the desire to be deceived as well.
> Rest, rest forever.
> You have beaten long enough. Nothing is worth
> Your smallest motion, nor the earth your sighs.
> This life is bitterness
> And vacuum, nothing else. The world is mud.
> From now on calm yourself.
> Despair for the last time. The only gift
> Fate gave our kind was death. Henceforth, heap scorn
> Upon yourself, Nature, the ugly force
> That, hidden, orders universal ruin,
> And the boundless emptiness of everything.

∾

163.

On the Likeness of a Beautiful Woman
Carved on her Sepulchral Monument

James Hervey's *Meditations among the Tombs* and Pope's *Elegy to the Memory of an Unfortunate Lady* have been nominated as possible influences on this poem, written at Naples in 1834-35. Although Leopardi appreciated eighteenth-century English poetry and had specifically read Pope when he was seeing Countess Malvezzi (who was translating *The Rape of the Lock)*, the poem is a highly romantic and Leopardian document. As elsewhere, Leopardi deals with the enigma of man, in whom perishability and striving are fused. But the poem is ultimately about art, and Leopardi anticipates Baudelaire in his fascination with the way Beauty relates to death and can spring from ugliness.

> And so you must have been;
> Who now are dust and skeleton in earth.
> Above the bones and dirt, this motionless
> And futile image of the beauty gone—
> The only sentinel of memory
> And grief—looks mutely on the flight of time.
> That tremble-starting gaze which sweetly fixed

Its object then as now it seems to do;
That curving mouth dispensing pleasure forth
As from a brimming urn;
The throat that once was circled with desire;
The loving hand which, roaming where it wished,
Would often feel the hand it squeezed grow cold;
That breast which made men visibly turn pale—
These things existed once. And now you are
But dirt and bones, a sad,
Outrageous sight a heavy stone must hide.

   To this does Fate reduce
The best similitude of heaven that earth
Can offer. Unending mystery of our being:
Today, Beauty—unutterable source
Of vast and highborn thoughts—dilates and thrives;
The dazzling light which pulses from the heart
Of timeless nature falls
Upon these lower sands,
Seeming to give the index and sure hope
Of more than human possibilities,
Of realms more fortunate and golden worlds.
And then tomorrow comes—
And at a touch the angel's lineaments
Become abomination,
And with them melt away
The corresponding glories they inspired.

   A skillful harmony
Creates in the entranced imagination,
By its own special force,
The noblest visions and infinite desires,
Whereby on luscious, arcane seas the mind
Of man may drift like some
Bold swimmer sporting in the ocean's heave.
But should a discord strike
On the attentive ear—
In one brief moment paradise is gone.

   Humanity, if you
Are so completely vile and vulnerable,
Of dust and shadow made,

How can you grope toward exaltation so?
And if you are in part
Of nobler birth, how then
Can such foul circumstance so lightly rouse
And curiously sate
The highest workings of your mind and heart?

∾

164.
Broom
or The Desert Flower

On April 25, 1835, Leopardi wrote his father, "I continue, thank God, to be quite well, even despite a period of bad weather that set in after a terrible eruption of Vesuvius which frightened all the city at the beginning of this month." About a year later, Leopardi wrote *La ginestra,* his spiritual testament. The poem has been debated. The excellent Italian critic Walter Binni sees it as the center of Leopardi's "new poetic" and his best effort. Whereas *Memories,* to Binni, is the apex of the idyllic poetry, *Broom* not only fuses poetry and philosophy in an "anti-idyllic" way but features a confident and heroic, rather than intimate, poetic voice.[2] Others, especially those of "pro-idyllic" or Crocean persuasion, have expressed severe reservations due to what they see as the labored prosiness of the work's philosophical verses.[3] Perhaps distinctions need to be made. Several passages seem to have spilled over from other polemical attacks on contemporary progress; these parts do seem too long, occasionally too prosaic, and at times even stridently self-pitying. Other—and fortunately dominant—sections rise to such poetic concision and majesty that the poem as a whole must be considered a major expression of the romantic period. Matthew Arnold singled out for praise the lines beginning "Often I sit alone at night . . . ," but he could have easily specified much of the rest of the poem.

Leopardi anticipated the substance of the work[4] as far back as November 16, 1826, when he wrote in the *Zibaldone:* "What a lovely observation of Hierocles in his *On Brotherly Love . . . ,* that since human life is like a constant war, in which we are attacked from outside things (by nature and fortune), our brothers, parents, and relatives are given to us as allies and helpers, etc." This may indeed be the first statement of the theme of fraternal love and its potential, an idea Leopardi extends outward in *Broom* to cover the entire human family. But it takes more than ideas to make poetry, and the key to this poem's art is in its artful objectification, in Leopardi's seizing upon splendid natural symbols to render his mature vision. They lay before him that last complete summer of his life: Vesuvius, the volcano that had effaced Pompeii in August of 79 A.D.; the desert slopes; and the broom-plants perfuming them.

As is usual with Leopardi—whom we have seen hovering ambiguously between the attractions of being and nonbeing, of expansion and shrinkage—the poem offers a paradox: he argues the smallness of man, almost lost in the sweep of cosmos, while urging a fraternal, dignified posture against the antihuman forces of that cosmos. He himself, however, undeniably dissolves that ambiguity. This, his last major utterance on our existence, is an affirmation of man, who is, in Kroeber's words, "finally more significant, even more powerful, than all the blank infinitude of natural space and time."[5] Some have detected in the poem's doctrine of human love the evidence of an incipient Marxism (Carducci whispered, "Let's keep our voices low—he was approaching socialism"[6]). But we can observe that the idea of earth as a place for suffering and love has obvious Christian overtones. Indeed, the image of the poet brooding at night over a world dominated by Vesuvius may recall that of Christ weeping over Jerusalem; and the Biblical inscription—in Greek—prefacing the poem suggests the profoundly timeless and oracular mood Leopardi was in when he wrote. Perhaps there is no one "ism" which can perfectly describe a poem that lines out a secular vision with such religious compassion; that assails modern idealism in accents appropriate to Greek tragedians and Hebrew prophets; that strips so much away from man and gives him so much back.

The phrase quoted ironically at the end of the first section is from Terenzo Mamiani's dedication to his 1832 *Sacred Hymns*.

> Καὶ ἠγάπησαν οἱ ἄνθρωποι μᾶλλον τὸ σκότος ἤ τὸ φῶς.
>
> "And men loved darkness rather than light."
>
> —John, iii, 19

Here on the bone-dry back
Of this tremendous mountain,
Vesuvius destroyer,
Companioned by no other tree or flower,
You broadly scatter solitary tufts,
O you sweet-smelling broom,
Contented with the desert. And I have seen
Your lovely shoots enrich the lonely plain
Around that ancient city
10   Which once ruled all the earth,
Whose grave and muted features still remind
The traveler of a great empire lost.
Again I see you blooming here, lover
Of doleful spots abandoned by the world,
You constant comrade of sad circumstance.
This waste, suffused throughout with barren ash
And coated with hard lava
That rings beneath the foot;
Where snakes build nests and twist themselves in sun,

20 And rabbits scurry to familiar burrows—
This once was happy, cared-for ground. The blades
Of wheat were gold, the sounds
Of lowing cattle played along the air.
Fine palaces were here
And gardens where the rich
Might bask in pleasure. And here were famous towns,
That the proud mountain, shooting streams of fire
From its roaring maw, wiped out
Together with their people.

30 Now one vast ruin exists
Where you take root, O gentle flower, and you
Send sweetly to the skies
(As though you felt the hurts of other beings)
A perfume that consoles the lonely waste.
Let him who would inflate our human lot
Come here and muse upon these sands, to see
How loving Nature ministers to us.
Let him behold and gauge
The power of mankind,

40 Whom this harsh Nurse, when he is unaware,
Can with the smallest flick in part destroy;
And with a scarcely greater motion—once
Again without a warning—
Can totally exterminate. Engraved
Upon these slopes is man's
"Magnificent, progressive destiny."

See your reflection here,
O proud and foolish age
Who have abandoned the clear path carved out

50 For us by years of reawakened thought—
Who stumbling backward
Trumpet your retrogression as a gain.
Your maunderings have made
The brilliant (if unlucky) gather round,
Like children smiling to a father's face,
And muttering to his back.
I will not sink to death
Encumbered by such shame
But will express the scorn within my heart,

60 Although I know oblivion awaits

The man who mocks his age.
I laugh at the bad fate we soon will share.
You dream of liberty
And yet you would enslave
Again the mind of man—
The thought which helped us rise from barbarism,
Alone encourages civility,
And guides us better in our general life.
You did not like the truth,
70   Of man's hard fate, the humble place assigned
By Nature to us all;
And so you turned a coward's back against
The truth-revealing light,
And darkly fleeing you declared him vile
Who sought to follow it,
And you considered noble only him
(Deluder or deluded, mad or shrewd)
Who elevated man above the stars.

A poor and weak-limbed man, but one possessed
80   Of magnanimity of mind, will not
Declare that he is rich
In gold and body both,
Or laughably affect to play the prince
Among his fellows;
But rather, without shame,
Acknowledges his beggared powers and purse
Are what they are, and quotes an honest price.
What can we call a man
Who, born to disappear and bred to pain,
90   Declares, "I was created to enjoy?"
And reeking vanity,
Fills page on witless page with promises
Of joy supreme and high-flung destinies
That heaven, much less earth,
Has never known—to people whom one wave
From a convulsèd sea,
One breath of poisoned air,
One subterranean shudder so destroys
That men must labor to remember them?
100   The noble man, instead,
Is he who dares to fix his mortal eyes

Upon our mutual lot,
And honestly stare truth sharp in the face,
Conceding all the doom
That fate has given us,
Our frail and insignificant estate;
Who in his misery stands great and strong,
And will not heap on woes already his
Fraternal hate and wrath,
110   The worst of human ills,
By blaming brothers for his suffering;
But lays the blame for his unhappiness
Where it belongs, on Her
The truly guilty one,
On Her, the mother of us all by birth—
By will transformed into a stepmother.
He calls her enemy,
As well she is, and so—
Believing that the human family
120   From the beginnings joined against her might—
He takes all men as his allies, all men
Embraces in deep love;
He offers and receives a friendly hand
Amid the frequent dangers and the pain
Of this their common war.
And would he take up arms
Against the insults of his kind, and strew
His neighbor's fields with trap and mine? But no,
For this would be insanity—as if
130   A man surrounded by the enemy
About to mount the fiercest of assaults
Should disregard the foe,
Lash out with bitter blows against his own,
And put to sword and flight
The legions of the warriors he loves.
When all men recognize
These truths as once they did,
When they recall the primal terror shared,
Which welded them into a social chain
140   Against this nature that is pitiless—
Then justice, piety,
And honest civil intercourse shall root
Themselves in better soil

209

Than this around us now,
From which the people's honor grows as strong
As honor can when rooted in the false.

Often I sit alone
At night by these deserted banks which seem
Like waves formed darkly by the hardened flow.
150   And over the sad land I see on high,
Aflame in the pure blue,
The many stars of heaven,
Which from afar mirror themselves in ocean
And make the whole world flash with circling sparks.
And when I fix my eyes
Upon those lights which seem mere points
Yet truly are immense enough to make
The earth and sea a dot compared to them—
To whom not only man
160   But this entire globe where man is nothing
Is utterly unknown; and when I see
Beyond them even farther, without end,
Those distant clustered stars resembling clouds,
For whom not merely man
And earth but the huge mass and infinite host
Of closer stars and our bright sun itself
Remain unknown, or seem
(As they to earth) a mote of cloudy light—
How then, O race of Man,
170   Do you appear to my imagination?
And when I call to mind
Your actual state on earth,
Suggested by this soil I tread upon,
And on the other hand
The title you confer upon yourself
Of sum and crown of All,
The way that, perched upon this grain of sand
Called Earth, you loved to dream
Of how the authors of this universe
180   Came down expressly for your sake to walk
Among you, passing time in sweet discourse;
And when I see you fabricate new myths
To vilify the wise who dare to doubt
Your progress, your supremacy of mind—

Then what should my mind think
Or my heart feel toward you
Unhappy children of mortality?
Should laughter or should pity dominate?

As when an apple falling from a tree,
190   Drawn down to earth by ripe autumnal weight,
Crushes the fragile homes
Carved in the yielding loam by a tribe of ants—
Who labored busily the summer long
With foresight to collect
Their riches and construct their careful works—
Annihilating all with one quick stroke;
So, falling from above,
From the mountain's thundering womb,
Hurled toward the utmost sky,
200   Ashes, pumice, rocks,
A ruin of night, enfused
With boiling lava streams,
Poured down the mountain's flank
And furious through the fields,
A burning, liquid mass
Of metals, boulders, sand
Descended, whelmed, and instantly destroyed
The towns along that shore washed by this sea.
And so above them now,
210   The nibbling goats and newly risen towns
Established on their tombs;
And the fierce mountain seems
To hold their prostrate walls beneath its foot.
Nature has no more heart
Or care for human seed than for the ants,
And if the butchery
Occurs for us more rarely than for them,
The reason is quite clear:
Men cannot match the ants' fertility.

220   Full eighteen hundred years
Have passed away since those thronged cities vanished,
Consumed by burning force.
The peasant now, who husbands carefully

His vines, which barely feed
On soil so dead and scorched,
Still throws a wary glance toward the fell peak
No gentler than before,
A thing of terror yet, that menaces
His children, him, and their impoverished field.
230 And often, on the roof
Of his poor hut, the wretch will sleepless lie
In the night's fitful air,
And frequently start up
To mark the dreaded flow
Which still boils from the inexhausted womb
And down the sandy slopes,
To shine above the shores
Of Capri, Naples' port, and Mergellina.
And if he sees the flow approach, or hears
240 From his deep well the sound
Of seething water,
He wakes his children, wakes his wife in haste,
And snatching what.they can, away they flee,
And from the distance they look back upon
Their home, their meager field—
Their only barrier against starvation—
Prey to the ruinous flood, which crackling comes,
Inexorably to cover all forever.
From old oblivion,
250 Extinct Pompeii returns
To heavenly light, her buried skeleton
Laid bare by avarice or piety;
In the deserted forum,
The traveler may stand among the rows
Of broken columns there,
And contemplate at length
The cloven smoking crest
Still threatening above the barren ruin;
And in the horror of the secret night,
260 Through vacant theaters,
Distorted temples,
And shattered houses where bats conceal their young—
Like the dark flickering
Of baleful torches in an empty palace—
Runs the shimmering of deadly lava,

That through the shadowed distance
Glows red and reddens all that lies around.
And so, oblivious of man, of names
That he ascribes to time,
270 Of generations gone and those to come,
Nature remains forever young, or so
She seems to us in her long-sweeping course.
While kingdoms reel and fall
And tongues and races pass, nothing she sees—
And man presumes to an eternity.

And you, O supple broom,
Who grace with fragrant clusters this bare land,
You too will soon succumb
To the cruel force of subterranean fire,
280 Returning, reaching out
With greed to cover all the fragile tufts.
Beneath that deadly burden, you will bow
That head so innocent,
Not stubbornly, but neither until then
Bent down to supplicate
In useless cowardice
The killer who will come.
Nor shall you swell with mad pride toward the stars
Or toward the wasteland here—
290 Your birthplace and your home by fortune's will
And not your own. In this you are more wise
And, ah, more strong than man:
You do not dream your fragile race endowed
By fate or you with immortality.

165. To Charles Lebreton (Paris)

Lebreton, a young French scholar and friend to De Sinner, had written to
Leopardi praising him as "the poet of all men of feeling." Leopardi's response
was written in French.

No, Monsieur, if I sought praises, yours would not be at all lost on
me. It is for souls such as yours, for tender, sensitive hearts like the

one speaking in your cordial letter, that poets write, and that I would have written if I had been a poet.

My good friend, M. De Sinner, has portrayed me to you in colors too flattering; he has attributed to me many ornaments. Watch out up there that you don't believe every word—his loyalty to me will lead you far from the truth. Tell him, I pray you, that despite the magnificient title of "works" my bookseller has seen fit to give my collection, I have never done real work. I have made only attempts, always considering them preludes, but my career has never gone beyond them . . . [Naples, late June, 1836].

∾

166.   *The Setting of the Moon*

Il tramonto della luna was composed in 1836 at about the same time as *Broom*. The poem needs little explication for those who have seen Leopardi identify poetry and illusion with the forces of life and light. As in the falling-apple passage of *Broom,* he here creates an effective Homeric metaphor, reminding us in his last poems who his favorite poet had always been. A tradition, deriving from Ranieri, holds that the last lines were dictated within hours of Leopardi's death. Given their quality, that seems unlikely.

As in the lonely night—
Above the silvered waters and the lands,
There where the soft winds play
And distant shadows shape
Themselves into a host of fair illusions;
Among the tranquil waves
And houses, hedges, branches, hills;
Now having touched the limits of the sky—
The moon descends beyond
The Alp or Apennine
Or down into the vast Tyrrenhian heart,
And all the colors of the world recede,
The shadows disappear
And one great darkness fuses vale and mountain,
While through the blinded night
The coachman, chanting his sad tune, salutes
The dying gleam which once had led his way;

So vanishes and fades
From our too human life the time of youth.
The shadows scatter now, those images

Of sweet illusions known;
And those old hopes on which
Our mortal nature used to lean depart.
The world remains, a dark and desert place.
And the lost traveler
Peers uselessly in the dense night to find
A reason for the road
He senses stretching out into the dark.
And he perceives that he,
The human, has become
A stranger on this earth no longer home.

For those above, our fate
Would have appeared too blessed, too full of joy,
If youth, whose every good derives from pain,
Had lasted all our lives;
Too mild the ordinance
Which sentences each creature born to death
Had they not introduced along his way
A stronger doom than terrible death itself.
And so the eternal ones
Invented the worst evil known, that fit
Creation of unaging souls—old age:
The state in which desire
Remains intact, our hopes become extinct,
The sources of our joys run dry, our pains
Increase, and good comes not again to us.

You little banks and hills,
Although the splendor in the western sky
Which silvered all the night has passed away,
You will not long be orphaned in the dark;
For from the other side, you soon will see
The heaven grow white again, the dawn begin,
And then the sun return,
Which burning brightly with tremendous fire
Shall flood with shining streams
Of light yourselves and the ethereal fields.
But human life, once flown our lovely youth,
Will never quicken to another light
Or know another dawn.
Widowed we shall remain until the end;

And in the night to come
The gods have raised a sign for us, the tomb.

❦

167. To Monaldo Leopardi (Recanati)

This was Leopardi's last letter.

Mio carissimo papà. It will be hard for you to believe this, but your dear letter of March 21, stamped here with an April 1 date, was delivered to me on May 11 together with two other letters stamped April 3. After receiving it, I was attacked for the first time by a real asthma that keeps me from walking, lying down, or sleeping, and I am forced to answer you by others' hands because my right eye may be going blind. . . .

The chief difficulty here is the cholera, which, as predicted, began again on the 13th of April and has augmented since then even though the government has tried to keep it quiet. People are afraid that as in Marseilles the second outburst will be worse than the first. In Marseilles it began in October and wasn't greatly destructive until it returned in April. . . . If I dodge the cholera and as soon as my health permits, I'll do everything possible at whatever time of the year to see you again, because I too am in haste, convinced now that the end of my life ordained by God cannot be far off. My physical sufferings, constant and incurable, have mounted with the years to such a pitch they can grow no further. I hope that once they overcome the fragile resistance offered by my dying body, they will lead me to the eternal rest for which I warmly call every day, not through heroism but because of the pain I am experiencing.

I tenderly thank you and Mamma for the gift of ten *scudi,* I kiss the hands of you both, I embrace my brothers, and I pray all of you to commend me to God, so that after seeing you again a good and prompt death will bring an end to my physical ills, which cannot otherwise heal. Your most loving son, Giacomo [Naples, May 27, 1837].

❦

Notes

GENERAL INTRODUCTION

1. Charles Sainte-Beuve, "Leopardi," *Revue des Deux Mondes,* 7 (1844), 556–84. For Nietzsche's remarks, see *We Philologists* and *The Joyful Wisdom,* Vols. VII and X of *The Complete Works of Friedrich Nietzsche,* ed. Oscar Levy (New York: Russell and Russell, 1909–11), p. 144; p. 126. For the other references in this paragraph, see George Santayana, "Foreword" to Iris Origo, *Leopardi: A Study in Solitude,* 2nd ed. (London: Hamish Hamilton, 1953), p. ix; Matthew Arnold, "Byron," in *The Complete Prose Works of Matthew Arnold,* ed. R. H. Super (Ann Arbor: University of Michigan Press, 1960–), IX, 217–37; Arthur Schopenhauer, "On the Vanity and Suffering of Life," Supplement to the Fourth Book of *The World as Will and Idea,* trans. R. B. Haldane and J. Kemp (New York: Scribner's, 1948), III, 401. Schopenhauer's expressed desire to have met Leopardi is discussed in Giovanni Mestica, *Studi leopardiani* (Florence: Le Monnier, 1901), p. 415.
2. All Leopardi quotations are taken from the five-volume edition *Tutte le opere di Giacomo Leopardi,* ed. Francesco Flora, 10th ed. (Milan: Mondadori, 1973). This edition, whose volumes are not numbered consecutively, is comprised of *Poesie e prose,* I and II; *Zibaldone di Pensieri,* I and II; and *Lettere.* The quotation here is from *Poesie e prose,* I, 143. As in the selections presented, I will refer to Leopardi's *Zibaldone* by using his own page numbers, which Flora shows.
3. Francesco De Sanctis, "La Nerina di Giacomo Leopardi," in *Nuovi saggi critici,* 19th ed. (Naples: Morano, 1903), p. 495.
4. Benedetto Croce, "Leopardi," in *Poesia e non poesia,* 7th ed. (Bari: Laterza, 1964), p. 102, said: "One remembers the disillusion that the Leopardian *Letters* produced when they came to light. Well then (we said), these doctrines to which we attributed speculative value were nothing other than the reaction to the individual's suffering and woe?" Croce's volume is also available in English as *European Literature in the Nineteenth Century,* trans. Douglas Ainslie (London: Chapman and Hall, 1925).
5. Thomson not only dedicated to Leopardi his first volume of poetry, *The City of Dreadful Night* (1880) but contributed a long memoir and translations of much prose to the *National Reformer* in 1867–68. These writings were later collected by Bertrand Dobell and published as *Essays, Dialogues and Thoughts of Giacomo Leopardi* (London: Routledge, 1905).

6. See the unsigned "Italian Literature since 1830," *London and Westminster Review*, 28 (October, 1837–January, 1838), 151.

7. For an example of their kind of "anthropological" work, see Mariano L. Patrizi, *Saggio psico-antropologico su Giacomo Leopardi e la sua famiglia* (Turin: Fratelli Bocca, 1896).

8. The original source of Tommaseo's language is unavailable to me. This and other attacks by him are cited by Origo, p. 171.

9. See Giovanni Ferretti, *Vita di Giacomo Leopardi* (Bologna: Zanichelli, 1945), p. 371. Vincenzo Gioberti, himself a prolific writer and sensitive to Leopardi's literary worth, wrote interestingly on him in *Del primato morale e civile degli italiani* (Brussels: Meline, 1843) and in *Il gesuita moderno* (Turin: Fontana, 1848).

10. Cesare Luporini, "Leopardi progressivo," in *Filosofi vecchi e nuovi* (Florence: Sansoni, 1947).

11. See Croce, *Poesia*, pp. 106–7.

12. "Song of the Night," *Blackwood's Edinburgh Magazine*, 124 (1878), 336.

13. "Works and Life of Giacomo Leopardi," *Quarterly Review*, 86 (1850), 295–336. Gladstone acknowledges Sainte-Beuve's article, but not that of G. H. Lewes, even though he obviously labored to differentiate his title from Lewes's recent "Life and Works of Giacomo Leopardi," *Fraser's Magazine*, 38 (1848), 659–69.

14. For Arnold's basic commentary (interestingly enough published in an 1881 essay on another poet), see the Byron essay cited above. A prime example of Leopardi's being identified with the "school" of philosophical pessimism is John Tulloch, "Pessimism," *Edinburg Review*, 149 (1879), 500–533.

15. In addition to Origo, already cited, see Geoffrey L. Bickersteth, ed. and trans., *The Poems of Leopardi* (Cambridge: Cambridge University Press, 1923); J. H. Whitfield, *Giacomo Leopardi* (Oxford: Basil Blackwell, 1954); Nicolas James Perella, *Night and the Sublime in Giacomo Leopardi* (Berkeley: University of California Press, 1970); G. Singh, *Leopardi and the Theory of Poetry* (Lexington: University of Kentucky Press, 1964); and Giovanni Carsaniga, *Giacomo Leopardi: The Unheeded Voice* (Edinburgh: University of Edinburgh Press, 1977).

16. See *Roma nel mille* (Florence: Le Monnier, 1875), p. 408. Carducci did much to spread the Countess's words by repeating this tale in his famous essay *Degli spiriti e delle forme nella poesia di Giacomo Leopardi* (Bologna: Zanichelli, 1898), pp. 30–31.

17. See Gladstone, pp. 334–35.

18. Giuseppe Chiarini, *Vita di Giacomo Leopardi* (Florence: Barbera, 1905), p. 40, said that "he was not aware that every bit of knowledge he was acquiring was an atom of life slipping away, every step he took toward immortality was a step toward the grave."

19. The question is reviewed incisively by Origo in Chaps. 14 and 15 ("Ranieri" and "Aspasia"). To balance the Ranieri contention regarding Leopardi's virginity, we have Leopardi's letters to Carlo from Rome (see

selections) which suggest that Leopardi had experienced some physical love at Recanati during adolescence. Carsaniga (pp. 98 ff.) argues on the basis of veiled poetic texts that Fanny succumbed out of pity to Leopardi at Florence in 1832. Leopardi's disgust on the topic of pederasty is expressed in *Zibaldone*, 4047.

20. Although it is difficult for any writer on Leopardi to avoid discussing his thought, and thus treatments are myriad, I found the most succinct coverage of the general development to be that of Sebastiano Timpanaro, "Il Leopardi e i filosofi antichi," in *Classicismo e illuminismo nell'ottocento italiano,* 2nd ed. (Pisa: Nistri-Lischi, 1969), pp. 183–228. An excellent longer treatment is that of Adriano Tilgher, *La filosofia di Leopardi* (Rome: Edizioni di Religio, 1940). Umberto Bosco's *Titanismo e pietà in Giacomo Leopardi* (Florence: Le Monnier, 1957) is a valuable essay on the heroic or "titanic" element in Leopardi. In English, J. H. Whitfield's entire book is the most helpful source on Leopardi's mind as a whole, although Bickersteth's introduction to his translations is also interesting.

21. *Zibaldone*, 453. The second quotation is from *Zibaldone*, 15.

22. Leopardi was influenced in his terminology by his Belgian friend A. Jacoppsen. See Whitfield, pp. 182–84.

23. From the *Dialogue of Nature and a Soul,* one of the *Operette.*

24. Carducci, p. 102.

25. English-language discussions on Leopardi's poetic theory can be found in Singh's book and in Perella, especially pp. 61–116. There is also a perceptive digest of some of the major ideas in René Wellek, *A History of Modern Criticism, 1750–1950,* III (New Haven: Yale University Press, 1965), 272–78.

26. Wellek, p. 274.

27. See Bickersteth, p. 317.

28. *Zibaldone*, 58.

29. M. H. Abrams, "Structure and Style in the Greater Romantic Lyric," in *Romanticism and Consciousness: Essays in Criticism,* ed. Harold Bloom (New York: Norton, 1970), pp. 201 ff.

30. Fernando Figurelli, *Giacomo Leopardi, poeta dell'idillio* (Bari: Laterza, 1941), p. 77.

31. Francesco Flora makes an eloquent case for the poetry of the *Operette* in *Poetica e poesia di Leopardi* (Milan: Malfasi, 1949), p. 158.

32. See Walter Binni, *La nuova poetica leopardiana* (Florence: Sansoni, 1947). Binni has probably done more than any other scholar to illuminate the character of the late "heroic" style.

33. Perella, pp. 69–70.

34. That Leopardi was primarily a moralist is now a truism among scholars. As might be expected, Francesco De Sanctis was one of the first to propose the idea forcefully. He pointed out that for Leopardi, "religion and philosophies have no other origin or basis than to give us an explanation of the world and accordingly determine our moral conduct. . . . It is not that he does not have his own metaphysic; but it is a simple

presupposition to his philosophy, which is directed chiefly to the practical life." See *Giacomo Leopardi,* ed. Walter Binni, Vol. III of *La letteratura italiana nel secolo XIX,* 2nd. ed. (Bari: Laterza, 1961), p. 199.

35. Karl Vossler, *Leopardi,* trans. T. Gnoli (Naples: Ricciardi, 1925), pp. 143–44.
36. Pasquale Gatti, *Esposizione del sistema filosofica di Giacomo Leopardi,* 2 vols. (Florence: Le Monnier, 1908), discusses not only the general outline of Leopardi's materialism but also the ways in which Leopardi anticipated such pragmatists as William James.
37. Bickersteth, p. 8.
38. Whitfield, p. 251. Also see Perella (p. 55), who says, "Leopardi oscillated between desire for death (oblivion or nothingness) and anguish at the idea of passing into nothingness."
39. I am here augmenting Whitfield's (p. 80) idea about the frequency of the word "magnanimous" in the *Operette.*
40. De Sanctis, "Schopenhauer e Leopardi: Dialogo tra A e D," in *Saggi Critici,* ed. Luigi Russo (Bari: Laterza, 1952), II, 159.
41. Croce, *Poesia,* pp. 113–14.

I. YOUNG LEOPARDI (to 1822)

1. These excerpts are from Flora, *Poesie e prose,* II, 470–81. For English-language discussions of this work (still untranslated into English), see Singh, pp. 21–39, and Perella, pp. 61 ff.
2. The excerpts from this work (again never translated into English) are from Flora, *Poesie e prose,* I, 673–86. This prose too was not published in Leopardi's lifetime.
3. The phrase is that of De Sanctis, *Giacomo Leopardi,* p. 86. Adriano Tilgher (pp. 156–57) gives the standard mystical interpretation when he says, "The poet forgets himself and the world: that is, more precisely, the barrier between the I and the Not-I falls, and he lives an experience of unity, of mystical shipwreck of the I into the all. . . ."
4. Perella, pp. 148–49. Perella's view seems convincing to me, as it squares with the text and with Leopardi's own thinking on the subject. Also see Karl Kroeber, *The Artifice of Reality: Poetic Style in Wordsworth, Foscolo, Keats, and Leopardi* (Madison: University of Wisconsin Press), pp. 96–97; Kroeber allows that if it is a mysticism at issue, it is a "mysticism of total realism."
5. For Kroeber's discussion of the poem see his *Artifice,* pp. 100–103. The most comprehensive work in English on the poem is that of Perella (pp. 1–60), who not only "places" the poem in respect to Leopardi's other writings, its probable sources, and its reception by critics but also makes a sensitive case for its unity and worth.
6. Carducci, p. 52.
7. Giuseppe De Robertis, *Saggio sul Leopardi* (Florence: Vallecchi, 1944), p. 99.
8. Kroeber, p. 103.
9. Bickersteth, p. 105.

10. This and the later quotation from Sainte-Beuve are from his article, pp. 570–71.
11. See Flora, *Poesie e prose*, I, 1037–45 for the complete essay.
12. Leopardi's two notes about the poem appear in Flora, *Poesie e prose*, I, 151, 447.

II. TO ROME AND BACK (1822–25)

1. This note can be found in Flora, *Poesie e prose*, I, 152.
2. See Flora, *Poesie e prose*, I, 1146.
3. After this sentence, Leopardi footnotes a long quotation from one Pedro de Cieza, who in his *Chronicles of Peru* (Anvers, 1554) testified to observing such cannibalism.
4. Leopardi cites in a note the *Revue Encyclopedique* (1825) regarding the wars of extermination waged by Indian tribes in North and South America.
5. Regarding the man who killed his children but left his dog to a friend, Leopardi notes cryptically, "This incident is true."
6. Whitfield interestingly relates this piece to Lucrètius' *De Rerum Natura* and to Byron's *Cain*. As for Leopardi's identification of nature with God, he sought occasionally—at least in his early notebook writings—to associate the two concepts (see *Zibaldone*, 393–96, for example).

III. THE CIRCUIT OF CITIES (1825–30)

1. The quoted language here is from Flora's discussion of the matter in *Poesie e prose*, I, lxxvi.
2. De Sanctis, *Nuovi saggi critici*, pp. 509–10.
3. Some Italian scholars think it the masterpiece, rather than *Broom*, *The Infinite*, or *To Sylvia*, the other apparent contenders. G. A. Levi, *Giacomo Leopardi* (Messina: Principato, 1931), p. 317, said, for example, that in the *Night-Song* Leopardi "put his hand to a poem truly worthy of eternity; to perhaps the greatest work of his life. . . ."
4. Bickersteth (p. 121) noted that while the shepherd of the poem dwells on his insignificance in the cosmos, "at the same time we are made to feel that he is greater than that universe through his 'incapability of being satisfied with it.' "

IV. FLORENCE AND NAPLES (1830–37)

1. See the journal entry for February 21, 1906, in *Letters of Wallace Stevens*, ed. Holly Stevens (New York: Knopf, 1966), p. 88.
2. Walter Binni, *La nuova poetica leopardiana*, pp. 191 ff.
3. See, for example, Giuseppe De Robertis's notes to the poem in his edition *Giacomo Leopardi: Canti* (Florence: Le Monnier, 1963), pp. 330–55.
4. I owe this observation to Timpanaro, pp. 224–25.
5. Kroeber, p. 64.
6. Carducci, p. 94.

Selected Bibliography

——

The amount of scholarship on Leopardi, especially in Italian, is prodigious. The following bibliography is intended only to indicate important book-length English-language scholarship, most of the basic translations available in English, and some of the eminent examples of Italian scholarship. The vast field of periodical literature is not represented, and some of the more tangential titles appearing in the above notes to this edition are not repeated here.

The definitive and probably most widely available bibliography is that published by Olschki of Florence as a continuing project. This work, which attempts to list foreign as well as Italian writings, has been issued in five parts, as follows: I: *Bibliografia leopardiana (to 1898)*, eds. G. Mazzatinti and M. Menghini (1931); II: *Bibliografia leopardiana (1898-1930)*, ed. Giulio Natali (1932); III: *Bibliografia leopardiana (1931-1951)*, eds. Giulio Natali and C. Musmarra (1953); IV: *Bibliografia analitica leopardiana (1952-1960)*, ed. Alessandro Tortoreto (1963); and V: *Bibliografia analitica leopardiana (1961-1970)*, eds. A. Tortoreto and C. Rotondi (1973).

STUDIES IN ENGLISH

Carsaniga, Giovanni. *Giacomo Leopardi: The Unheeded Voice.* Edinburgh: Edinburgh University Press, 1977.

Kroeber, Karl. *The Artifice of Reality: Poetic Style in Wordsworth, Foscolo, Keats, and Leopardi.* Madison: University of Wisconsin Press, 1964.

Origo, Iris. *Leopardi: A Study in Solitude,* 2nd. ed. London: Hamish Hamilton, 1953.

Perella, Nicolas James. *Night and the Sublime in Giacomo Leopardi.* Berkeley: University of California Press, 1970.

Singh, G. *Leopardi and the Theory of Poetry.* Lexington: University of Kentucky Press, 1964.

Whitfield, J. H. *Giacomo Leopardi.* Oxford: Basil Blackwell, 1954.

ENGLISH TRANSLATIONS

Barricelli, Jean-Pierre. *Giacomo Leopardi: Poems.* New York: Las Americas, 1963.

Bickersteth, Geoffrey L. *The Poems of Leopardi.* Cambridge: Cambridge University Press, 1923.

Caserta, Ernesto. *Giacomo Leopardi: The War of the Mice and the Crabs.* Chapel Hill: University of North Carolina Department of Romance Languages, 1976.

Cliffe, Francis H. *The Poems of Leopardi*. London: Remington, 1893.

Edwardes, Charles. *Essays and Dialogues of Giacomo Leopardi*. London: Trübner, 1882.

Flores, Angel (gen. ed.). *Leopardi: Poems and Prose*. Bloomington: Indiana University Press, 1966.

Maxwell, Major-General Patrick. *Essays, Dialogues and Thoughts of Count Giacomo Leopardi*. London: W. Scott, 1893.

Morrison, J. M. *The Poems ("Canti") of Giacomo Leopardi*. London: Gay and Bird, 1900.

Origo, Iris, and John Heath-Stubbs. *Giacomo Leopardi: Selected Prose and Poetry*. Oxford: Oxford University Press, 1966.

Thomson, James. *Essays, Dialogues and Thoughts of Giacomo Leopardi*. London: Routledge, 1905.

Townsend, Frederick. *Poems of Giacomo Leopardi*. New York: Putnam's, 1887.

Whitfield, J. H. *Leopardi's Canti Translated into English Verse*. Naples: G. Scalabrini, 1962.

STUDIES IN ITALIAN

Bigongiari, Piero. *L'elaborazione della lirica leopardiana*. Florence: Le Monnier, 1948.

Binni, Walter. *La nuova poetica leopardiana*. Florence: Sansoni, 1947.

Bosco, Umberto. *Titanismo e pietà in Giacomo Leopardi*. Florence: Le Monnier, 1957.

Carducci, Giosue. *Degli spiriti e delle forme nella poesia di Giacomo Leopardi*. Bologna: Zanichelli, 1898.

Cecchetti, Giovanni. *Leopardi e Verga, sette studi*. Florence: La Nuova Italia, 1962.

Chiarini, Giuseppe. *Vita di Giacomo Leopardi*. Florence: Barbera, 1905.

Croce, Benedetto. "Leopardi," in *Poesia e non poesia*, 7th ed. Bari: Laterza, 1964.

De Robertis, Giuseppe. *Saggio sul Leopardi*. Florence: Vallecchi, 1944.

De Sanctis, Francesco, *Giacomo Leopardi*, ed. Walter Binni, Vol. III of *La letteratura italiana nel secolo XIX*, 2nd ed. Bari: Laterza, 1961.

――――. "La prima canzone di Giacomo Leopardi," "La Nerina di Giacomo Leopardi," and "Le Nuove canzoni di Giacomo Leopardi," in *Nuovi saggi critici*, 19th ed. Naples: Morano, 1903.

――――. "Schopenhauer e Leopardi: Dialogo tra A e D," in Vol. II of *Saggi Critici*, ed. Luigi Russo. Bari: Laterza, 1952.

Ferretti, Giovanni, *Vita di Giacomo Leopardi*. Bologna: Zanichelli, 1945.

Figurelli, Fernando. *Giacomo Leopardi, poeta dell'idillio*. Bari: Laterza, 1941.

Flora, Francesco. *Poetica e poesia di Leopardi*. Milan: Malfasi, 1949.

Frattini, Alberto. *Il problema dell'esistenza in Leopardi*. Milan: Gastaldi, 1950.

Galimberti, Cesare. *Linguaggio del vero in Leopardi*. Florence: Olschki, 1959.

Gatti, Pasquale. *Esposizione del sistema filosofico di Giacomo Leopardi*, 2 vols. Florence: Le Monnier, 1906.

Gentile, Giovanni. *Poesia e filosofia di Giacomo Leopardi*. Florence: Sansoni, 1939.

——.*Manzoni e Leopardi*. Milan: Treves, 1928.

Graf, Arturo. *Foscolo, Manzoni, Leopardi*. Turin: Loescher, 1898.

Levi, G. A. *Giacomo Leopardi*. Messina: Principato, 1931.

Luporini, Cesare. "Leopardi progressivo," in *Filosofi vecchi e nuovi*. Florence: Sansoni, 1947.

Mestica, Giovanni. *Studi leopardiani*. Florence: Le Monnier, 1901.

Saponaro, Michele. *Leopardi*. Milan: Garzanti, 1941.

Solmi, Sergio. *Scritti leopardiani*. Milan: All'insegna del pesce d'oro, 1969.

Tilgher, Adriano. *La filosofia di Leopardi*. Rome: Edizioni di Religio, 1940.

Timpanaro, Sebastiano. "Il Leopardi e i filosofi antichi," in *Classicismo e illuminismo nell'ottocento italiano*, 2nd ed. Pisa: Nistri-Lischi, 1969.

Vossler, Karl. *Leopardi*. Trans. T. Gnoli. Naples: Ricciardi, 1925. German original pub. Munich: Musarian Verlag, 1923.

Zumbini, Bonaventura. *Studi sul Leopardi*, 2 vols. Florence: Barbera, 1920-24.

APPENDIX:

ITALIAN ORIGNALS OF POEMS

L'Infinito

(The Infinite, p. 44)

Sempre caro mi fu quest'ermo colle,
E questa siepe, che da tanta parte
Dell'ultimo orizzonte il guardo esclude.
Ma sedendo e mirando, interminati
Spazi di là da quella, e sovrumani
Silenzi, e profondissima quiete
Io nel pensier mi fingo; ove per poco
Il cor non si spaura. E come il vento
Odo stormir tra queste piante, io quello
Infinito silenzio a questa voce
Vo comparando: e mi sovvien l'eterno,
E le morte stagioni, e la presente
E viva, e il suon di lei. Così tra questa
Immensità s'annega il pensier mio:
E il naufragar m'è dolce in questo mare.

Alla luna

(To the Moon, p. 48)

O graziosa luna, io mi rammento
Che, or volge l'anno, sovra questo colle
Io venia pien d'angoscia a rimirarti:
E tu pendevi allor su quella selva
Siccome or fai, che tutta la rischiari.
Ma nebuloso e tremulo dal pianto
Che mi sorgea sul ciglio, alle mie luci
Il tuo volto apparia, che travagliosa
Era mia vita: ed è, nè cangia stile,
O mia diletta luna. E pur mi giova
La ricordanza, e il noverar l'etate
Del mio dolore. Oh come grato occorre
Nel tempo giovanil, quando ancor lungo
La speme e breve ha la memoria il corso,
Il rimembrar delle passate cose,
Ancor che triste, e che l'affanno duri!

La sera del dì di festa

(Sunday Evening, p. 53)

Dolce e chiara è la notte e senza vento,
E queta sovra i tetti e in mezzo agli orti
Posa la luna, e di lontan rivela
Serena ogni montagna. O donna mia,
Già tace ogni sentiero, e pei balconi
Rara traluce la notturna lampa:
Tu dormi, che t'accolse agevol sonno
Nelle tue chete stanze; e non ti morde
Cura nessuna; e già non sai nè pensi
Quanta piaga m'apristi in mezzo al petto.
Tu dormi: io questo ciel, che sì benigno
Appare in vista, a salutar m'affaccio,
E l'antica natura onnipossente,
Che mi fece all'affanno. A te la speme
Nego, mi disse, anche la speme; e d'altro
Non brillin gli occhi tuoi se non di pianto.
Questo dì fu solenne: or da' trastulli
Prendi riposo; e forse ti rimembra
In sogno a quanti oggi piacesti, e quanti
Piacquero a te: non io, non già ch'io speri,
Al pensier ti ricorro. Intanto io chieggo
Quanto a viver mi resti, e qui per terra
Mi getto, e grido, e fremo. Oh giorni orrendi
In così verde etate! Ahi, per la via
Odo non lunge il solitario canto
Dell'artigian, che riede a tarda notte,
Dopo i sollazzi, al suo povero ostello;
E fieramente mi si stringe il core,
A pensar come tutto al mondo passa,
E quasi orma non lascia. Ecco è fuggito
Il dì festivo, ed al festivo il giorno
Volgar succede, e se ne porta il tempo
Ogni umano accidente. Or dov'è il suono
Di que' popoli antichi? or dov'è il grido
De' nostri avi famosi, e il grande impero
Di quella Roma, e l'armi, e il fragorio
Che n'andò per la terra e l'oceano?
Tutto è pace e silenzio, e tutto posa
Il mondo, e più di lor non si ragiona.

Nella mia prima età, quando s'aspetta
Bramosamente il dì festivo, or poscia
Ch'egli era spento, io doloroso, in veglia,
Premea le piume; ed alla tarda notte
Un canto che s'udia per li sentieri
Lontanando morire a poco a poco,
Già similmente mi stringeva il core.

Bruto minore

(Brutus, p. 64)

Poi che divelta, nella tracia polve
Giacque ruina immensa
L'italica virtute, onde alle valli
D'Esperia verde, e al tiberino lido,
Il calpestio de' barbari cavalli
Prepara il fato, e dalle selve ignude
Cui l'Orsa algida preme,
A spezzar le romane inclite mura
Chiama i gotici brandi;
Sudato, e molle di fraterno sangue,
Bruto per l'atra notte in erma sede,
Fermo già di morir, gl'inesorandi
Numi e l'averno accusa,
E di feroci note
Invan la sonnolenta aura percote.

Stolta virtù, le cave nebbie, i campi
Dell'inquiete larve
Son le tue scole, e ti si volge a tergo
Il pentimento. A voi, marmorei numi,
(Se numi avete in Flegetonte albergo
O su le nubi) a voi ludibrio e scherno
È la prole infelice
A cui templi chiedeste, e frodolenta
Legge al mortale insulta.
Dunque tanto i celesti odii commove
La terrena pietà? dunque degli empi
Siedi, Giove, a tutela? e quando esulta
Per l'aere il nembo, e quando
Il tuon rapido spingi,
Ne' giusti e pii la sacra fiamma stringi?

Preme il destino invitto e la ferrata
Necessità gl'infermi
Schiavi di morte: e se a cessar non vale
Gli oltraggi lor, de' necessarii danni
Si consola il plebeo. Men duro è il male
Che riparo non ha? dolor non sente
Chi di speranza è nudo?

Guerra mortale, eterna, o fato indegno,
Teco il prode guerreggia,
Di cedere inesperto; e la tiranna
Tua destra, allor che vincitrice il grava,
Indomito scrollando si pompeggia,
Quando nell'alto lato
L'amaro ferro intride,
E maligno alle nere ombre sorride.

Spiace agli Dei chi violento irrompe
Nel Tartaro. Non fora
Tanto valor ne' molli eterni petti.
Forse i travagli nostri, e forse il cielo
I casi acerbi e gl'infelici affetti
Giocondo agli ozi suoi spettacol pose?
Non fra sciagure e colpe,
Ma libera ne' boschi e pura etade
Natura a noi prescrisse,
Reina un tempo e Diva. Or poi ch'a terra
Sparse i regni beati empio costume,
E il viver macro ad altre leggi addisse;
Quando gl'infausti giorni
Virile alma ricusa,
Riede natura, e il non suo dardo accusa?

Di colpa ignare e de' lor proprii danni
Le fortunate belve
Serena adduce al non previsto passo
La tarda età. Ma se spezzar la fronte
Ne' rudi tronchi, o da montano sasso
Dare al vento precipiti le membra,
Lor suadesse affanno;
Al misero desio nulla contesa
Legge arcana farebbe
O tenebroso ingegno. A voi, fra quante
Stirpi il cielo avvivò, soli fra tutte,
Figli di Prometeo, la vita increbbe;
A voi le morte ripe,
Se il fato ignavo pende,
Soli, o miseri, a voi Giove contende.

E tu dal mar cui nostro sangue irriga,
Candida luna, sorgi,
E l'inquieta notte e la funesta
All'ausonio valor campagna esplori.
Cognati petti il vincitor calpesta,
Fremono i poggi, dalle somme vette
Roma antica ruina;
Tu sì placida sei? Tu la nascente
Lavinia prole, e gli anni
Lieti vedesti, e i memorandi allori;
E tu su l'alpe l'immutato raggio
Tacita verserai quando ne' danni
Del servo italo nome,
Sotto barbaro piede
Rintronerà quella solinga sede.

Ecco tra nudi sassi o in verde ramo
E la fera e l'augello,
Del consueto obblio gravido il petto,
L'alta ruina ignora e le mutate
Sorti del mondo: e come prima il tetto
Rosseggerà del villanello industre,
Al mattutino canto
Quel desterà le valli, e per le balze
Quella l'inferma plebe
Agiterà delle minori belve.
Oh casi! oh gener vano! abbietta parte
Siam delle cose; e non le tinte glebe,
Non gli ululati spechi
Turbò nostra sciagura,
Nè scolorò le stelle umana cura.

Non io d'Olimpo e di Cocito i sordi
Regi, o la terra indegna,
E non la notte moribondo appello;
Non te, dell'atra morte ultimo raggio,
Conscia futura età. Sdegnoso avello
Placàr singulti, ornàr parole e doni
Di vil caterva? In peggio
Precipitano i tempi; e mal s'affida
A putridi nepoti
L'onor d'egregie menti e la suprema

De' miseri vendetta. A me dintorno
Le penne il bruno augello avido roti;
Prema la fera, e il nembo
Tratti l'ignota spoglia;
E l'aura il nome e la memoria accoglia.

Alla primavera
o delle favole antiche

(To Spring, p. 68)

Perchè i celesti danni
Ristori il sole, e perchè l'aure inferme
Zefiro avvivi, onde fugata e sparta
Delle nubi la grave ombra s'avvalla;
Credano il petto inerme
Gli augelli al vento, e la diurna luce
Novo d'amor desio, nova speranza
Ne' penetrati boschi e fra le sciolte
Pruine induca alle commosse belve;
Forse alle stanche e nel dolor sepolte
Umane menti riede
La bella età, cui la sciagura e l'atra
Face del ver consunse
Innanzi tempo? Ottenebrati e spenti
Di febo i raggi al misero non sono
In sempiterno? ed anco,
Primavera odorata, inspiri e tenti
Questo gelido cor, questo ch'amara
Nel fior degli anni suoi vecchiezza impara?

Vivi tu, vivi, o santa
Natura? vivi e il dissueto orecchio
Della materna voce il suono accoglie?
Già di candide ninfe i rivi albergo,
Placido albergo e specchio
Furo i liquidi fonti. Arcane danze
D'immortal piede i ruinosi gioghi
Scossero e l'ardue selve (oggi romito
Nido de' venti): e il pastorel ch'all'ombre
Meridiane incerte ed al fiorito
Margo adducea de' fiumi
Le sitibonde agnelle, arguto carme
Sonar d'agresti Pani
Udì lungo le ripe; e tremar l'onda
Vide, e stupì, che non palese al guardo
La faretrata Diva
Scendea ne' caldi flutti, e dall'immonda
Polve tergea della sanguigna caccia

237

Il niveo lato e le verginee braccia.

Vissero i fiori e l'erbe,
Vissero i boschi un dì. Conscie le molli
Aure, le nubi e la titania lampa
Fur dell'umana gente, allor che ignuda
Te per le piagge e i colli,
Ciprigna luce, alla deserta notte
Con gli occhi intenti il viator seguendo,
Te compagna alla via, te de' mortali
Pensosa immaginò. Che se gl'impuri
Cittadini consorzi e le fatali
Ire fuggendo e l'onte,
Gl'ispidi tronchi al petto altri nell'ime
Selve remoto accolse,
Viva fiamma agitar l'esangui vene,
Spirar le foglie, e palpitar segreta
Nel doloroso amplesso
Dafne o la mesta Filli, o di Climene
Pianger credè la sconsolata prole
Quel che sommerse in Eridano il sole.

Nè dell'umano affanno,
Rigide balze, i luttuosi accenti
Voi negletti ferìr mentre le vostre
Paurose latebre Eco solinga,
Non vano error de' venti,
Ma di ninfa abitò misero spirto,
Cui grave amor, cui duro fato escluse
Delle tenere membra. Ella per grotte,
Per nudi scogli e desolati, alberghi,
Le non ignote ambasce e l'alte e rotte
Nostre querele al curvo
Etra insegnava. E te d'umani eventi
Disse la fama esperto,
Musico augel che tra chiomato bosco
Or vieni il rinascente anno cantando,
E lamentar nell'alto
Ozio de' campi, all'aer muto e fosco,
Antichi danni e scellerato scorno,
E d'ira e di pietà pallido il giorno.

Ma non cognato al nostro
Il gener tuo; quelle tue varie note
Dolor non forma, e te di colpa ignudo,
Men caro assai la bruna valle asconde.
Ahi ahi, poscia che vote
Son le stanze d'Olimpo, e cieco il tuono
Per l'atre nubi e le montagne errando,
Gl'iniqui petti e gl'innocenti a paro
In freddo orror dissolve; e poi ch'estrano
Il suol nativo, e di sua prole ignaro
Le meste anime educa;
Tu le cure infelici e i fati indegni
Tu de' mortali ascolta,
Vaga natura, e la favilla antica
Rendi allo spirto mio; se tu pur vivi,
E se de' nostri affanni
Cosa veruna in ciel, se nell'aprica
Terra s'alberga o nell'equoreo seno,
Pietosa no, ma spettatrice almeno.

Ultimo canto di Saffo

(The Last Song of Sappho, p. 73)

Placida notte, e verecondo raggio
Della cadente luna; e tu che spunti
Fra la tacita selva in su la rupe,
Nunzio del giorno; oh dilettose e care
Mentre ignote mi fur l'erinni e il fato,
Sembianze agli occhi miei; già non arride
Spettacol molle ai disperati affetti.
Noi l'insueto allor gaudio ravviva
Quando per l'etra liquido si volve
E per li campi trepidanti il flutto
Polveroso de' Noti, e quando il carro,
Grave carro di Giove a noi sul capo,
Tonando, il tenebroso aere divide.
Noi per le balze e le profonde valli
Natar giova tra' nembi, e noi la vasta
Fuga de' greggi sbigottiti, o d'alto
Fiume alla dubbia sponda
Il suono e la vittrice ira dell'onda.

Bello il tuo manto, o divo cielo, e bella
Sei tu, rorida terra. Ahi di cotesta
Infinita beltà parte nessuna
Alla misera Saffo i numi e l'empia
Sorte non fenno. A' tuoi superbi regni
Vile, o natura, e grave ospite addetta,
E dispregiata amante, alle vezzose
Tue forme il core e le pupille invano
Supplichevole intendo. A me non ride
L'aprico margo, e dall'eterea porta
Il mattutino albor; me non il canto
De' colorati augelli, e non de' faggi
Il murmure saluta: e dove all'ombra
Degl'inchinati salici dispiega
Candido rivo il puro seno, al mio
Lubrico piè le flessuose linfe
Disdegnando sottragge,
E preme in fuga l'odorate spiagge.

Qual fallo mai, qual sì nefando eccesso
Macchiommi anzi il natale, onde sì torvo
Il ciel mi fosse e di fortuna il volto?
In che peccai bambina, allor che ignara
Di misfatto è la vita, onde poi scemo
Di giovanezza, e disfiorato, al fuso
Dell'indomita Parca si volvesse
Il ferrigno mio stame? Incaute voci
Spande il tuo labbro: i destinati eventi
Move arcano consiglio. Arcano è tutto,
Fuor che il nostro dolor. Negletta prole
Nascemmo al pianto, e la ragione in grembo
De' celesti si posa. Oh cure, oh speme
De' più verd'anni! Alle sembianze il Padre,
Alle amene sembianze eterno regno
Diè nelle genti; e per virili imprese,
Per dotta lira o canto,
Virtù non luce in disadorno ammanto.

Morremo. Il velo indegno a terra sparto,
Rifuggirà l'ignudo animo a Dite,
E il crudo fallo emenderà del cieco
Dispensator de' casi. E tu cui lungo
Amore indarno, e lunga fede, e vano
D'implacato desio furor mi strinse,
Vivi felice, se felice in terra
Vissi nato mortal. Me non asperse
Del soave licor del doglio avaro
Giove, poi che perìr gl'inganni e il sogno
Della mia fanciullezza. Ogni più lieto
Giorno di nostra età primo s'invola.
Sottentra il morbo, e la vecchiezza, e l'ombra
Della gelida morte. Ecco di tante
Sperate palme e dilettosi errori,
Il Tartaro m'avanza; e il prode ingegno
Han la tenaria Diva,
E l'altra notte, e la silente riva.

Alla sua donna

(To His Lady, p. 89)

Cara beltà che amore
Lunge m'inspiri o nascondendo il viso,
Fuor se nel sonno il core
Ombra diva mi scuoti,
O ne' campi ove splenda
Più vago il giorno e di natura il riso;
Forse tu l'innocente
Secol beasti che dall'oro ha nome,
Or leve intra la gente
Anima voli? o te la sorte avara
Ch'a noi t'asconde, agli avvenir prepara?

Viva mirarti omai
Nulla speme m'avanza;
S'allor non fosse, allor che ignudo e solo
Per novo calle a peregrina stanza
Verrà lo spirto mio. Già sul novello
Aprir di mia giornata incerta e bruna,
Te viatrice in questo arido suolo
Io mi pensai. Ma non è cosa in terra
Che ti somigli; e s'anco pari alcuna
Ti fosse al volto, agli atti, alla favella,
Saria, così conforme, assai men bella.

Fra cotanto dolore
Quanto all'umana età propose il fato,
Se vera e quale il mio pensier ti pinge,
Alcun t'amasse in terra, a lui pur fora
Questo viver beato:
E ben chiaro vegg'io siccome ancora
Seguir loda e virtù qual ne' prim'anni
L'amor tuo mi farebbe. Or non aggiunse
Il ciel nullo conforto ai nostri affanni;
E teco la mortal vita saria
Simile a quella che nel cielo india.

Per le valli, ove suona
Del faticoso agricoltore il canto,
Ed io seggo e mi lagno

Del giovanile error che m'abbandona;
E per li poggi, ov'io rimembro e piagno
I perduti desiri, e la perduta
Speme de' giorni miei; di te pensando,
A palpitar mi sveglio. E potess'io,
Nel secol tetro e in questo aer nefando,
L'alta specie serbar; che dell'imago,
Poi che del ver m'è tolto, assai m'appago.

Se dell'eterne idee
L'una sei tu, cui di sensibil forma
Sdegni l'eterno senno esser vestita,
E fra caduche spoglie
Provar gli affanni di funerea vita;
O s'altra terra ne' superni giri
Fra' mondi innumerabili t'accoglie,
E più vaga del Sol prossima stella
T'irraggia, e più benigno etere spiri;
Di qua dove son gli anni infausti e brevi,
Questo d'ignoto amante inno ricevi.

A Silvia

(To Sylvia, p. 158)

Silvia, rimembri ancora
Quel tempo della tua vita mortale,
Quando beltà splendea
Negli occhi tuoi ridenti e fuggitivi,
E tu, lieta e pensosa, il limitare
Di gioventù salivi?

Sonavan le quiete
Stanze, e le vie dintorno,
Al tuo perpetuo canto,
Allor che all'opre femminili intenta
Sedevi, assai contenta
Di quel vago avvenir che in mente avevi.
Era il maggio odoroso: e tu solevi
Così menare il giorno.

Io gli studi leggiadri
Talor lasciando e le sudate carte,
Ove il tempo mio primo
E di me si spendea la miglior parte,
D'in su i veroni del paterno ostello
Porgea gli orecchi al suon della tua voce,
Ed alla man veloce
Che percorrea la faticosa tela.
Mirava il ciel sereno,
Le vie dorate e gli orti,
E quinci il mar da lungi, e quindi il monte.
Lingua mortal non dice
Quel ch'io sentiva in seno.

Che pensieri soavi,
Che speranze, che cori, o Silvia mia!
Quale allor ci apparia
La vita umana e il fato!
Quando sovviemmi di cotanta speme,
Un affetto mi preme
Acerbo e sconsolato,
E tornami a doler di mia sventura.
O natura, o natura,

Perchè non rendi poi
Quel che prometti allor? perchè di tanto
Inganni i figli tuoi?

Tu pria che l'erbe inaridisse il verno,
Da chiuso morbo combattuta e vinta,
Perivi, o tenerella. E non vedevi
Il fior degli anni tuoi;
Non ti molceva il core
La dolce lode or delle negre chiome,
Or degli sguardi innamorati e schivi;
Nè teco le compagne ai dì festivi
Ragionavan d'amore.

Anche peria fra poco
La speranza mia dolce: agli anni miei
Anche negaro i fati
La giovanezza. Ahi come,
Come passata sei,
Cara compagna dell'età mia nova,
Mia lacrimata speme!
Questo è quel mondo? questi
I diletti, l'amor, l'opre, gli eventi
Onde cotanto ragionammo insieme?
Questa la sorte dell'umane genti?
All'apparir del vero
Tu, misera, cadesti: e con la mano
La fredda morte ed una tomba ignuda
Mostravi di lontano.

Le ricordanze

(Memories, p. 165)

Vaghe stelle dell'Orsa, io non credea
Tornare ancor per uso a contemplarvi
Sul paterno giardino scintillanti,
E ragionar con voi dalle finestre
Di questo albergo ove abitai fanciullo,
E delle gioie mie vidi la fine.
Quante immagini un tempo, e quante fole
Creommi nel pensier l'aspetto vostro
E delle luci a voi compagne! allora
Che, tacito, seduto in verde zolla,
Delle sere io solea passar gran parte
Mirando il cielo, ed ascoltando il canto
Della rana rimota alla campagna!
E la lucciola errava appo le siepi
E in su l'aiuole, susurrando al vento
I viali odorati, ed i cipressi
Là nella selva; e sotto al patrio tetto
Sonavan voci alterne, e le tranquille
Opre de' servi. E che pensieri immensi,
Che dolci sogni mi spirò la vista
Di quel lontano mar, quei monti azzurri,
Che di qua scopro, e che varcare un giorno
Io mi pensava, arcani mondi, arcana
Felicità fingendo al viver mio!
Ignaro del mio fato, e quante volte
Questa mia vita dolorosa e nuda
Volentier con la morte avrei cangiato.

Nè mi diceva il cor che l'età verde
Sarei dannato a consumare in questo
Natio borgo selvaggio, intra una gente
Zotica, vil; cui nomi strani, e spesso
Argomento di riso e di trastullo,
Son dottrina e saper; che m'odia e fugge,
Per invidia non già, che non mi tiene
Maggior di se, ma perchè tale estima
Ch'io mi tenga in cor mio, sebben di fuori
A persona giammai non ne fo segno.
Qui passo gli anni, abbandonato, occulto,

Senz'amor, senza vita; ed aspro a forza
Tra lo stuol de' malevoli divengo:
Qui di pietà mi spoglio e di virtudi,
E sprezzator degli uomini mi rendo,
Per la greggia ch'ho appresso: e intanto vola
Il caro tempo giovanil; più caro
Che la fama e l'allor, più che la pura
Luce del giorno, e lo spirar: ti perdo
Senza un diletto, inutilmente, in questo
Soggiorno disumano, intra gli affanni,
O dell'arida vita unico fiore.

Viene il vento recando il suon dell'ora
Dalla torre del borgo. Era conforto
Questo suon, mi rimembra, alle mie notti,
Quando fanciullo, nella buia stanza,
Per assidui terrori io vigilava,
Sospirando il mattin. Qui non è cosa
Ch'io vegga o senta, onde un'immagin dentro
Non torni, e un dolce rimembrar non sorga.
Dolce per se; ma con dolor sottentra
Il pensier del presente, un van desio
Del passato, ancor tristo, e il dire: Io fui.
Quella loggia colà, volta agli estremi
Raggi del dì; queste dipinte mura,
Quei figurati armenti, e il Sol che nasce
Su romita campagna, agli ozi miei
Porser mille diletti allor che al fianco
M'era, parlando, il mio possente errore
Sempre, ov'io fossi. In queste sale antiche,
Al chiaror delle nevi, intorno a queste
Ampie finestre sibilando il vento,
Rimbombaro i solazzi e le festose
Mie voci al tempo che l'acerbo, indegno
Mistero delle cose a noi si mostra
Pien di dolcezza; indelibata, intera
Il garzoncel, come inesperto amante,
La sua vita ingannevole vagheggia,
E celeste beltà fingendo ammira.

O speranze, speranze, ameni inganni
Della mia prima età! sempre, parlando,

Ritorno a voi; che per andar di tempo,
Per variar d'affetti e di pensieri,
Obbliarvi non so. Fantasmi, intendo,
Son la gloria e l'onor; diletti e beni
Mero desio; non ha la vita un frutto,
Inutile miseria. E sebben vóti
Son gli anni miei, sebben deserto, oscuro
Il mio stato mortal, poco mi toglie
La fortuna, ben veggo. Ahi, ma qualvolta
A voi ripenso, o mie speranze antiche,
Ed a quel caro immaginar mio primo;
Indi riguardo il viver mio sì vile
E sì dolente, e che la morte è quello
Che di cotanta speme oggi m'avanza;
Sento serrarmi il cor, sento ch'al tutto
Consolarmi non so del mio destino.
E quando pur questa invocata morte
Sarammi allato, e sarà giunto il fine
Della sventura mia; quando la terra
Mi fia straniera valle, e dal mio sguardo
Fuggirà l'avvenir; di voi per certo
Risovverrammi; e quell'imago ancora
Sospirar mi farà, farammi acerbo
L'esser vissuto indarno, e la dolcezza
Del dì fatal tempererà d'affanno.

E già nel primo giovanil tumulto
Di contenti, d'angosce e di desio,
Morte chiamai più volte, e lungamente
Mi sedetti colà su la fontana
Pensoso di cessar dentro quell'acque
La speme e il dolor mio. Poscia, per cieco
Malor, condotto della vita in forse,
Piansi la bella giovanezza, e il fiore
De' miei poveri dì, che sì per tempo
Cadeva: e spesso all'ore tarde, assiso
Sul conscio letto, dolorosamente
Alla fioca lucerna poetando,
Lamentai co' silenzi e con la notte
Il fuggitivo spirto, ed a me stesso
In sul languir cantai funereo canto.

Chi rimembrar vi può senza sospiri,
O primo entrar di giovinezza, o giorni
Vezzosi, inenarrabili, allor quando
Al rapito mortal primieramente
Sorridon le donzelle; a gara intorno
Ogni cosa sorride; invidia tace,
Non desta ancora ovver benigna; e quasi
(Inusitata maraviglia!) il mondo
La destra soccorrevole gli porge,
Scusa gli errori suoi, festeggia il novo
Suo venir nella vita, ed inchinando
Mostra che per signor l'accolga e chiami?
Fugaci giorni! a somigliar d'un lampo
Son dileguati. E qual mortale ignaro
Di sventura esser può, se a lui già scorsa
Quella vaga stagion, se il suo buon tempo,
Se giovanezza, ahi giovanezza, è spenta?

O Nerina! e di te forse non odo
Questi luoghi parlar? caduta forse
Dal mio pensier sei tu? Dove sei gita,
Che qui sola di te la ricordanza
Trovo, dolcezza mia? Più non ti vede
Questa Terra natal: quella finestra,
Ond'eri usata favellarmi, ed onde
Mesto riluce delle stelle il raggio,
È deserta. Ove sei, che più non odo
La tua voce sonar, siccome un giorno,
Quando soleva ogni lontano accento
Del labbro tuo, ch'a me giungesse, il volto
Scolorarmi? Altro tempo. I giorni tuoi
Furo, mio dolce amor. Passasti. Ad altri
Il passar per la terra oggi è sortito,
E l'abitar questi odorati colli.
Ma rapida passasti; e come un sogno
Fu la tua vita. Ivi danzando; in fronte
La gioia ti splendea, splendea negli occhi
Quel confidente immaginar, quel lume
Di gioventù, quando spegneali il fato,
E giacevi. Ahi Nerina! In cor mi regna
L'antico amor. Se a feste anco talvolta,
Se a radunanze io movo, infra me stesso

Dico: o Nerina, a radunanze, a feste
Tu non ti acconci più, tu più non movi.
Se torna maggio, e ramoscelli e suoni
Van gli amanti recando alle fanciulle,
Dico: Nerina mia, per te non torna
Primavera giammai, non torna amore.
Ogni giorno sereno, ogni fiorita
Piaggia ch'io miro, ogni goder ch'io sento,
Dico: Nerina or più non gode; i campi,
L'aria non mira. Ahi tu passasti, eterno
Sospiro mio: passasti: e fia compagna
D'ogni mio vago immaginar, di tutti
I miei teneri sensi, i tristi e cari
Moti del cor, la rimembranza acerba.

La quiete dopo la tempesta

(The Calm after the Storm, p. 169)

Passata è la tempesta:
Odo augelli far festa, e la gallina,
Tornata in su la via,
Che ripete il suo verso. Ecco il sereno
Rompe là da ponente, alla montagna;
Sgombrasi la campagna,
E chiaro nella valle il fiume appare.
Ogni cor si rallegra, in ogni lato
Risorge il romorio
Torna il lavoro usato.
L'artigiano a mirar l'umido cielo,
Con l'opra in man, cantando,
Fassi in su l'uscio; a prova
Vien furo la femminetta a còr dell'acqua
Della novella piova;
E l'erbaiuol rinnova
Di sentiero in sentiero
Il grido giornaliero.
Ecco il Sol che ritorna, ecco sorride
Per li poggi e le ville. Apre i balconi,
Apre terrazzi e logge la famiglia:
E, dalla via corrente, odi lontano
Tintinnio di sonagli; il carro stride
Del passeggier che il suo cammin ripiglia.

Si rallegra ogni core.
Sì dolce, sì gradita
Quand'è, com'or, la vita?
Quando con tanto amore
L'uomo a' suoi studi intende?
O torna all'opre? o cosa nova imprende?
Quando de' mali suoi men si ricorda?
Piacer figlio d'affanno;
Gioia vana, ch'è frutto
Del passato timore, onde si scosse
E paventò la morte
Chi la vita abborria;
Onde in lungo tormento,
Fredde, tacite, smorte,

Sudàr le genti e palpitàr, vedendo
Mossi alle nostre offese
Folgori, nembi e vento.

O natura cortese,
Son questi i doni tuoi,
Questi i diletti sono
Che tu porgi ai mortali. Uscir di pena
È diletto fra noi.
Pene tu spargi a larga mano; il duolo
Spontaneo sorge: e di piacer, quel tanto
Che per mostro e miracolo talvolta
Nasce d'affanno è gran guadagno. Umana
Prole cara agli eterni! assai felice
Se respirar ti lice
D'alcun dolor: beata
Se te d'ogni dolor morte risana.

Il sabato del villaggio

(The Village Saturday, p. 171)

La donzelletta vien dalla campagna,
In sul calar del sole,
Col su fascio dell'erba; e reca in mano
Un mazzolin di rose e di viole,
Onde, siccome suole,
Ornare ella si appresta
Dimani, al dì di festa, il petto e il crine.
Siede con le vicine
Su la scala a filar la vecchierella,
Incontro là dove si perde il giorno;
E novellando vien del suo buon tempo,
Quando ai dì della festa ella si ornava,
Ed ancor sana e snella
Solea danzar la sera intra di quei
Ch'ebbe compagni dell'età più bella.
Già tutta l'aria imbruna,
Torna azzurro il sereno, e tornan l'ombre
Giù da' colli e da' tetti,
Al biancheggiar della recente luna.
Or la squilla dà segno
Della festa che viene;
Ed a quel suon diresti
Che il cor si riconforta.
I fanciulli gridando
Su la piazzuola in frotta,
E qua e là saltando,
Fanno un lieto romore:
E intanto riede alla sua parca mensa,
Fischiando, il zappatore,
E seco pensa al dì del suo riposo.

Poi quando intorno è spenta ogni altra face,
E tutto l'altro tace,
Odi il martel picchiare, odi la sega
Del legnaiuol, che veglia
Nella chiusa bottega alla lucerna,
E s'affretta, e s'adopra
Di fornir l'opra anzi il chiarir dell'alba.

253

Questo di sette è il più gradito giorno,
Pien di speme e di gioia:
Diman tristezza e noia
Recheran l'ore, ed al travaglio usato
Ciascun in suo pensier farà ritorno.

Garzoncello scherzoso,
Cotesta età fiorita
È come un giorno d'allegrezza pieno,
Giorno chiaro, sereno,
Che precorre alla festa di tua vita.
Godi, fanciullo mio; stato soave,
Stagion lieta è cotesta.
Altro dirti non vo'; ma la tua festa
Ch'anco tardi a venir non ti sia grave.

Canto notturno di un pastore errante dell'Asia

(Night-Song of a Wandering Shepherd of Asia, p. 172)

Che fai tu, luna, in ciel? dimmi, che fai,
Silenziosa luna?
Sorgi la sera, e vai,
Contemplando i deserti; indi ti posi.
Ancor non sei tu paga
Di riandare i sempiterni calli?
Ancor non prendi a schivo, ancor sei vaga
Di mirar queste valli?
Somiglia alla tua vita
La vita del pastore.
Sorge in sul primo albore;
Move la greggia oltre pel campo, e vede
Greggi, fontane ed erbe;
Poi stanco si riposa in su la sera:
Altro mai non ispera.
Dimmi, o luna: a che vale
Al pastor la sua vita,
La vostra vita a voi? dimmi: ove tende
Questo vagar mio breve,
Il tuo corso immortale?

Vecchierel bianco, infermo,
Mezzo vestito e scalzo,
Con gravissimo fascio in su le spalle,
Per montagna e per valle,
Per sassi acuti, ed alta rena, e fratte,
Al vento, alla tempesta, e quando avvampa
L'ora, e quando poi gela,
Corre via, corre, anela,
Varca torrenti e stagni,
Cade, risorge, e più e più s'affretta,
Senza posa o ristoro,
Lacero, sanguinoso; infin ch'arriva
Colà dove la via
E dove il tanto affaticar fu volto:
Abisso orrido, immenso,
Ov'ei precipitando, il tutto obblia.
Vergine luna, tale
È la vita mortale.

Nasce l'uomo a fatica,
Ed è rischio di morte il nascimento.
Prova pena e tormento
Per prima cosa; e in sul principio stesso
La madre e il genitore
Il prende a consolar dell'esser nato.
Poi che crescendo viene,
L'uno e l'altro il sostiene, e via pur sempre
Con atti e con parole
Studiasi fargli core,
E consolarlo dell'umano stato:
Altro ufficio più grato
Non si fa da parenti alla lor prole.
Ma perchè dare al sole,
Perchè reggere in vita
Chi poi di quella consolar convenga?
Se la vita è sventura,
Perchè da noi si dura?
Intatta luna, tale
È lo stato mortale.
Ma tu mortal non sei,
E forse del mio dir poco ti cale.

Pur tu, solinga, eterna peregrina,
Che sì pensosa sei, tu forse intendi
Questo viver terreno,
Il patir nostro, il sospirar, che sia;
Che sia questo morir, questo supremo
Scolorar del sembiante,
E perir dalla terra, e venir meno
Ad ogni usata, amante compagnia.
E tu certo comprendi
Il perchè delle cose, e vedi il frutto
Del mattin, della sera,
Del tacito, infinito andar del tempo.
Tu sai, tu certo, a qual suo dolce amore
Rida la primavera,
A chi giovi l'ardore, e che procacci
Il verno co' suoi ghiacci.
Mille cose sai tu, mille discopri,
Che son celate al semplice pastore.

Spesso quand'io ti miro
Star così muta in sul deserto piano,
Che, in suo giro lontano, al ciel confina;
Ovver con la mia greggia
Seguirmi viaggiando a mano a mano;
E quando miro in ciel arder le stelle;
Dico fra me pensando:
A che tante facelle?
Che fa l'aria infinta, e quel profondo
Infinto seren? che vuol dir questa
Solitudine immensa? ed io che sono?
Così meco ragiono: e della stanza
Smisurata e superba,
E dell'innumerabile famiglia;
Poi di tanto adoprar, di tanti moti
D'ogni celeste, ogni terrena cosa,
Girando senza posa,
Per tornar sempre là donde son mosse;
Uso alcuno, alcun frutto
Indovinar non so. Ma tu per certo,
Giovinetta immortal, conosci il tutto.
Questo io conosco e sento,
Che degli eterni giri,
Che dell'esser mio frale,
Qualche bene o contento
Avrà fors'altri; a me la vita è male.

O greggia mia che posi, oh te beata,
Che la miseria tua, credo, non sai!
Quanta invidia ti porto!
Non sol perchè d'affanno
Quasi libera vai;
Ch'ogni stento, ogni danno,
Ogni estremo timor subito scordi;
Ma più perchè giammai tedio non provi.
Quando tu siedi all'ombra, sovra l'erbe,
Tu se' queta e contenta;
E gran parte dell'anno
Senza noia consumi in quello stato.
Ed io pur seggo sovra l'erbe, all'ombra,
E un fastidio m'ingombra
La mente, ed uno spron quasi mi punge

Sì che, sedendo, più che mai son lunge
Da trovar pace o loco.
E pur nulla non bramo,
E non ho fino a qui cagion di pianto.
Quel che tu goda o quanto,
Non so già dir; ma fortunata sei.
Ed io godo ancor poco,
O greggia mia, nè di ciò sol mi lagno.
Se tu parlar sapessi, io chiederei:
Dimmi: perchè giacendo
A bell'agio, ozioso,
S'appaga ogni animale;
Me, s'io giaccio in riposo, il tedio assale?

　　Forse s'avess'io l'ale
Da volar su le nubi,
E noverar le stelle ad una ad una,
O come il tuono errar di giogo in giogo,
Più felice sarei, dolce mia greggia,
Più felice sarei, candida luna.
O forse erra dal vero,
Mirando all'altrui sorte, il mio pensiero:
Forse in qual forma, in quale
Stato che sia, dentro covile o cuna,
È funesto a chi nasce il dì natale.

A se stesso

(To Himself, p. 202)

Or poserai per sempre,
Stanco mio cor. Perì l'inganno estremo
Ch'eterno io mi credei. Perì. Ben sento,
In noi di cari inganni,
Non che la speme, il desiderio è spento.
Posa per sempre. Assai
Palpitasti. Non val cosa nessuna
I moti tuoi, nè di sospiri è degna
La terra. Amaro e noia
La vita, altro mai nulla; e fango è il mondo.
T'acqueta omai. Dispera
L'ultima volta. Al gener nostro il fato
Non donò che il morire. Omai disprezza
Te, la natura, il brutto
Poter che, ascoso, a comun danno impera,
E l'infinita vanità del tutto.

Sopra il ritratto di una bella donna
Scolpito nel monumento sepolcrale della medesima

(On the Likeness of a Beautiful Woman, p. 203)

Tal fosti: or qui sotterra
Polve e scheletro sei. Su l'ossa e il fango
Immobilmente collocato invano,
Muto, mirando dell'etadi il volo,
Sta, di memoria solo
E di dolor custode, il simulacro
Della scorsa beltà. Quel dolce sguardo,
Che tremar fe, se, come or sembra, immoto
In altrui s'affisò; quel labbro, ond'alto
Par, come d'urna piena,
Traboccare il piacer; quel collo, cinto
Già di desio; quell'amorosa mano,
Che spesso, ove fu porta,
Sentì gelida far la man che strinse;
E il seno, onde la gente
Visibilmente di pallor si tinse,
Furo alcun tempo: or fango
Ed ossa sei: la vista
Vituperosa e trista un sasso asconde.
Così riduce il fato
Qual sembianza fra noi parve più viva
Immagine del ciel. Misterio eterno
Dell'esser nostro. Oggi d'eccelsi, immensi
Pensieri e sensi inenarrabil fonte,
Beltà grandeggia, e pare,
Quale splendor vibrato
Da natura immortal su queste arene,
Di sovrumani fati,
Di fortunati regni e d'aurei mondi
Segno e sicura spene
Dare al mortale stato:
Diman, per lieve forza,
Sozzo a vedere, abominoso, abbietto
Divien quel che fu dianzi
Quasi angelico aspetto,
E dalle menti insieme
Quel che da lui moveva
Ammirabil concetto, si dilegua.

Desiderii infiniti
E visioni altere
Crea nel vago pensiere,
Per natural virtù, dotto concento;
Onde per mar delizioso, arcano
Erra lo spirto umano,
Quasi come a diporto
Ardito notator per l'Oceano:
Ma se un discorde accento
Fere l'orecchio, in nulla
Torna quel paradiso in un momento.

Natura umana, or come,
Se frale in tutto e vile,
Se polve ed ombra sei, tant'alto senti?
Se in parte anco gentile,
Come i più degni tuoi moti e pensieri
Son così di leggeri
Da sì basse cagioni e desti e spenti?

La ginestra
o il fiore del deserto

(Broom, p. 205)

Καὶ ἠγάπησαν οἱ ἄνθρωποι μᾶλλον τὸ σκότος ἤ τὸ φῶς.

E gli uomini vollero piuttosto le tenebre che la luce.
—GIOVANNI, III, 19.

Qui su l'arida schiena
Del formidabil monte
Sterminator Vesevo,
La qual null'altro allegra arbor nè fiore,
Tuoi cespi solitari intorno spargi,
Odorata ginestra,
Contenta dei deserti. Anco ti vidi
De' tuoi steli abbellir l'erme contrade
Che cingon la cittade
La qual fu donna de' mortali un tempo,
E del perduto impero
Par che col grave e taciturno aspetto
Faccian fede e ricordo al passeggero.
Or ti riveggo in questo suol, di tristi
Lochi e dal mondo abbandonati amante,
E d'afflitte fortune ognor compagna.
Questi campi cosparsi
Di ceneri infeconde, e ricoperti
Dell'impietrata lava,
Che sotto i passi al peregrin risona;
Dove s'annida e si contorce al sole
La serpe, e dove al noto
Cavernoso covil torna il coniglio;
Fur liete ville e colti,
E biondeggiàr di spiche, e risonaro
Di muggito d'armenti;
Fur giardini e palagi,
Agli ozi de' potenti
Gradito ospizio; fur città famose
Che coi torrenti suoi l'altero monte
Dall'ignea bocca fulminando oppresse
Con gli abitanti insieme. Or tutto intorno
Una ruina involve,
Dove tu siedi, o fior gentile, e quasi
I danni altrui commiserando, al cielo

Di dolcissimo odor mandi un profumo,
Che il deserto consola. A queste piagge
Venga colui che d'esaltar con lode
Il nostro stato ha in uso, e vegga quanto
È il gener nostro in cura
All'amante natura. E la possanza
Qui con giusta misura
Anco estimar potrà dell'uman seme,
Cui la dura nutrice, ov'ei men teme,
Con lieve moto in un momento annulla
In parte, e può con moti
Poco men lievi ancor subitamente
Annichilare in tutto.
Dipinte in queste rive
Son dell'umana gente
Le magnifiche sorti e progressive.

Qui mira e qui ti specchia,
Secol superbo e sciocco,
Che il calle insino allora
Dal risorto pensier segnato innanti
Abbandonasti, e volti addietro i passi,
Del ritornar ti vanti,
E procedere il chiami.
Al tuo pargoleggiar gl'ingegni tutti,
Di cui lor sorte rea padre ti fece,
Vanno adulando, ancora
Ch'a ludibrio talora
T'abbian fra se. Non io
Con tal vergogna scenderò sotterra;
Ma il disprezzo piuttosto che si serra
Di te nel petto mio,
Mostrato avrò quanto si possa aperto:
Bench'io sappia che obblio
Preme chi troppo all'età propria increbbe.
Di questo mal, che teco
Mi fia comune, assai finor mi rido.
Libertà vai sognando, e servo a un tempo
Vuoi di nuovo il pensiero,
Sol per cui risorgemmo
Della barbarie in parte, e per cui solo
Si cresce in civiltà, che sola in meglio

Guida i pubblici fati.
Così ti spiacque il vero
Dell'aspra sorte e del depresso loco
Che natura ci diè. Per questo il tergo
Vigliaccamente rivolgesti al lume
Che il fe palese: e, fuggitivo, appelli
Vil chi lui segue, e solo
Magnanimo colui
Che se schernendo o gli altri, astuto o folle,
Fin sopra gli astri il mortal grado estolle.

Uom di povero stato e membra inferme
Che sia dell'alma generoso ed alto,
Non chiama se nè stima
Ricco d'or nè gagliardo,
E di splendida vita o di valente
Persona infra le gente
Non fa risibil mostra;
Ma se di forza e di tesor mendico
Lascia parer senza vergogna, e noma
Parlando, apertamente, e di sue cose
Fa stima al vero uguale.
Magnanimo animale
Non credo io già, ma stolto,
Qual che nato a perir, nutrito in pene,
Dice, a goder son fatto,
E di fetido orgoglio
Empie le carte, eccelsi fati e nove
Felicità, quali il ciel tutto ignora,
Non pur quest'orbe, promettendo in terra
A popoli che un'onda
Di mar commosso, un fiato
D'aura maligna, un sotterraneo crollo
Distrugge sì che avanza
A gran pena di lor la rimembranza.
Nobil natura è quella
Che a sollevar s'ardisce
Gli occhi mortali incontra
Al comun fato, e che con franca lingua,
Nulla al ver detraendo,
Confessa il mal che ci fu dato in sorte,
E il basso stato e frale;

Quella che grande e forte
Mostra se nel soffrir, nè gli odii e l'ire
Fraterne, ancor più gravi
D'ogni altro danno, accresce
Alle miserie sue, l'uomo incolpando
Del suo dolor, ma dà la colpa a quella
Che veramente è rea, che de' mortali
Madre è di parto, e di voler matrigna.
Costei chiama inimica; e incontro a questa
Congiunta esser pensando,
Siccome è il vero, ed ordinata in pria
L'umana compagnia,
Tutti fra se confederati estima
Gli uomini, e tutti abbraccia
Con vero amor, porgendo
Valida e pronta ed aspettando aita
Negli alterni perigli e nelle angosce
Della guerra comune. Ed alle offese
Dell'uomo armar la destra, e laccio porre
Al vicino ed inciampo,
Stolto crede così, qual fora in campo
Cinto d'oste contraria, in sul più vivo
Incalzar degli assalti,
Gl'inimici obbliando, acerbe gare
Imprender con gli amici,
E sparger fuga e fulminar col brando
Infra i propri guerrieri.
Così fatti pensieri
Quando fien, come fur, palesi al volgo,
E quell'orror che primo
Contra l'empia natura
Strinse i mortali in social catena,
Fia ricondotto in parte
Da verace saper, l'onesto e il retto
Conversar cittadino,
E giustizia e pietade, altra radice
Avranno allor che non superbe fole,
Ove fondata probità del volgo
Così star suole in piede
Quale star può quel ch'ha in error la sede.

Sovente in queste rive,
Che, desolate, a bruno
Veste il flutto indurato, e par che ondeggi,
Seggo la notte; e su la mesta landa
In purissimo azzurro
Veggo dall'alto fiammeggiar le stelle,
Cui di lontan fa specchio
Il mare, e tutto di scintille in giro
Per lo vòto seren brillare il mondo.
E poi che gli occhi a quelle luci appunto,
Ch'a lor sembrano un punto,
E sono immense, in guisa
Che un punto a petto a lor son terra e mare
Veracemente; a cui
L'uomo non pur, ma questo
Globo ove l'uomo è nulla,
Sconosciuto è del tutto; e quando miro
Quegli ancor più senz'alcun fin remoti
Nodi quasi di stelle
Ch'a noi paion qual nebbia, a cui non l'uomo
E non la terra sol, ma tutte in uno,
Del numero infinite e della mole,
Con l'aureo sole insiem, le nostre stelle
O sono ignote, o così paion come
Essi alla terra, un punto
Di luce nebulosa; al pensier mio
Che sembri allora, o prole
Dell'uomo? E rimembrando
Il tuo stato quaggiù, di cui fa segno
Il suol ch'io premo; e poi dall'altra parte,
Che te signora e fine
Credi tu data al Tutto, e quante volte
Favoleggiar ti piacque, in questo oscuro
Granel di sabbia, il qual di terra ha nome,
Per tua cagion, dell'universe cose
Scender gli autori, e conversar sovente
Co' tuoi piacevolmente, e che i derisi
Sogni rinnovellando, ai saggi insulta
Fin la presente età, che in conoscenza
Ed in civil costume
Sembra tutte avanzar; qual moto allora,
Mortal prole infelice, o qual pensiero

Verso te finalmente il cor m'assale?
Non so se il riso o la pietà prevale.

 Come d'arbor cadendo un picciol pomo,
Cui là nel tardo autunno
Maturità senz'altra forza atterra,
D'un popol di formiche i dolci alberghi,
Cavati in molle gleba
Con gran lavoro, e l'opre
E le ricchezze che adunate a prova
Con lungo affaticar l'assidua gente
Avea provvidamente al tempo estivo,
Schiaccia, diserta e copre
In un punto; così d'alto piombando,
Dall'utero tonante
Scagliata al ciel profondo,
Di ceneri e di pomici e di sassi
Notte e ruina, infusa
Di bollenti ruscelli,
O pel montano fianco
Furiosa tra l'erba
Di liquefatti massi
E di metalli e d'infocata arena
Scendendo immensa piena,
Le cittadi che il mar là su l'estremo
Lido aspergea, confuse
E infranse e ricoperse
In pochi istanti: onde su quelle or pasce
La capra, e città nove
Sorgon dall'altra banda, a cui sgabello
Son le sepolte, e le prostrate mura
L'arduo monte al suo piè quasi calpesta.
Non ha natura al seme
Dell'uom più stima o cura
Che alla formica: e se più rara in quello
Che nell'altra è la strage,
Non avvien ciò d'altronde
Fuor che l'uom sue prosapie ha men feconde.

 Ben mille ed ottocento
Anni varcàr poi che spariro, oppressi
Dall'ignea forza, i popolati seggi,

E il villanello intento
Ai vigneti, che a stento in questi campi
Nutre la morta zolla e incenerita,
Ancor leva lo sguardo
Sospettoso alla vetta
Fatal, che nulla mai fatta più mite
Ancor siede tremenda, ancor minaccia
A lui strage ed ai figli ed agli averi
Lor poverelli. E spesso
Il meschino in sul tetto
Dell'ostel villereccio, alla vagante
Aura giacendo tutta notte insonne,
E balzando più volte, esplora il corso
Del temuto bollor, che si riversa
Dall'inesausto grembo
Su l'arenoso dorso, a cui riluce
Di Capri la marina
E di Napoli il porto e Mergellina.
E se appressar lo vede, o se nel cupo
Del domestico pozzo ode mai l'acqua
Fervendo gorgogliar, desta i figliuoli,
Desta la moglie in fretta, e via, con quanto
Di lor cose rapir posson, fuggendo,
Vede lontan l'usato
Suo nido, e il picciol campo,
Che gli fu dalla fame unico schermo,
Preda al flutto rovente,
Che crepitando giunge, e inesorato
Durabilmente sovra quei si spiega.
Torna al celeste raggio
Dopo l'antica obblivion l'estinta
Pompei, come sepolto
Scheletro, cui di terra
Avarizia o pietà rende all'aperto;
E dal deserto foro
Diritto infra la file
Dei mozzi colonnati il peregrino
Lunge contempla il bipartito giogo
E la cresta fumante,
Che alla sparsa ruina ancor minaccia.
E nell'orror della secreta notte
Per li vacui teatri,

Per li templi deformi e per le rotte
Case, ove i parti il pipistrello asconde,
Come sinistra face
Che per vòti palagi atra s'aggiri,
Corre il baglior della funerea lava,
Che di lontan per l'ombre
Rosseggia e i lochi intorno intorno tinge.
Così, dell'uomo ignara e dell'etadi
Ch'ei chiama antiche, e del seguir che fanno
Dopo gli avi i nepoti,
Sta natura ognor verde, anzi procede
Per sì lungo cammino
Che sembra star. Caggioni i regni intanto,
Passan genti e linguaggi: ella nol vede:
E l'uom d'eternità s'arroga il vanto.

   E tu, lenta ginestra,
Che di selve odorate
Queste campagne dispogliate adorni,
Anche tu presto alla crudel possanza
Soccomberai del sotterraneo foco,
Che ritornando al loco
Già noto, stenderà l'avaro lembo
Su tue molli foreste. E piegherai
Sotto il fascio mortal non renitente
Il tuo capo innocente:
Ma non piegato insino allora indarno
Codardamente supplicando innanzi
Al futuro oppressor; ma non eretto
Con forsennato orgoglio inver le stelle,
Nè sul deserto, dove
E la sede e i natali
Non per voler ma per fortuna avesti;
Ma più saggia, ma tanto
Meno inferma dell'uom, quanto le frali
Tue stirpi non credesti
O dal fato o da te fatte immortali.

Il tramonto della luna

(The Setting of the Moon, p. 214)

Quale in notte solinga,
Sovra campagne inargentate ed acque,
Là 've zefiro aleggia,
E mille vaghi aspetti
E ingannevoli obbietti
Fingon l'ombre lontane
Infra l'onde tranquille
E rami e siepi e collinette e ville;
Giunta al confin del cielo,
Dietro Apennino od Alpe, o del Tirreno
Nell'infinito seno
Scende la luna; e si scolora il mondo;
Spariscon l'ombre, ed una
Oscurità la valle e il monte imbruna;
Orba la notte resta,
E cantando, con mesta melodia,
L'estremo albor della fuggente luce,
Che dianzi gli fu duce,
Saluta il carrettier dalla sua via;

Tal si dilegua, e tale
Lascia l'età mortale
La giovinezza. In fuga
Van l'ombre e le sembianze
Dei dilettosi inganni; e vengon meno
Le lontane speranze,
Ove s'appoggia la mortal natura.
Abbandonata, oscura
Resta la vita. In lei porgendo il guardo,
Cerca il confuso viatore invano
Del cammin lungo che avanzar si sente
Meta o ragione; e vede
Che a se l'umana sede,
Esso a lei veramente è fatto estrano.

Troppo felice e lieta
Nostra misera sorte
Parve lassù, se il giovanile stato,
Dove ogni ben di mille pene è frutto,

270

Durasse tutto della vita il corso.
Troppo mite decreto
Quel che sentenzia ogni animale a morte,
S'anco mezza la via
Lor non si desse in pria
Della terribil morte assai più dura.
D'intelletti immortali
Degno trovato, estremo
Di tutti i mali, ritrovàr gli eterni
La vecchiezza, ove fosse
Incolume il desio, al speme estinta,
Secche le fonti del piacer, le pene
Maggiori sempre, e non più dato il bene.

Voi, collinette e piagge,
Caduto lo splendor che all'occidente
Inargentava della notte il velo,
Orfane ancor gran tempo
Non resterete; che dall'altra parte
Tosto vedrete il cielo
Imbiancar novamente, e sorger l'alba:
Alla qual poscia seguitando il sole,
E folgorando intorno
Con sue fiamme possenti,
Di lucidi torrenti
Inonderà con vio gli eterei campi.
Ma la vita mortal, poi che la bella
Giovinezza sparì, non si colora
D'altra luce giammai, nè d'altra aurora.
Vedova è insino al fine; ed alla notte
Che l'altre etadi oscura,
Segno poser gli Dei la sepoltura.

A NOTE ON THE AUTHOR

Since 1965 Ottavio Mark Casale has been a professor of English at Kent State University, where he has taught courses in American, British, and comparative literature. His professional interests include publications and papers on Edgar Allan Poe, American transcendentalism, and Giacomo Leopardi as well as extensive university administrative experience. His career has included a Woodrow Wilson Fellowship at the University of Michigan; an appointment as Fulbright Senior Lecturer in American literature at the University of Pisa, Italy; and a National Endowment for the Humanities Translation Grant. Professor Casale received his B.A. degree from Kent State University and his M.A. and Ph.D. degrees from the University of Michigan.